# THE FABRIC OF LIFE

AF657074

# THE FABRIC OF LIFE

## On the Songs of the Mystic Kabir

**OSHO**

PAN

This edition published 2022 by Pan
an imprint of Pan Macmillan Publishing India Private Limited
707 Kailash Building
26 K. G. Marg New Delhi 110001
www.panmacmillan.co.in

Pan Macmillan, The Smithson, 6 Briset St., Farringdon, London EC1M 5NR
Associated companies throughout the world
www.panmacmillan.com

ISBN 978-93-95624-37-4

Copyright © 1976, 2022 OSHO International Foundation, www.osho.com/copyrights

All rights reserved. No part of this book may be reproduced or transmitted in any form or by any means, electronic or mechanical, including photocopying, recording, or by any information storage and retrieval system, without prior written permission from OSHO International Foundation.

Originally published in Hindi as *Suno Bhai Sadho*, by Osho. The complete OSHO text archive can be found via the online OSHO Library at www.osho.com/Library

Photos of Osho: Copyright © OSHO International Foundation

The sutras Osho comments on are translated by Yoga Pratap Bharati, copyright © OSHO International Foundation

OSHO® and OSHO Vision® are registered trademarks and trademarks of OSHO International Foundation, used under license. www.osho.com/trademarks

3 5 7 9 8 6 4 2

This book is sold subject to the condition that it shall not, by way of trade or otherwise, be lent, re-sold, hired out, or otherwise circulated without the publisher's prior consent in any form of binding or cover other than that in which it is published and without a similar condition including this condition being imposed on the subsequent purchaser.

Typeset in Joanna MT Std by Manmohan Kumar
Printed and bound in India by Replika Press Pvt. Ltd.

# Contents


*Preface* vii

*A Note about Language* ix

1. Chasing Dreams 1
2. The Desert or the Ocean 44
3. Cutting the Chains 80
4. Wordless Silence 111
5. The Fabric of Life 156
6. Love Is an Invitation 192
7. Lifting the Veil 227
8. Don't be Asleep while Awake 263
9. The Tenth Door 305
10. The Silence of the Inner Sky 338

*About Osho* 380

Osho International Meditation Resort 383

Books by Osho in English 386

For More Information 390

# Preface

Kabir is one of the greatest mystics of the world. Meditate on Kabir – pay attention to him, to what he says. He is a very simple man, not learned in any way – all that he says is out of his experience. He is not a scholar, he does not know anything about the Vedas and the Koran and the Bible. All that he says is out of his own existential experience. He is not a theoretician or a philosopher; he is a poet. And not only a poet, he is a mystic poet; the difference is that the poet sometimes has glimpses of God, and then he falls back again – rare moments of flight.

In India we have a saying that if you love the poetry of a poet, never go to see him because you will be disappointed. You will find a very ordinary man – even more ordinary than ordinary people. Or you may find somebody ugly – and he has been talking so beautifully. And you will find somebody vulgar, immoral, obscene – and his poetry was so spiritual. The saying is right: if you love the poetry, forget the poet, never go to see him. Because the poet only jumps – in rare moments of insight he flies high, he's turned on, some visions descend in him… And then he is closed again, turned off; then he is an ordinary man. Only sometimes, like lightning, poetry comes to him.

That is the difference between a poet and a mystic poet. A mystic poet has arrived. It is not a flight of his imagination, it is not just a vision – now it is his very life. He breathes in God, he lives in God, he lives like God, he *is* God. So when he says something, it is not just accidental; when he says something, it is from his very core.

Kabir is a mystic poet. Listen to his melody, sing his song; and if you have understood, then become a little more aware. And don't look for the forest! There are only trees, there is no forest – *forest* is just a collective noun, an abstraction. There is no God high in the heaven; there are gods and gods and gods – the tree god, the rock god, the river god, the man god, the woman god – there are gods and gods and gods, but there is no God.

This whole existence is divine. Love the trees, if you want to know something about the forest. Love people, if you want to know anything about God. Each particular manifestation can become a window, a door. Don't be too obsessed by words – the word *God* is not God, the word *love* is not love, and the word *fire* of course is not fire. Drop words, and move more and more towards the existential.

Feel more, rather than thinking. Through feeling, your prayer will arise. And through feeling, one day you will be dissolved. When you are dissolved, God is.

Osho
*The Divine Melody*

# A Note about Language

Spoken Words: Osho's books are not "written" but rather are transcribed from recordings of his talks. These talks are extemporaneous, without reference to notes other than copies of questions, stories or scriptures he has been asked to comment upon, or jokes he might use to drive home a particular point. He has asked his editors to preserve that quality of the spoken word in his printed books.

Pronouns: When hearing him speak, it is quite clear to the listener that generally when Osho talks about "man" he is referring to "human beings." His use of "he" as a default pronoun simply serves an ease and flow of speaking – in no way does it imply that "she" (or "they") is being dismissed or disregarded.

Osho's unique vantage point is good to keep in mind:

*A meditator is neither a man nor a woman,*
*because meditation has nothing to do with your body;*
*neither does it have anything to do with your mind.*
*In meditation you are simply and purely consciousness.*
*And consciousness is neither male nor female.*

~Osho

# 1
# Chasing Dreams

**I know Maya is a great deceiver.**
**Formless, carrying a noose in her hand,**
**she wanders around, speaking with a sweet tongue.**
**She takes the form of Kamala with Keshava, and Bhavani with Shiva.**
**She works as an idol for the priest, and is the water at the holy places.**
**She is Yogini with the yogi, and in the King's palace she is the queen.**
**To some, she is a diamond; to some, she is a broken cowrie shell.**
**She is bhakti for the devotee, and the Brahmani of Brahma.**

Kabir says: **Listen, O sadhu! All this is an indescribable story.**

Kabir is unique. He gives hope to everyone – it is difficult to find a more ordinary person than Kabir. If Kabir can reach, then everyone can. Kabir is an utterly simple man; so even a simple-hearted person can have hope. Kabir is illiterate, which shows that being educated has nothing to do with truth. There is no way to know what caste or community he belonged to – maybe he was born into a Muslim family and was raised in a Hindu family. So caste and community have nothing to do with godliness.

Kabir lived as a householder. He was a weaver by profession, and so he would weave clothes and sell them in the marketplace. He never left home to go to the Himalayas. Godliness can be realized even at home, there is no need to go to the Himalayas. Kabir did not renounce anything – yet he found everything. So, leaving something behind cannot be a precondition for achieving. There is no precondition that you have to leave something behind in order to achieve something.

There is nothing extraordinary about Kabir's life. To be extraordinary may be an embellishment for the ego, but it cannot reflect the beauty of one's being. Kabir is not rich, neither is he knowledgeable, respected, educated or highly cultured. If a person like Kabir can attain the ultimate, there is no reason why you should be disappointed. Hence, Kabir gives much hope.

If Buddha has attained, it does not assure you that you will attain too. If you truly understand Buddha, you may feel disheartened because Buddha had so many achievements to his credit before his attainment. Buddha was an emperor and it is not much of a surprise when an emperor gives up his riches. Only one who has everything can really see the futility of it all.

For a poor man it is very difficult to give up his possessions. How can someone know the futility of something he doesn't have? Buddha could see it, but how will *you* be able to know? Before realizing the futility of anything, you need to have at least some experience of it. How can you say being wealthy is meaningless? Are you wealthy? You have always lived in poverty, you have always lived in a hut – how can you say it is no fun living in a palace? And, even if you said such a thing, it would be the truth someone else has realized; it would not be your voice coming from within. And deep down money will continue to keep a hold on you. So if you really understand Buddha, you will be totally at a loss.

Buddha says there is nothing to women but bones and marrow. But he is saying this after having seen many beautiful women – whom you may have seen only on the movie screen. There is a vast distance between you and such beautiful women. You can be very easily attracted to these women; you would be ready to give up everything to get them. It would require tremendous awareness to know the futility of that which has never been yours.

Kabir is poor and yet he knows this truth: having wealth is futile. Kabir has one simple wife and yet he realizes that all glamour, all pomp and show, all physical beauty are nothing but projections of the mind.

So it is very arduous for a poor man to attain liberation, arduous for the simple reason that he will have to compensate for his lack of experience by becoming aware; he will have to replace his lack of experience with meditation. You would also have escaped from the palace if you had had all that Buddha had – because you would also come to see that there is nothing more to achieve. The moment your hopes, your desires, fall away, you will see there is nothing for you in the future – the palace will look empty.

Man lives through his ambitions, his ambition to attain greater and greater heights tomorrow – and so he goes on chasing. But once the last stop on the journey is reached, where else is there to go? What else will you do if you don't renounce everything? Then the palace becomes either a reason for commiting suicide or for self-transformation. But Kabir doesn't have a palace.

Buddha is a genius. He was given the highest possible training available. He was well versed in scriptures. He had excellent command on language; he had a sharp intellect; he was the son of an emperor. So he was highly educated in every way.

Kabir grew up on the streets. There is no record of his parents. He may have been an illegitimate child. Perhaps after his birth his mother left him at a roadside. That's why nothing is known about his mother. He did not come from a noble family. In a way, he was born on the street and was raised on the streets – as if it was his fate to be a beggar.

So if this beggar could see the futility of wealth, you can see it too. You cannot expect to learn this from Buddha, there is a huge gap between him and you. You can worship him – but it would be difficult for you to be like Buddha, you would need to go through many lives. But there is no gap between Kabir and you. Perhaps he is standing way behind you in the queue, and if Kabir, standing so far behind, can reach there is no reason why you cannot.

Kabir can be a great inspiration. So, first keep this in mind. That's why I call Kabir an extraordinary person. Mahavira is the son of an emperor, so are Krishna, Rama and Buddha. They all came from palaces. Kabir came straight from the streets, he has nothing to do with palaces. Kabir has said clearly: I have never touched pen and paper.

It gives a lot of confidence to see that even such an illiterate person, who could not even sign his name, attained godliness. If you have not realized, then it is because of you; don't ever blame the circumstances. Whenever you feel like blaming the conditions, always remember Kabir. At least you know who your parents are, you have a home, you were not born on the streets. You are able to sign your name. You must have had some education; you have some ability to keep accounts. You must have read a little from the *Vedas*, the *Koran*, the *Gita*. You may not be a great scholar, but you must be a learned person of some measure.

So, whenever you begin to reason "Buddha could reach because he had everything in his favor, but how can I, in my circumstances?" remember Kabir. Following Buddha, a person may lose his equilibrium; he may feel he won't be able to make it. Kabir helps bring the person back to a more balanced state;

with Kabir the scales are again in balance. So Kabir is more of a help than Buddha. Buddha can be of help to a few people; Kabir is like a wide highway. Buddha's path is very narrow, only a few people can reach and attain through it.

The language Buddha uses is exclusively his own. It is a language which is used by exceptionally few people. Every word is precious, every word carries a subtle meaning. Kabir's language is everyman's language – it is the language of an illiterate person. If you fail to understand Kabir, then you won't be able to understand anything. If Kabir is understood, then nothing further remains to be understood. And the more you come to understand Kabir, the more you will find that enlightenment has nothing to do with your circumstances.

Enlightenment depends on your inner longing. It can happen anywhere: in a hut, in a palace, in the marketplace, in the Himalayas. It can happen to an educated mind and it can happen to an illiterate mind. It can happen to the poor, to the rich, to a pundit or to an uneducated person. Circumstances have nothing whatsoever to do with it.

The words of Kabir that we will be following in this meditation camp are entitled *Suno Bhai Sadho* – listen, O sadhu. In his expressions, somewhere or other, he always addresses the sadhu. Let us understand this form of address before we enter the sutras of Kabir.

A person can ask in three ways. One is like a child, out of curiosity, asking just for the sake of it. There is no need, no longing, there is no particular reason; just a mental itch. A question comes to mind and is asked immediately. If he gets the answer, it is fine; he never bothers to ask again – just like children do. When they are walking down the road, they ask: what is this? And if you say it is a tree, they will ask: what's a tree? Why are trees green? Why does the sun rise in the morning, why not at night? But there is no particular interest in listening to your answer. By the time you answer their first question, they are ready with the next one. They won't press you, even if you do not answer. Whether you answer or not is irrelevant to them.

The child asks just for the sake of asking. The child is only making use of his brain. Just as when he starts walking for the first time, he tries again and again, though not necessarily to reach anywhere. At this point he has no particular place to reach, he just enjoys walking. He simply makes use of his feet and feels very happy; he is just thrilled that he can walk. The walking is not related to reaching any destination; it is only a matter of practicing. Similarly, when a child begins to speak, he speaks just for the sake of it, just for practice. There is no particular meaning to what he says. Once he has learned how to ask, then he asks for the sake of asking – there is no real question in it, only curiosity.

So there are those who, out of curiosity, ask childish questions even about God. It doesn't matter to them if they get an answer or not. And whatever answer they may be given, will make no difference to their lives. They will live the same way, whether they believe in God or not.

This is really strange: whether a person is a theist or an atheist, his life remains unchanged. Can you say whether someone is a theist or an atheist just by looking at his life? No. In fact you have to ask whether the person is a theist or an atheist. One finds not an iota of difference in the behavior of either of them. If one is dishonest, so is the other. They are both the same, there is no difference whatsoever. One believes in God, the other does not believe in God. Such a great belief does not leave even a little imprint on life – it leaves not even a slight mark on life! One is as dishonest in business as the other; one is as much a liar as the other. Neither the believer can be trusted nor the nonbeliever. Shouldn't faith make some difference in life? If it doesn't, then such faith is worthless. Then the faith must have been born out of curiosity, then it is childish. Such childish faith should be completely dropped.

So, curiosity is on the surface. Secondly: as you go a little deeper, it becomes inquiry. Inquiry is not just about asking – there is a search for an answer, but the search is intellectual, it is not existential. The search is thought-centered, not life-centered. Anyone who is filled with inquiry is certainly sincere in his desire to find an answer. But once he finds it, he will intellectualize it, he will store it in his memory; he will become more informed. His knowledge will grow, but he will not grow in the way he behaves, there will be no growth in his life. The answer will not transform the individual. The person will remain the same – though he will be more informed. Inquiry is a product of intellect.

Then, there is a third level called *mumuksha*, the desire to attain the ultimate freedom. *Mumuksha* means the inquiry is not intellectual, it is existential. The inquiry is not in order to accumulate more information. One inquires because all of life is at stake. The question is asked because the very answer will show where to go, what to do, how to live.

For example, a thirsty man asks where he can find water. This is not a simple inquiry. Someone is lying in a desert, thirsty, and asks, "Where is some water?" At that moment each and every pore is asking the question, it is not arising from his intellect. At that moment, he is not interested in having a scientific definition of water. If someone asks him why he keeps asking about water… Doesn't he know that water is $H_2O$? Why doesn't he make use of science? The formula is clear: two parts of hydrogen and one part of oxygen makes water – $H_2O$! But for the person who is thirsty, it makes no difference how water is formed. That is not the question. His question is not to find out what water is; it is not an inquiry to increase his knowledge about water. His whole life is at stake. If he does not get water in the next moment, death is certain. His whole life depends on water. It's a matter of life and death for him.

*Mumuksha* means the inquiry has hit the center. Now the question is not whether God exists or not – a childish question. The question is also not asked the way philosophers raise questions of an intellectual type and then start looking for the answer in scriptures. Someone who is thirsty will not go to the scriptures to find what water is like. A thirsty person goes in search of a lake. Anyone who is really thirsty seeks a man of wisdom from whom he can drink and quench his thirst. He does not want knowledge, he seeks the knower.

A *mumukshu* seeks a master, an inquirer looks for a scripture, a curious man asks anyone. Kabir calls the one who is a *mumukshu* a sadhu. That's why his every word has been addressed keeping this fact in mind: *Suno bhai sadho* – listen, O sadhu. *Sadhu* means one who is interested in sadhana, in spiritual work; one who is a seeker. *Sadhu* means one who is earnest about transforming himself, to work for the good, to live the truth – in other words, one who is interested in being a sadhu.

This word *sadhu* is so wonderful. Because of its overuse it has become distorted. *Sadhu* means one who is simple, straight, innocent, natural. *Sadhu* has great connotations and nuances. And, being simple, straight, innocent, natural is what sadhana, spirituality, is all about. Hence, Kabir says: O sadhu, a naturally attained samadhi, superconsciousness, is better. Be natural, be simple, take it easy.

It will be good to understand this a little, because we come across many people who became complex just in their effort to become simple. They started with the idea of becoming simple but ended up becoming complicated.

I have a friend. People call him a sadhu, but I call him a non-sadhu because he is not at all simple. If you offer him milk in the morning, the first thing he asks is whether it is cow's milk or buffalo milk, because he does not drink buffalo milk. He is a chaste Hindu, he drinks only cow's milk. Not just cow's milk, but milk from a white cow. He has found in some scripture that milk given by a white cow is the purest, and that, too, only if it has been drawn very recently; he believes some harmful alteration happens in the milk if it is left standing for some time. Similarly, he takes only recently prepared ghee, purified butter because, according to him, the scriptures say if it is left standing for some time it goes through some harmful alteration.

He drinks only that water that is brought from the well by someone wearing wet clothes, because that is the only way that the water can be considered absolutely pure. How can one rely on dry clothes? They may have been touched by an untouchable, they may have been washed by the washerman or sent to the laundry – and that is not right. The person has to take a bath at the well, with his clothes on, so that he will be clean, his clothes will be clean, and only then can he draw water from the well and take it to someone.

He eats only food that is cooked by a brahmin. And, the effort he puts into all of this… He remains occupied for twenty-four hours. During those twenty-four hours he finds not a single minute to remember God, the whole time is consumed in matters relating to meals. He had started out trying to become simple, but he has ended up being so complicated that life has become a hell. And when he visits someone as a guest, the host, who otherwise may never have prayed to God, begins praying to get rid of him.

Ordinarily, if a sadhu stays in your house as a guest, you will have only one thing to pray for: that he may leave again soon – because he wakes up at three o'clock in the night. Not only does he wake up, he wakes up the entire family. He not only wakes up at an auspicious time in the early morning but begins chanting the mantra Om so loudly that you can't sleep.

And, you can't tell him he is doing something wrong because he is not really doing anything wrong. If he is chanting Om early in the morning, he is in a way doing you a favor.

So even a person who is in pursuit of simplicity ends up becoming difficult. Obviously, something is wrong: we have no understanding of what it means to be simple. To be simple means you begin to live moment to moment, naturally – not under any discipline – because discipline is a complicated thing. So when you are hungry, you have your meal. Whatever you get, you accept it quietly. When you wake up, you consider that moment to be the *brahmamuhurta*, the auspicious moment. When you feel sleepy, you take it as a message from existence, and when you come out of your sleep you take it that existence wants you to wake up. You don't do anything on your own, you leave everything to existence – "Thy will be done" – because whatsoever you do, you will make things complicated. After all, whatever you do, you will do through the mind, and the mind is a mechanism that creates complications. It will generate some trouble, which then keeps on growing. Then there will be no end to it.

Those whom you call sadhus become more like non-sadhus than sadhus because the essential meaning of *sadhu* – simplicity, innocence – gets lost. We have devised new meanings for *simplicity*. By *simplicity* we mean that a simple person is one who lives with one loincloth. But did you know that someone who lives with only one loincloth becomes as attached to it as an emperor does to his whole kingdom? Obviously, because then there is nothing else to be attached to, so the entire focus of the person's attachment is on his loincloth.

It is not a question of either the loincloth or the kingdom; it is a question of attachment. An emperor's attachment is spread out, it is divided. A beggar's attachment is narrow; it is centered only at one point. And if you observe closely, you will find that a beggar's attachment is more dangerous because it is undivided, condensed and intense. Everything is put at stake for just one thing. The beggar will commit suicide if he loses his loincloth because for him it means everything. So what appears to be simplicity has great complexity hidden underneath.

Kabir calls that one a sadhu who is really ordinary and simple. Although Kabir attained enlightenment, attained nirvana, realized the ultimate truth, he continued weaving cloth. He had hundreds of devotees. They said, "This does not look good, that a self-realized person such as yourself goes on weaving cloth the whole day – and then goes to the market to sell it. We feel so embarrassed."

Kabir said, "If existence does not feel any shame in weaving this vast samsara, why should a poor man like me feel ashamed of doing such a small thing? If existence can weave such a vast world… Existence is a weaver, and I am a weaver too. I am a slightly smaller weaver, existence is a slightly bigger weaver. And if it hasn't given up and run away from weaving, why should I? I have left everything to existence, whatever its wish may be. So far, I haven't received any word from it to stop weaving."

Right until the end of his life, even into his old age, he continued to sell in the marketplace. But there was a big difference in his selling, there was a certain simplicity. While weaving the cloth he would sing Rama's name. A warp from this side, a weft from the other side, and he would keep on chanting Rama. When a person like Kabir infuses the song of Rama in the warp and woof of the cloth, the very quality of the cloth changes, as if he were weaving Rama himself in the cloth. Hence, Kabir says: "I have woven a very fine sheet of cloth." And he says he has woven it with great love and devotion.

When he used to go to the marketplace, addressing a customer he would say, "Rama, I have woven this piece just for you, and I have worked on it very carefully." He never addressed a customer as anything other than "Rama." He would say, "This customer is Rama. I have especially woven this for Rama. This customer is not just any customer, and Kabir is not just any businessman."

Kabir continued with his vocation and became simple. He did not work separately on simplicity because it becomes complex if you practice it separately. Simplicity cannot be practiced; the very understanding makes one simple.

Kabir left himself totally in the hands of existence. For example, people used to gather around him in the morning for the chanting of devotional songs. And Kabir would urge them not to leave without taking a meal. His wife and children were very worried: how to manage all this? They went on borrowing money and got heavily into debt. Every night Kabir's son, Kamaal, would tell him, "This is enough. Now don't invite anyone else tomorrow." Kabir would reply, "If existence makes me say it, what can I do? Shall I listen to you or to existence? The day existence stops making me speak… Actually, who is really the one who is saying it? I don't do anything on my own, but why are you so bothered? If existence makes arrangements for everything else, it will take care of this too."

But there came a limit. One day Kamaal became angry and said, "Enough is enough! Do you now expect us to go and steal?"

Kabir replied, "You fool. Why didn't you think of this before?"

Kamaal thought that perhaps Kabir didn't follow what he meant. So he said: "Did you understand what I was saying? I am saying, shall we go and start stealing? How else can we manage?"

Kabir said, "Everything belongs to existence. What is stealing and what is non-stealing? – whatever its will is! But why didn't you think of this before?"

Kamaal was an extraordinary man. He thought, "Let's put this to the test." So he said, "Okay, I'll set out and go stealing, but you will have to accompany me."

Kabir immediately got up. This will be difficult for us to understand, because we have absolutely no idea what a simple man is like. The sadhus we know keep telling us that stealing is a sin, that non-stealing is a virtue. The sadhus we know would have said, "You idiot. You are going to hell and you want to drag me along as well?"

But Kabir got up. This simplicity is very sweet – as if there was no difference between stealing and non-stealing, between good and evil. If everything belongs to existence, then why make any distinction? Only the clever mind creates division. When one becomes simple, where is the room for any division? So, Kabir immediately stood up. It will be difficult for you to understand Kabir's inner world, because you also carry divisions in your mind. You will also feel, "What is going on here? Is Kabir really in favor of stealing?"

When Kabir got up, Kamaal felt at a loss. He thought maybe this was just a joke. But, after all, he was Kabir's son and now things had to be brought to a conclusion. So he entered a house by making a hole in the wall. Kabir remained outside. After breaking into the house, Kamaal went in and dragged out a sack of wheat. Somehow he managed to push the sack through the hole, but as he started climbing out people in the house woke up. The reason they woke up was that Kabir asked in a loud voice, "You fool, did you take permission from the people in the house? It is fine that you are stealing, but have you told the people living in the house? Make a little noise so that they can wake up and know that they have been robbed!"

Here is a simple man for whom all distinctions have disappeared.

Listening to the noise and this conversation, the people of the house woke up. And as Kamaal was climbing out of the hole he had made in the wall, someone grabbed his feet from behind. So Kamaal said: "What shall we do now? Now please cut my head off so that at least there will be no scandal."

Kabir said: "That's great! You have come up with a great idea right on time." And the story goes on to say that before chopping off his head, Kabir said to Kamaal: "I will cut off your head, but the whole thing will not remain a secret – existence will know it. But since you have suggested it, I will do it."

It may appear to us that this man is not only a thief but a killer, too. But Kabir knows that nothing dies. If a man doesn't become a killer by pulling your jacket away from you, then how can he be a killer by separating you from your head? If the body is nothing but a worn piece of cloth, then Kabir is not a killer. This is exactly what Krishna is explaining to Arjuna in the Gita: "Don't be worried, the spirit never dies even when the body is killed. It never dies by killing, it is never cut even when cutting, it never burns even when burning." That's what Kabir is saying.

So, he cut off Kamaal's head and said: "Since you are asking, I will cut your head off, but it will not remain a secret, it will be known because existence knows everything. So be it, whatever it wills."

Looking at the body, the people of the house suspected it was Kamaal's body but without the head! It is a strange story. They knew Kabir used to pass by to go to the river to take a bath, singing devotional songs and dancing, accompanied by his couple of hundred devotees. So they hung Kamaal's body in front of their house thinking that perhaps, seeing his son, Kabir's face might reflect something different. And the devotees must have known the whole story by then, so somebody might certainly make some comments.

But something else happened. When Kabir and the procession reached the house, Kabir stopped and said: "Look. Kamaal is hanging on a pole. Poor fellow, he used to join us every day, but he won't be able to today. We must do our chanting near him." The story goes that when they started chanting, Kamaal's dead hands started clapping!

No one dies. Death is an impossibility. You die because you believe in death, and you die because you don't know there is no death. Life energy is present all around.

And Kabir had told him: "You fool, I had warned you before. This will not remain a secret. Stealing is one thing, but existence knows everything. Now it has revealed the secret."

Hence, Kabir would tell his disciples, "I always say: move along according to the will of existence."

The highest truth in life is when all distinctions disappear: distinctions between good and bad, the saint and Satan, day and night, life and death, light and darkness. When one has dropped all the differences between good and evil, he can truly be known as a sadhu. We call someone a sadhu who is in favor of light and is against darkness; the one who is in favor of good and against evil. We call that one a sadhu who is a saint, and not a Satan. But basically our sadhu is nothing but a projection of our mind, he is not Kabir's sadhu.

Kabir's sadhu is the one for whom all differences have disappeared. He lives in an undivided state. For him there is no longer any duality, he lives in the state of non-dualism, he has attained oneness. In that oneness how can there be a saint or a Satan? How can there be a gentleman and a scoundrel? What will be a sin or a virtue there? All distinctions are maya, illusion. The very distinctions are the root of maya.

Someone who is lost in divisions will become complicated. A man who lives in non-duality is truly a sadhu – he is simple, he is ordinary. He never chooses on his own; he never brings in his own desire. He simply flows, just like one floats in the river without swimming. He is willing to go where the river takes him, and wherever he reaches will be his destination. Even if the river drowns him in the middle, for him that will be the shore.

And Kabir says again and again, "Listen, O sadhu!" He is pointing at the one within you who is simple and innocent. How will you find that simple and innocent one? Will you have to do any complicated spiritual practice, do yoga postures, stand on your head or chant mantras for hours? If you have to do something to find it, then remember it is not simple and innocent. Because, it is basically a matter of understanding, it is a matter of awareness.

When you realize that all is one, simplicity manifests on its own accord. Hence, Kabir insists on effortless enlightenment. Effortless means that which you will not be required to achieve through practice.

*Sadhu* means that which flowers out of understanding; for which no effort is made, no strain is taken. Whichever way you are, wherever you are, the door opens without you moving an inch. Because the moment you make a move, complications will arise. So that which is attained out of effort cannot be spontaneous.

"Listen, O sadhu" – and here I am also addressing the hidden sadhu within you. Inside you, the intellect is the essence of complexity, and the heart is the essence of simplicity. The heart knows neither good nor bad. The heart is without arithmetic. The heart does not know the skill of cutting, the heart is not a pair of scissors. The heart knows the art of uniting. The heart works like a needle and a thread.

Once, someone presented a pair of golden scissors to Farid...

Farid was Kabir's contemporary. They met once. It was a really sweet meeting. Both stayed together for two days but kept silent. Not a word was exchanged between the two. Both hugged each other, both sat together and had a good laugh. Kabir went to welcome Farid at the edge of the village and went again to give him a send-off. But for two days not a word was spoken between the two. The disciples of both said: "What's the matter? We got bored, we got tired, we had high hopes that we would hear some conversation, learn something. Two days have been wasted."

Farid said: "One who speaks is ignorant. If I had spoken, I would have been seen as ignorant; if Kabir had spoken, he would have been seen as ignorant."

Kabir told his disciples: "There was nothing to talk about because we both know; both of us have known oneness. Now who is there to speak to? Who is there to listen? And there is no point in repeating, making a meaningless effort, when we both already know. Farid is exactly where I am. We both are nobodies. For you, we were two, for us we were just one. You wanted us to have a dialogue, but if we had done that we would have looked like fools. Actually, it would have been only a monologue. The other was not there, who could I have talked to?"

There can be discussion if two ignorant people meet, a lot in fact. There can be a discussion if a meeting takes place between a wise man and an ignorant man – although not much is understood. But how can there be any conversation when two wise men meet? Absolutely nothing is said, and yet everything is understood. Not a word is heard, and yet all is understood. But two ignorant people get into a lot of discussion, a lot is heard, too much noise happens, but nothing is understood.

A wise man and an ignorant person also talk. If the ignorant one is willing, he can gain much from such talk. If he is a little open, if he has some heart quality and is not all intellect, a few seeds can sprout in his heart.

Once someone gave Farid a pair of golden scissors as a gift. Farid said: "Please forgive me, but what will I do with these scissors? We are not in the business of cutting, our business is that of mending. If you really wish to give something, then bring a needle and thread."

Real saints are in the business of mending, uniting. The heart is in the business of uniting. The intellect's business is to divide. Priests divide, saints unite. The world is divided today because of the priests – there are three hundred religions, all because of the priests. The priest looks for the minutest difference. Real saints look for the indivisible; they look for that which unifies the two divisions. Priests look for that which is the divisive factor between the two. But the real conflict is not between the saint and the non-saint; the real conflict is between the saint and the priest. The real conflict is not between the saint and the sinner; it is between the saint and the priest.

Religions are born through saints and the priests destroy them. And as soon as a religion is born, the priests overpower it.

The heart that you carry within constitutes saintliness. Why? – because the heart inside you is untrained. Intellect has received training; the intellect has been created by the society. Existence has made the heart. There is no way to educate the heart, there is no university where your heart can be educated. No method has yet been discovered for teaching love – and we are fortunate that no such method has yet been found. There will be no greater misfortune than the day it is found. Then that day you will turn into a machine. Your intellect has already become mechanical, but your heart is a little less mechanical. Existence still beats in your heart. Existence still echoes in your heart. Your intellect, on the other hand, is absolutely mechanical and is a creation of society.

You won't be able to attain godliness through the intellect. That's the reason why no one can reach there with the help of scriptures. One reaches through the heart, through love, through prayer, through trust. It is your heart that is being addressed when *sadhu* is being talked about. So, don't think about what is being said here, just try to understand. The heart understands, intellect thinks – and there is no meeting point between the two. Intellect gives big arguments; heart has the ability to see. The heart has eyes, while intellect merely gropes like a blind man. Intellect is like a blind man's stick, which is used to figure out the way. The heart is able to see, it doesn't need to figure out. Logical arguments are useless; the heart sees and finds the way.

*Listen, O sadhu!* means "Listen through your heart; listen with simplicity. Don't listen through logic and thinking, listen with feelings and love." Only one who listens this way will be able to understand.

Let's now look at Kabir's words. Pay attention to each word and let it penetrate your heart.

***I know Maya is a great deceiver.***

What does maya mean? That which makes "one" look like "two" is the essence of maya. For example, you get drunk, and you see a man coming toward you on the street but it appears to you that two men are coming; you begin to see two houses instead of one; you see two doors instead of one.

Once, Mulla Nasruddin was seeing off a friend. They kept drinking till late into the night. And when it was time to say good-bye, the street was deserted and the night was dark. The friend asked Nasruddin for directions.

Nasruddin said, "Just remember one thing about the road: when you go a hundred steps you will see two roads. Make sure you turn left, because there is no road on the right side, it just appears so. I am telling you this based on my experience, because many times I took the right turn and got lost. There is just no road on that side."

Once, Mulla Nasruddin was sitting in a pub explaining something to his son. He said, "Look, son. There are four people sitting in that corner, when you begin to see them as eight understand it is time to stop drinking, and then just start walking home."

His son said, "But father, I see only two people."

Nasruddin had already had too much.

When you are drunk, you shake within and because of that you find objects outside shaking too. When you are drunk, you get divided into two.

There is one element within you which can never get drunk – your consciousness can never become unconscious. The intoxicant enters your body, your mind, but it can never enter your soul. As soon as the intoxicant goes inside you, you get divided into two parts – your soul is separate, your body and mind are separate. In fact, body and mind are actually one, there is not much difference between the two. They are gross and subtle manifestations respectively of the same element. So when you get divided within, everything begins to tremble. When you begin to tremble inside, everything begins to tremble outside.

Maya is an intoxicant. Kabir says, "Maya is a great deceiver. I have come to know that Maya is a great deceiver and because of it there are two of everything."

***Formless, carrying a noose in her hand,***
***she wanders around, speaking with a sweet tongue.***
***She takes the form of Kamala with Keshava, and Bhavani with Shiva.***

Try to understand this concept.

Rama is accompanied by Sita, Krishna is with Radha, Shiva is with Bhavani, Vishnu is with Lakshmi. Hindus have given a lot of thought to choosing these symbols. It is because of you, because you are divided into two. The divine cannot be one for you. In your intoxicated state and because of it, your inner shaking, the maya within you – the element of illusion – makes you see Shiva and Bhavani as two. The moment your shaking stops, suddenly you will find Shiva and Bhavani becoming one. That's what the statue of Ardhanarishwar shows. The moment your trembling stops, you will see the two disappearing: Lakshmi disappears into Vishnu, Vishnu disappears into Lakshmi. Only one remains.

The two are because of you, because you are unsteady. Who is making you tremble? Although you have not had a drink, you are a drunkard. And you have taken many different kinds of drinks of which you have no knowledge.

You are drunk with attachment, you are drunk with infatuation, you are drunk with ego, you are drunk with envy, jealousy, ambition, hatred, anger and greed – who knows how many kinds of drinks you have consumed? A drink means that which makes you unconscious. Alcohol is sold not just in bottles, alcohol is available in every part and particle of life. It is available everywhere if you want to go and grab it.

An alcoholic drink is something that makes you tremble within. An alcoholic drink means that which causes such unconsciousness that it makes it difficult for you to see properly, your eyes lose the ability to see, or you begin to see that which is not there at all; or, you begin to see that which never was. When you are filled with anger, you begin to see something else.

For example, you fall in love with a woman, or a woman falls in love with a man. So when you fall in love with a woman she looks very beautiful. It feels as if never before has such a beauty appeared in the world, that she is unmatched. Till yesterday, the woman was just ordinary; you had seen her many times on the road. What happened suddenly today? A little attachment has grown within you. An attraction has arisen inside you. Some kind of drunkenness has overtaken you.

The woman is the same as she was yesterday. She cannot suddenly become beautiful today. Something has changed inside *you*. You have gone a little cuckoo. Today the woman is looking supremely beautiful. But what you are seeing today is not real. What you are seeing today is nothing but an extension of your dream. The woman has become like a screen and you are watching your own dream projected on it.

Stay with her for a few days, get married to her, and soon the dream will begin to wither away because dreams cannot go on for long. The very characteristic of dreams is that sometimes they are and sometimes they are not. Nobody can see a dream for twenty-four hours. Also, no one can remain drunk for twenty-four hours. And there is no way to stay drunk forever.

Only truth can remain forever, not a dream. Within a few days the woman begins to look ordinary. Although you go on stretching the dream, you also realize the dream is coming close to crumbling apart. It can hardly continue for even a month or two. And when the dream falls into pieces a feeling of aversion, sadness, depression surrounds you. Now you look at the same woman with sadness and in a state of depression and she becomes ordinary. Once she was way up at the top and now she falls down into a ditch. Before her body appeared to be made of gold, now she stinks. Before you never saw her perspire – you couldn't see her sweating – now her body gives off a foul odor. Before everything was smelling good, now everything is stinking. Now you will see her in anger and with hatred and the woman will look very ugly. But the woman is the same – or the man is the same – nothing has changed in this regard. All the change is happening inside you.

Kabir says: "*I know Maya is the great deceiver.*" Maya is the trick within you which makes you unconscious. Maya is the system which makes you fall asleep. Maya is the process of your dreaming.

Let's say someone is crazy after money. You cannot imagine that craziness if you are not so crazy. What does he get from making so much of money? You should look at his eyes when he opens his safe; he looks at money like a lover looks at his beloved. No poet has ever looked with such ecstasy at the beauty of his poetic world as a person mad after money does on seeing the contents of his safe. You should look into his eyes at that moment, how they glitter, how many dreams float around.

If you are mad after money and you see the Kohinoor lying on the street, you will lose all your senses. And the Kohinoor is just a stone. But everything will change inside you. The Kohinoor will create a situation that awakens all the dormant intoxicants inside you. And then, what you see in the Kohinoor will be your projection; the Kohinoor doesn't have it.

Whatsoever you see in the world is not there. It is all your projection. Look how much a greedy person covets a position or runs after status! People run after such things like crazy.

One night Mulla Nasruddin was returning home. It was the rainy season and it was drizzling. On the way he met the local politician of the town. He said: "Nasruddin, how come you are out without an umbrella?"

Nasruddin didn't want to say he had no umbrella and that these days he couldn't afford one either. Nasruddin said: "This is a spiritual practice, this is meditation, it gives a great experience. God is showering and you, you idiot, are standing with your umbrella up? Is this the way? Close your umbrella and just see; it will be a great revelation. God will reveal great truths!"

The politician didn't believe him, but then he thought: "What is the harm in doing it?"

Next day he returned very angry. He said: "Nasruddin, there is a limit to making fun of someone. I had a fever the whole night. I did exactly as you had said. When everyone went to bed, I went outside and stood in the rain. Nothing happened except that the water went down my neck into my clothes. I felt cold and began shivering. I asked myself what kind of stupid thing I was doing. Am I an idiot or have I gone mad?"

Nasruddin said: "Is this not a tiny revelation? Such an experience, at just the first attempt! Is this a small achievement? Keep on practicing and you will have many more such experiences."

Man cannot find God on the outside unless his inner condition changes, because otherwise whatever he finds will be nothing but that same unconscious world. Whatsoever you see, will, after all, be seen through *your* eyes. Whatsoever you achieve, *you*, after all, will be the achiever. The real issue is not that of searching for God, the real issue is that of getting over the inner unconsciousness. Wherever an unconscious man goes, he will face nothing but unconsciousness.

If maya disappears from within, if the inner sleep and dreams disappear, you will attain God right where you are. He surrounds you. There is no one except him. It is really a miracle how you have escaped him. How you have lost him is indeed a miracle. Certainly you are in a deep sleep.

Someone asked, "Who is a sadhu?"

I replied, "One who is awake is a sadhu."

"And who is a non-sadhu?"

"One who is asleep."

You have within a system for waking up and also a system for going to sleep. You have within the potential for seeing the dream and also for knowing the truth. You can wake up and you can go to sleep – both potentialities are within you. Maya is the potentiality to go to sleep.

You watch a dream at night. In order to see a dream one thing is needed – and that is that you go to sleep. It is difficult to see a dream while awake. In order to see a dream one needs to be asleep. And the way you are seeing the world now: you see God in money; you see beauty in blood, bones and marrow; you see in food the whole juice of life; in clothes you see the whole art of weaving; you see meaning in the meaningless; you don't know what is meaningful – all this shows one thing very clearly: you are asleep and dreaming.

*I know Maya is the great deceiver.* Maya is not some kind of a philosophical doctrine. The philosophers grabbed it and made great doctrines out of it. And they have created a great confusion. If you were to read these philosophers, it would be very difficult for you to figure out what actually maya is because they have given different interpretations. Someone says, maya is God's power; somebody else says, maya is God's shadow. And they are in great difficulty. For example, Shankaracharya has great difficulty in explaining where maya comes from; because, if everything is *brahman*, then from where is maya born? He has no answer. There cannot be an answer.

But if you look closely, maya is a psychological concept. It is not a philosophical concept. Maya has nothing to do with *brahman*, with existence. Maya is concerned with you. Maya is *your* shadow, not *brahman*'s. And maya is another name for your inner unconsciousness. So, as you become conscious within, as you become more alert and able to witness, maya will begin to disappear.

If maya is a fundamental component of *brahman*, then how would you be able to let it go? Then how would you wake up? If maya were part of *brahman*, how would you be able to destroy it? No, maya is part of you. So don't get involved in the discussion of *brahman*. Until the maya within you breaks down, you won't be able to know *brahman*. Maya is a very significant word. Maya means exactly what *magic* means. The root word is the same.

You have within you an amazing capacity to invent dreams. For example, you are walking down a dark street, you are afraid – afraid of the darkness, afraid of being alone, afraid of the unknown road: you are trembling with fear. Fear is a part of maya. When the leaves shake, you think someone is approaching. You interpret the sound of moving leaves as someone's footsteps – all because of your fear. Had it been daytime, had there been daylight, had there been people on the street, you would not have worried about the leaves making a sound. But now, the dry leaves are moving in the wind, you stop immediately, startled – it feels like someone is coming. It is not even necessary that the leaves move – if there is enough fear, even your own footsteps in the lonely street make you feel as if someone is following you.

Go to the cemetery some day and see for yourself. You will see so many things that are actually not there, and you will see them so vividly that you will find your own presence powerless and their presence much stronger. And if you run away out of fear, the more afraid you will be, the more…

Have you ever noticed? If you pass through a cemetery and you do not know it is a cemetery, nothing will happen. No ghosts will appear on the road. No drums will sound. No light will appear. No lamp will move from one end to another. If you don't know it is a cemetery, you will pass through it merrily. And if you are told it is a cemetery, though actually it may not be, you will get into trouble.

A friend of mine would always boast about his being fearless. Someone who boasts about not being afraid knows that he is fearful, otherwise no need to boast. We always boast about the opposite.

Once he was my guest and I asked him: "Are you not even afraid of ghosts?"

He said: "Why should I be afraid of ghosts? They are all part of imagination. I am not afraid of anybody. Bring ghosts in front of me."

I said: "Wait, you have come at the right time."

He got a little scared. He said: "What do you mean?"

I said: "The house in front of us is a hangout for ghosts. I will arrange for your bed to be put there. No one else will be there, just the ghosts and you."

He laughed a little but now his laughter was hollow. He said: "I am not afraid...but why should I go there?"

I said: "If you are not afraid, then what is the fear in going there?"

Now he was caught! He said: "Okay!" But then he became very sad.

No one had ever heard of there being ghosts in the house in front – there were none. But an oil merchant used the house as a depot for storing empty containers. So no one really lived there. But empty containers make a sound in summer – because of the heat they expand in the day and shrink at night. And there were about a thousand or two thousand containers stored in the house. So the sound would pass from one container to another. A wonderful play of "ghosts" used to take place in that house.

So I arranged for a bed to be put in the house on the second floor, escorted my friend to the bed and went back home. Around two o'clock at night I heard a loud noise of shouting and screaming. My friend, standing on the balcony, was going totally crazy and shouting, "Save me!"

I asked: "What are you afraid of? I have left the key with you, come down and get out."

He said: "I will have to pass through the same room where the ghosts are having fun."

It became quite a problem; how to get him down? He asked for a ladder. So a ladder was brought, but he was trembling so much that he fell off the ladder. I tried to convince him there was nothing in the house, but he said: "I cannot believe it. It is just not possible to believe nothing is there. With my own eyes I have seen ghosts continuously coming out of one container and entering into another."

Now he doesn't boast, at least not in front of me. And since then he has become a great believer in ghosts. I told him there was really nothing in the house. I explained the whole thing to him: that the containers make a noise.

He said: "Just forget it. It was a different matter before I experienced it. Now I am talking from my own experience."

This experiencing is maya. And, when elderly people speak about this world from their own experience, it too is maya; it is this type of experience. Only the experience of a person who has awakened from maya is meaningful. All other experiences are of this type. Such an experience has no value because it is born out of your imagination, out of your inner unconsciousness.

Hence, Kabir says: I know, Maya is a great deceiver. Formless, carrying a noose in her hand, she wanders around, speaking with a sweet tongue. She takes the form of Kamala with Keshava, and Bhavani with Shiva. He is saying, what greater miracle can there be than the one which is without attribute. You are without any attribute, you are brahman, you are the ultimate energy of the universe – formless, pure. What greater miracle can there be? Maya has hooked onto the attribute-less and is moving with it hand in hand.

*I know Maya is a great deceiver. ...speaking with a sweet tongue.* Maya's words are very sweet. They are bound to be, otherwise how could she have hooked so many people! She supplies very pleasant dreams. She creates a great show all around. The dream becomes so profound, so psychedelic, that you cannot stop. You have to go on the journey. You have to go in search of dreams.

Everyone is chasing his own dreams. But you will never realize these dreams because they don't exist at all. At the end you will find yourself empty-handed and sad. You will finally come to realize that even after attaining everything your hands are still empty, just as having not attained anything your hands are also empty. Ultimately you will see: death approaches and all dreams disappear and you wasted a valuable opportunity given to you in life.

You could have known truth, instead you kept chasing dreams. Children run after butterflies, but if you watch closely you will find even adults chasing butterflies. The butterflies may have changed – because adults are more experienced – but the chase never changes. The chasing after butterflies continues. We ask a little child if he has gone crazy, what will he do if he catches a butterfly? But what are adults running after? What are *you* running after? Once you were a child and caught butterflies. Your children will become adults and then they will ask their children why they are chasing after butterflies. But the fact remains that grown-ups too keep chasing butterflies.

If one needs to choose, children's butterflies seem more realistic than those of the adults. The grown-ups are running after banknotes, they are running after status; Delhi is their salvation, they are on their way to Delhi! Money is their soul, they are counting money. Children collect rocks and stones; grown-ups collect diamonds and jewelry – what's the difference? There is no difference at all between ordinary rocks and diamonds. If there were no human being on the earth, what difference would there be between an ordinary stone and the Kohinoor? Would the Kohinoor be able to say with arrogance, "I am special"? But even great emperors…

Ranjeet Singh owned the Kohinoor. After his death Queen Victoria had her eyes on it: she wanted to have it by any means. Victoria had everything. Her Empire was so big that the sun never set on it. But the Kohinoor was hurting her heart like a wound. And to tease her, Ranjeet Singh used to hang the Kohinoor on his horse. He would not wear it, he would hang it around the horse's neck.

After Ranjeet Singh's death, as his son was still a minor, Victoria called him over to England. He could not be the king until he became an adult, so until then the British Empire took over the responsibility for his education. The boy used to tell people: "The real interest is in the Kohinoor, not in me and the woman is a thief." And the Kohinoor was finally stolen. The British Empire took the Kohinoor under the excuse that the boy was still a minor and might lose it. The Kohinoor was never returned after that.

Victoria had everything and yet she kept an eye on the stone. Even grown-ups collect rocks and stones. The butterflies that children collect are at least alive: your butterflies are absolutely dead. But the chase continues because maya is the same. The same maya is within children as in the grown-ups. Until you wake up, until you are awakened and born again, whatsoever you do will be stupid. Everything that comes out of maya will be stupid.

It is important to understand one thing clearly: when I talk about maya I have nothing to do with the doctrine of maya and *brahman*. Kabir too has nothing to do with any doctrine. Maya is the process of becoming unconscious inside yourself, it is the state of your being asleep. You are living in the state of a somnambulist. And you are surrounded by dreams.

So meditation is useful. Because meditation is the technique to destroy maya: how you can wake up so that maya can be shattered into pieces. And if you see the world after waking up, you won't find the world at all, you will see *brahman*. You will not be able to see the truth as long as maya is within you.

*Formless, carrying a noose in her hand, she wanders around, speaking with a sweet tongue.* She has a very sweet tongue, she traps everyone with it. When you hear the sound of a rupee coin, how sweet it sounds! When you see the beauty in the face of a woman, how sweet it looks. When you are attracted to status, how sweet the status appears. Later all becomes bitter, but the beginning is very sweet. It is the same as taking sugarcoated pills – we are willing to take the poison just as long as it has a little touch of maya in it. Later all the poison becomes apparent, but by then it is too late.

Remember: the experience which first gives happiness and then is followed by misery, know that it has come out of maya; and the opposite: the experience which feels painful in the beginning but is followed by happiness, know that it has not come out of maya.

The definition of spiritual fire, *tapa*, is where pain comes first, followed by happiness. And the definition of sensual gratification is simply where pleasure in the beginning is followed by misery. Happiness – the servant of maya – will always be there to welcome you, but misery is hiding behind. In going through the spiritual fire, in pursuing spiritual discipline when you are full of search for the truth – when you are filled with the desire to attain liberation and keep going – first you will find it painful. If you get too scared of facing that pain, you will never wake up from maya. But if you accept the pain, then soon that pain disappears and the doors to the greatest happiness open up.

Choosing pain consciously is to go through spiritual fire. Chasing happiness is like chasing butterflies. And the funny thing is: those who run after happiness find misery and those who accept misery become worthy of bliss. This equation needs to be understood very clearly because without understanding this equation maya cannot be destroyed, you cannot escape its sweet tongue. It creates a sweet dream.

***She takes the form of Kamala with Keshava, and Bhavani with Shiva.***
***She works as an idol for the priest, and is the water at the holy places.***

***She is Yogini with the yogi, and in the King's palace she is the queen.***
***To some, she is a diamond; to some, she is a broken cowrie shell.***
***She is a bhakti for the devotee, and the Brahmani of Brahma.***

Kabir says: ***Listen, O sadhu! All this is an indescribable story.***

Kabir is saying, "I am telling you something that cannot be told, it is an indescribable story. It cannot be told because you can talk about only such things which are logical. It is difficult to talk about things that are totally against logic."

Language is the vehicle for logic. Only that which is logical can be explained through it. But this story sounds unreasonable: that you are suffering because of your own doing. One may say this cannot be possible, we want happiness; how can we become miserable because of our own doing? That's why we always say we get misery from others. The husband is getting it from the wife, the wife is getting it from the husband; the son is unhappy because of the father, the father is miserable because of the son. We always think we are miserable because of others, this sounds logical. Why would we become miserable through our own doing? We want happiness.

This story is indeed beyond description. You are miserable because you want happiness. This is totally illogical, but that's the truth. As long as you seek happiness, you will be miserable. And the day you become agreeable to misery, you will be free from getting it. The story is really indescribable.

It will look contradictory. If someone says you have gone astray because you are searching, if someone says if you stop you will find it – this will look very contradictory. A very inexpressible thing indeed! But that's the truth. As long as you keep running, you won't find it because that which you are seeking is hidden within you. As long as you keep running, you will keep wandering because you yourself is what you are looking for.

Where do you think you will end up, running? And the more you run, the more you will forget yourself in excitement. Stop!

This story is incommunicable. Those who stop, find it. It is a paradox. Logic will not agree with it. What will logic say? Logic will say: if you run and still don't find it, then run a little faster. The arithmetic is clear. If despite running after it you do not get it, then it means the speed is not enough – you need to run faster. Or, if you do not find it even by running after it, then that means the direction is wrong. Then find the right direction. Logic will say: change direction, increase the speed, and somehow reach there. But, if the place you want to reach, your destination, is hiding right inside you then regardless of which direction you may go – any direction – it will be the wrong direction. Because it has nothing to do with which direction you go in. Inside you...

We have never considered the inner direction. Generally, people say there are ten directions. I say there are eleven. Ten are outside – eight all around, one below, one above. And what about the direction leading you inside? But geography never counts it. We have left it out and where we have left it out is the place to find it.

That which you are looking for is hiding inside you. You are searching for yourself. So, regardless of which direction you choose, all directions will prove wrong; whichever path you may choose, you are bound to go astray. And it is not a question of running slowly or fast. No matter how fast you may run, the faster you run the farther away you will go.

Stop! Drop all directions! Drop all the ten directions! Stay where you are! Stay inside exactly where you are. Leave all paths. This is what being natural means. No path, no effort, nowhere to go, no running, asanas, exercise, spiritual discipline – nothing. Just stop quietly where you are. All that you are searching for is hiding right there.

Maya is nothing but the chase; to stop is to attain *brahman*. The moment you stop, you will find it. If you choose to run, then you will have to move in thoughts. While running, help from the mind is necessary. Mind is a machine; it shows the way, it shows the difficulties on the path. It creates the ways and means for how to tread the path. Mind will be needed if you want to make the journey. And the longer the journey you want to take the more the mind will be needed. Mind has to be dropped, only then will you be able to achieve.

Mind is maya. The moment mind stops, there is no longer any journey to be taken – not even a pilgrimage. The moment you become silent and settled down inside, not a ripple of thought arises, know that you have reached. You have reached the destination. And then you will laugh about how much you ran to find it. Then you will laugh, realizing it was because of your running that you were not able to find it. Then you will laugh at what a fool you were: *you* were the cause of misery and you thought others were giving it to you.

As long as you believe others are the cause of your misery, you are bound to go astray. No one else is responsible for your misery except your own way of living. The way you live is wrong – it is wrapped in maya.

Just think: you are robbed. A robber came and stole your money. Do you think the robber gave you a lot of misery? What misery can a robber give you? You were miserable because of your attachment to money. If you had not been attached and the robber had stolen your money, would that have made you miserable? In that case you would have felt happy and relieved to have been freed from that burden. Perhaps you would have thanked the thief for taking away the load. But because there is attachment to money, the thief causes misery.

Let us say: your wife dies, you weep and cry aloud. Did death give you the pain? You say: Oh God, why are you so hard on me? You say: What a misfortune and why has it happened to me? Why not to others? Why me? I offer my prayers every day, I go to the temple, I read the Gita, I read the Koran and I go to the mosque and pray five times – and this is what I get!

Is God giving you pain? Is fate giving you pain or is your attachment causing the pain? You were tied to the woman and you believed she was your happiness. Now that the woman is no longer alive you ask how you are going to find happiness. This is the reason why you are suffering.

Remember, whenever you are miserable it is all because of you. And the moment this awareness that you are the cause of misery becomes intense, you will begin to put an end to the process that brings misery. But if you wish to be miserable, then that's a different matter. Go ahead and walk on that path, but then don't complain; don't tell anyone you are suffering because of someone else. Then it will be your preference. If you want to be miserable, then that's alright. But then no complaint. If you don't want to be miserable, then try to understand the basic reasons causing misery.

Someone calls you a bad name and you get angry. You say: it is clear, if this man had not abused me, I would neither have been angry nor would I have been unhappy. No one gets angry just because someone calls him a bad name. You become angry because you are carrying an ego, which gets hurt when you are abused. You have created an egoistic view of yourself: here I am, a well-respected person, and this man is insulting me; he is ruining my reputation. The ego gets hurt when you are abused. But if there is no ego inside, then the invective will pass by like a breeze. You will remain untouched.

Just think: this must have happened to you many times. Your foot gets hurt and then the whole day you are hurt in the same place again and again. You bump into a ladder or a man bumps into you. You pass by a chair and the chair hurts you. You wear shoes and the shoes hurt you. You go for a shower and the water troubles you. Something or other goes on happening. And you wonder because this never happened any day before. Now that you are hurt the whole world seems to be interested in hurting you.

No, the world is not interested in hurting you. This was happening every day but there was no wound to get hurt, So you never felt it. Every day you hit against the chair on this same spot, your shoes used to touch the same spot. Every day your son would come home, climb onto your feet, but because there was no wound you never felt it. Today you are feeling it.

Someone calls you a bad name; you get hurt because the ego is like a wound inside you. Someone praises you and you are delighted; someone condemns you and you are dejected. What kind of slavery is this? And no one else is responsible for this; you alone are responsible. As you keep looking deeply into the miseries in your life, you will find that somewhere you alone are responsible. That's where maya is. Drop all that which is causing you pain, remove it. If someone abuses you, tell him you are very thankful for it and then get rid of the wound at the place where you are hurt.

Kabir has said: keep your critics close, give them a place in your home. Just go and bring home the man who calls you a bad name. Tell him: "My friend, stay close to me. If you stay away, then who knows, you may abuse me or you may not; we may meet each other or we may not. So better stay here in my house, I will prepare a room for you." Make a beautiful place for him to stay with you so that he may always be around you and you continue to experience your ego.

And the main thing is dropping the ego. The real issue is how to bring some change within. But how will you change? If you make the other responsible then you will never look within yourself.

This inner blindness is called maya. And this maya takes many forms. There is no end to how many forms it can take.

It takes whatever form you want it to take because maya is a dream. It is not made of matter, which you would find difficult to give a form to.

So, Kabir says, if the statue itself turns into maya for a devotee, then he holds it with great care.

I was once a guest. As I came out to take a bath and was crossing a room, I saw the *Guru Granth Sahib*, the book of Nanak's teachings, and nearby I saw a metal mug and a toothbrush. I was a little puzzled seeing the metal mug and the toothbrush there. My host explained these had been kept there for *Guru Granth Sahib* to brush his teeth in the morning. There was just the book, not even a statue. The toothbrush was for the book *Guru Granth Sahib*.

One could have somehow understood it if it had been a statue. Even that is stupid, because someone has made the statue, you have bought it at the market and you put the metal mug and the toothbrush near it. But to keep them beside a book is going too far. It has gone so far because the name of the book is *Guru Granth Sahib*. The book is personified by using the word *sahib*. So *Guru Granth Sahib* will be offered food; will be put to bed; will be woken up.

Kabir says: "She is bhakti for the devotee. She is Yogini with the yogi, and in the King's palace she is the queen. She works as an idol for the priest, and is water at the holy places. She has taken on many forms in the world." The problem is: whatever you become fond of, whatever your attachment is, wherever your blindness finds its way, wherever you feel emotional, immediately maya will take form. Now you become emotional about the book and the book turns into maya. You become emotionally attached to me and that will turn into maya. Then you will be in trouble because of me. Wherever maya will be, the trouble is bound to begin. Wake up!

*I know Maya is a great deceiver!* Wake up! See within yourself how many and what kinds of forms *you* have created – you, yourself! Only understanding is needed, no need to break these forms. The moment you will come to understand, you will laugh seeing the mug and the toothbrush in front of *Guru Granth Sahib*. The moment you will have an understanding, you will laugh at how you are kneeling with folded hands and talking to the statue in the temple. You are a fool. Who are you talking to?

People get angry, unhappy or happy with the statue. This is very interesting. You ask for employment for your son. If, by coincidence, he finds a job you become happy. You talk to the statue. You say: "You have been very kind; without you nothing would have happened, the boy has got a job." If he doesn't find a job, you become angry and get ready to throw the statue away.

I have seen people who, in anger, have thrown a statue into a well, because so many days had passed with praying, worshipping, but no one cared, no one satisfied them.

I know a man who was once an atheist but then became a theist. I asked him: "What happened? You were such an atheist!"

He said: "I had to believe. My son was not finding a job, every effort was made. I tried to please people, a bribe was given; nothing worked. Finally, when there was no way left I went to the temple and there I said if my son gets a job within fifteen days, I will become your devotee forever. Now I have become a devotee of Lord Hanuman."

How is poor Lord Hanuman responsible for finding a job for his son? There is no connection. Lord Hanuman has not opened some kind of employment agency. And even if he opened one, he would rather employ monkeys than men! Everyone has his own relatives to look after.

I told this man: "You don't even look like a monkey."

He said: "What do you mean?"

I said: "Lord Hanuman will take care of you! You are unnecessarily taking yourself to be so important."

This is the reason why the man became a theist. Now, as a devotee, every Tuesday he receives the offerings made in the temple. But the man cannot be trusted; because if the son loses his job, he will get angry. If the wife dies and Lord Hanuman doesn't save her… How many times can Lord Hanuman come to his rescue? He will bring a thousand and one problems. And the moment he finds his work is not done… This man is not trustworthy at all. His devotion is part and parcel of maya. His prayer and worship are fake.

Where there is desire how can there be any worship or prayer? Wherever there is desire, there is lust. Lust has nothing whatsoever to do with prayer. And the moment lust disappears, then what is left for prayer? For what would you offer your prayer when your whole life becomes a prayer? What then remains to be done separately? You live with a prayerful heart, filled with gratitude… The whole world is giving you so much, more than you want. What existence has given you is manifold more than you are worthy of. What worthiness can you claim? You have been awarded life, isn't that enough? You need a job first, only then will you worship? You have been given such great potential to wake up, to attain consciousness so that you may become enlightened – isn't that enough for you? You first need employment, only then will you express your gratitude?

The devotee feels: whatever has been given is more than I need. A non-devotee's prayer is: whatever I have is not enough, I need more. If you think in such terms, you will find more non-devotees in temples than devotees because for a devotee the whole existence is a temple. Wherever he is, there is the temple. And whatsoever he is doing is prayer.

Kabir has said: whatsoever I do is worship. No one ever saw Kabir going to a temple. That's why the priests and the pundits of Varanasi never gave him recognition. At the time of his death Kabir asked that he be taken to Magahar. The legend is that people who die in Varanasi attain liberation and people who die in Magahar are reborn as donkeys.

Kabir lived his whole life in Varanasi, but before dying he asked his disciples: "Take me to Magahar. I don't want to die in Varanasi. Because what's so special about dying in Varanasi and reaching heaven? I want to go to heaven dying in Magahar." Just a joke made by Kabir. He was a man of courage. He was a man who had great trust. If you trust existence, then what difference does it make if you die in Varanasi or in Magahar?

People go to Varanasi to die. They live in Magahar like donkeys and die in Varanasi in the hope of reaching heaven. Kabir lived in Varanasi like a saint and went to Magahar to die. People think: live whichever way you want but die in Varanasi. They believe: live as you please, but at the time of death remember Rama and drink water from the Ganges – that's all.

You are very clever, very smart. Even your religion is nothing but an extension of your smartness. You believe, live, whichever way you like – with maya – but when dying evoke the name of Rama. But remember, you won't even be able to utter the name of Rama because what will come out at the time of death is all that which you have lived during your life. Alone, the whole essence of your life will go along with you at the moment of death.

So the priests repeat the name of Rama in the ear of a dying man. The dying man himself is in no state to utter Rama's name. In fact, in his mind he is accumulating maya. He is taking account of what he got in life and complaining about what he did not get. In his mind, he is preparing to enter the new world, to enter the new womb. He is doing this so that he may complete what has remained incomplete in this life. He could fill the iron safe which has remained empty; he could have the woman he should have had but did not get; he could attain what he wanted but did not. He is collecting within all the possible seeds of maya.

Before leaving the body his soul will collect all the seeds of maya so that the journey may continue after entering a new womb. And the priest is a hired man. The man who is hired to repeat Rama's name in his ears is thinking about the five rupees he will earn for doing so. This is very interesting. The dying man is collecting maya inside. And the man who is repeating Rama's name in his ears is calculating the maya he is going to get – and in between poor Rama is caught.

Kabir is right when he says: *Formless, carrying a noose in her hand, she wanders around, speaking with a sweet tongue.* All seem to be caught in the noose – the temple priests, priests at the holy places, the worshippers. Maya's forms change but not the trap. Wherever you find yourself trapped, search within and you will find maya. And wherever you find the trap, slowly start cutting through it with understanding. I am saying *with understanding* because you may cut it without understanding too. Often people cut through it without understanding, then the matter remains unfinished. Then a new trend starts. You may run away from one wife but somewhere you will find another. You may leave home but end up in an ashram. You were once attached to your home, now you will be attached to the ashram.

Never pluck anything unripe, you cannot pluck something which is not yet ripe. Hence I say, *with understanding*. With understanding means when it is ripe. Try to understand as deeply as you can. Why am I trapped? What is the trap? Why am I chained? Where is the source of this bondage inside me? Go deep within, find the cause, and in every possible way get a good understanding of the cause. The moment you gain the understanding, the cause will disappear. You won't need to pluck anything. For example, a leaf ripens, dries, then even with a small puff of wind it is sure to fall. You won't need an ax to cut it. Often people use an ax to cut. Your so-called monks and mendicants are of this type. They use an ax to cut and a wound is left. Now they try to heal the wound by running after a new situation. The chase remains the same; there is no difference. Names change, forms change, and maya finds a place for it again.

Make it ripe! Be mature! Be aware! Understand! Understanding! Don't be in a hurry. Existence is not in any haste; you also don't need to be in any haste. Patiently allow the understanding to go deep. As you gain more clarity, as you begin to see the pain is not in someone calling you a bad name but rather it is in your ego, then try to understand your ego. The day you come to this understanding, you will find that a dry leaf which was hanging loose has dropped. As soon as it drops, you are free. We ...*know Maya is a great deceiver.*

Kabir says: *Listen, O sadhu. All this is an indescribable story.* We begin with this sutra. The whole story is inexplicable, it cannot be told. And yet, Kabir has described it with great sweetness, with great clarity. He has put it very frankly. There is no web of logic around it. What he has said is very straightforward. His words are those of an illiterate man. Don't create a web of logic; try to understand Kabir directly. If what Kabir feels reaches inside you, you won't have to do anything to attain samadhi.

Understanding is enough. Understanding is the revolution. Understanding is the transformation.

You have to do something because understanding is not proving sufficient. Then you have to do meditation, get into spiritual practice because understanding is not proving to be enough. If there is enough understanding, then nothing remains to be done. Kabir has said: "Everything happens without doing." *Everything happens without doing* – nothing has to be done. But this does not mean you don't have to do anything; you will have to do a lot. Doing all that, your capacity of understanding will grow.

Participate fully in the various meditations that will be conducted in this meditation camp. By doing so you will begin to have, for a few moments, a glimpse of that ultimate state Kabir is pointing to. But if you spare yourself even a little, you will miss. Try to drown yourself totally in meditation. Make every possible effort from your side and leave the rest to existence. If nothing happens even after this, then you are not responsible.

From your side make every effort, then leave it to existence; but don't leave it to existence making only a half-hearted effort from your side. Existence extends a helping hand only when you have made total effort; before that there is no point.

Some travelers were on a journey in a boat. There was a mystic in the boat too. A terrible storm appeared and the boat was about to sink. Everyone started praying on their knees. There was screaming and shouting, "God, save us!" Seeing that only the mystic was sitting silently, everyone was puzzled.

The storm disappeared. Travelers surrounded the mystic and said, "We were expecting something else from you. You are a monk, you should have prayed. While we were all praying, you simply sat there. What's the matter?"

The mystic said, "Until we have finished doing what *we* can do we are not entitled to pray. Existence extends its hand only when we have totally made use of our hands. While there is still something left to be done, existence is not needed."

So drown yourself totally in meditation. If you leave nothing undone, suddenly you will find the hand of existence above your head. Suddenly you will feel you have been uplifted. Suddenly you will find someone carrying you, some boat taking you to the other shore. Everything happens without doing, not before that. First make sure to complete it from your side, after that existence starts working.

Enough for today.

# 2
# The Desert or the Ocean

*Mind and maya are the same,*
*Maya resides in mind.*
*The entire world is confused;*
*to whom shall I go and explain it?*
*You fenced the farm, but it devoured the farm itself.*
*The entire world is puzzled;*
*how shall I explain it?*
*The mind knows everything, and yet still it does the wrong thing.*
*What kind of cleverness is it,*
*that though holding a lamp you fall into a well?*

*The mind is the ocean, and the mind is the wave as well.*
*Many unconscious thoughts are drowned in the waves.*
*Only those who have a discerning heart can understand this, says Kabir.*
*You have lost it through the mind.*
*Now you can only find it through the mind.*
*Mind cannot exist without the mind.*
*A mind, when it becomes a no-mind,*
*is like an egg in which the whole brahman is hidden.*

***The mind is Gorakh and the mind is Govind too.***
***And the same mind is like the Aughad mendicant.***
***One who guards the mind with awareness, and is watchful,***
***automatically becomes the creator.***
***Body yoga is done by one and all, but no one does mind yoga.***
***Once the mind becomes yoga, all else is easily attainable.***
***The mind has become as clean and pure as the water of Ganges.***
***Now the Lord follows you, calling, "Kabir, Kabir!"***

As I said yesterday, maya is not a philosophical doctrine associated with *brahman*. Rather it is a process connected with the mind. Maya is not an ontological matter; it is actually a philosophical matter. So those who look for the principle of maya in scriptures, those who try to work it out by engaging in logical arguments, will miss understanding what maya is. And how can one who has not known maya, ever know *brahman*? How can one who has not known what illusion is ever know what truth is? One who has not understood rightly what darkness is can hardly understand what light is. Only having known what is wrong does one come closer to truth. Truth comes closer as one begins to recognize untruth. There is no other way. The moment one rightly recognizes untruth, suddenly the doors of truth open up.

So the first thing is recognition: where have I gone wrong? Where is the doubt? Where is the confusion? Where have I gone astray? Forget about the destination. Come to understand rightly how you wandered away – suddenly you have arrived home. Don't worry about what the truth is. You won't be able to know it at this point. As long as you are connected with falsehood, there is no way of knowing the truth. As long as *you* are false, how will you be able to know the truth? And what is the way to find truth within? For that, first you will have to recognize what is false.

For example, you visit a physician. He doesn't worry about your health; he is concerned about the disease. His concern is to locate the disease. He diagnoses the disease. It is meaningless to worry about health. If the disease is diagnosed correctly, if the disease is figured out, then it can be eliminated. And when the disease no longer remains, that is indeed health. There is no way of capturing health directly. That is why you may go through all the medical books in the world but you won't come across any definition of what health is. There cannot be any definition of health. There is no way it can be confined in words.

The word *swasthya* for health in Sanskrit is very significant. It means one who is seated in himself. To be rooted in oneself is to be healthy. One who has gone astray from himself is unhealthy. One who has moved away from his center is diseased, and one who has returned to his center is healthy. Being healthy means to be in one's original state. But in order to be in one's original state one has to recognize the disease. The diagnosis is not that of health, it is of the disease. The treatment is not of health, it is of the ailment. And when there is no disease, when you are free from disease, then you are healthy.

There is no way to attain *brahman*. *Brahman* is a state of supreme health. It is possible to understand maya, because it is a disease. And as the diagnosis becomes clear, as your eyes begin to recognize maya, it will start disappearing.

Make sure you understand one thing more. A physician has to make a diagnosis and then give treatment too. But in the case of treating the soul, the diagnosis itself is the remedy. Once the malady is recognized, you are free from it. Then there is no need to give any medicine because the disease is due to illusion. For example, suppose you are walking down a dark road and you see a tree stump along the way that looks like a man – who may be a robber – standing there. The closer you come, the illusion begins to disappear. And if you carried a lamp, you would know instantly that it is a tree stump. Would you then ask how you can get rid of the illusion of a man standing there? No, the moment you recognize the tree stump you are free from the illusion that a man is standing on the road.

The way to attain truth is to recognize the false rightly – there is not even a path to truth. In fact, the moment you recognize the false, truth is instantly attained. So Kabir is first talking about maya, about what maya is.

The first sutra:

***Mind and maya are the same,***
***Maya resides in mind.***
***The entire world is confused;***
***to whom shall I go and explain it?***

So many doctrines about maya have been created; the entire history of India's past is full of them. That is why Kabir says: *The entire world is confused; to whom shall I go and explain it?*

To whom to go and explain it? People are engaged in great debates. They are thinking big, working on great doctrines about maya. They are gathering arguments from the scriptures so they can say, "Your doctrine is wrong, mine is right." *To whom shall I go and explain it?* "The whole world is confused," says Kabir. The matter is very simple; there is no need to look for maya anywhere else. *Mind and maya are the same* – maya is nothing but an extension of the mind.

*Maya resides in the mind.* And you need not destroy maya. The moment you recognize, it merges in the mind itself. Maya is a distortion of the mind; it is the mind's abnormal state. So what is the disease? Even to have a disease, you need to be alive. A dead man never has any disease. The dead enjoy great benefits: they never fall ill; they are never afraid of becoming sick; they don't have to knock on the door of a doctor; they never have to go through the trouble of falling sick. The dead have gained a lot. Now they cannot die again, and so they have no fear of dying.

So one thing is necessary for a disease to exist – to be healthy is to be alive, illness cannot strike without life. That means illness is a distorted form of life. As if life got tangled up somewhere; as if life has somehow gone astray; as if the life current turned in the direction of a desert instead of flowing toward the ocean. And yet, it is still a current of life – whether it goes toward the ocean or toward the desert. Going toward the desert will be straying; the desert will suck your life energy, it will make you impotent, weak. Nothing will be achieved; you will simply wander around, fall – and ultimately get destroyed. Meeting the ocean is the achievement.

One needs to give some thought to this. The river disappears in the desert; it never finds the ocean. It disappears in the ocean too, but then it benefits the ocean. In both cases the disappearance is inevitable. In both cases one needs to erase oneself. But in the one case, by erasing nothing is achieved, while in the other case, by erasing one attains everything.

It is true: one gets lost in the mundane world, but one needs to lose oneself in the divine too. Losing oneself in the mundane world is like a river disappearing in the desert. The river goes dry, begins to rot, screams and shouts, wants to be free from this ordeal, but finds no way out and fragments into thousands of streams. The river is sucked up by the desert. It neither reaches a destination nor does it achieve anything. It does not dance like it does when merging with the ocean. That ultimate moment of ecstasy never comes; the river disappears into nothing, without any purpose, sad and restless.

The river disappears in the ocean too. The phenomenon of disappearance is the same, but the disappearance in the ocean has its own charm. The joy in this disappearance is simply unique. Such disappearance is without any hurt or pain, because although the river vanishes on the one hand, on the other it becomes vast. In fact, it is not losing anything but rather gaining something. The river will certainly disappear as a river, as an insignificant and narrow stream. It will no longer have banks; its old name and form will be gone. But all of it will now be replaced by vastness – the river will have become an ocean. Until then it was small, now it will be boundless. Until then it was confined, now it will be unconfined. Until then it was within limits, now it will be limitless.

Man, human life, also disappears in two ways. First, take maya. Maya means a desert where no matter how much you do, you gain nothing; you keep on running but reach nowhere; you make a lot of noise but there is no melody in life; you struggle a lot but achieve no victory – you end up facing defeat after defeat. Samsara, the world, is nothing but a story of lost battles. Whosoever enters into it, returns defeated. Of course, one gets dissolved into it but that is more like rotting.

You can place a seed on a rock; it will surely cease to exist as a seed – but without sprouting. You may press the same seed down into the soil; here too, it will no longer remain a seed, but, although on the one hand, it disappears, on the other a sprout will appear. It will now live like a bud, but will survive no more as a seed – it will become a gigantic tree. You can, of course, let the seed rot, that is maya. You can also turn the seed into a tree, that is *brahman* – both are hidden within you.

Maya means your going astray. And, your coming back on track is what *brahman* is all about. Just as the illness is yours, so is good health yours. It is good to diagnose your illness so that you may not go astray.

*Mind and maya are the same, Maya resides in the mind.* So once you come to realize it, then what happens to maya? Where does it disappear to? Your energy, which had gone astray, gets back on track. It begins to flow toward the ocean: maya has been absorbed in the mind. For example, you get angry; anger is maya, because in anger you lose something, and gain nothing. You can make this a litmus test: that which makes you lose something inside you and find nothing; that which destroys something inside you and creates nothing; that which causes the seed within you to rot rather than sprout; whenever the river, instead of becoming an ocean dries up – make these your criteria for understanding that this is all maya.

Destructiveness is a disease. Creativity is healthy. When you get angry, you lose energy – but do you gain anything except sorrow and disappointment? You cry and scream, you become sad; and in becoming sad you lose energy – it dries up in the desert. What do you really gain? Have flowers ever bloomed in sadness? Does sadness ever bring a dance to your life? When you hate somebody you certainly waste energy, but then what do you gain in return? What do you achieve?

So always make this a touchstone within yourself: will what I am going to do lead me to the desert or to the ocean? And if it is leading you to the desert, then be alert – that is not your path, that is straying away. What will happen if you do not get angry? The energy saved by not getting angry, where will it go? It will get absorbed in the mind. When you refrain from anger, and when the energy which otherwise is lost through anger gets released, it again returns to the mind. The very energy that reverts to the mind is compassion. The energy which was getting wasted in the desert was anger. But the energy which was prevented from getting lost in the desert – and was absorbed within yourself – when it merges with the ocean, is compassion.

Anger and compassion are two names of the same energy. Anger is the diseased state of the same energy which in its healthy state is the energy of compassion. Hate and love are two manifestations of the same energy. When the energy of hate gets reabsorbed in you, infinite love arises. You cannot find anyone more loving than the enlightened ones. You can hardly find anyone more loving than Christ and Krishna. In them you see hatred absorbed; not lost in the desert but merged with the ocean. The seed found the soil.

So whenever you do anything, keep this as a litmus test for yourself because maya is intrinsically attached to you – in each and every act of yours. There is disease in your every pore so you will need to be alert at every point; you will have to free every cell of your being from maya.

*Mind and maya are the same, Maya resides in mind. The entire world is confused; to whom shall I go and explain it?* Kabir says, people are engaged in great debate, they are involved in heavy scriptural discussion, they are trying to prove this and they are trying to disprove that. And the fact is: "Mind and maya are the same." They don't see that this is how you are. Certainly, it is a wrong way to be, but that is exactly what you are. Maya is your wrong way to be; *brahman* is your right way to be. And remember: never try to be like *brahman*, because there is no way to seek it directly. You just need to escape from maya and *brahman* will be attained. So all sadhana, all spiritual discipline is through negation, *via negativa* – negation of maya, disease, perverse behavior. Once there is no perversity, the energy automatically becomes virtuous.

**You fenced the farm, but it devoured the farm itself.**
**The entire world is puzzled;**
**how shall I explain it?**

People protect their farm by creating a fence around it. The mind is also a fence for your protection. But you may create a hedge, which then spreads over the entire farm. So instead of saving the farm, it might simply destroy it. The hedge is meant for the farm's protection, but you may do the fencing in such a way that the hedge may turn into a little forest, leaving no space on the farm to grow anything.

Mind is like the hedge; it is useful as a fence. But if it were to swallow you, if you were to become nothing but the mind, then what would be the point in having a fence when the farm itself is no longer there? Often it happens, and this is the second sutra about maya.

In life, it so happens that the hedge devours the farm and people never come to know about it. Understand this: to live you need bread, you need shelter. You need some kind of security, some comfort – these are very essential. But then for his whole life somebody just goes on building a home, he keeps himself busy making the house larger and larger. The time never comes when he can actually live in the house, reside in the house – that moment never comes. You need bread, clothes, for which some money is required. But then, somebody just gets busy accumulating money; he forgets that the money was just a hedge. The money became the farm. The hedge gobbled up the very farm.

There is a certain need for money and the need has a limit. No need is limitless; but craving is limitless. Needs are very small – you need bread, you need water, you need clothes. If people were only to look at their needs, there would not be a single person hungry, there would not be anyone poor and wretched – because needs have a limit. Birds and animals are able to meet their needs, how strange that man is not able to. Although trees have no feet to go anywhere, they take care of their needs. They remain standing in one place, yet their needs are fulfilled. Birds and animals are able to fulfill their needs even though they don't have much intellect or a university education. Why is man not able to fulfill his needs? It looks as though something has gone wrong somewhere.

Needs are fine; but desires are dangerous. What is the difference? A need is like the hedge; desires are like the hedge taking over the entire field. Your needs can be fulfilled but your desires can never be. To stop needing is intelligence. To keep following desire is insanity – then there is no end to it. Just look at people.

I know a man who owns seven houses. He earns thousands of rupees in rent. But for himself he has rented a small room, which he lives in. He has a bicycle that he uses for the purpose of collecting the rent. He resides in that small room and takes his meals in a restaurant.

Once I got a chance to stay in one of his bungalows. This man would come and collect his rent every month. I was the guest of a friend who lived in one of those bungalows. I asked about the man. He laughed and said, "He is the landlord."

The clothes he was wearing had holes, his bicycle seemed like an antique piece – everybody could hear the rattling sound of the bicycle approaching from far away. Just by looking at him no one would know he owned seven houses. The price of those seven houses is approximately two hundred thousand rupees. He collects thousands of rupees in rent every month but for his room he pays five rupees a month. The hedge has devoured that man's life!

Once it happened…

A retired military doctor was staying in front of my house. He had never married. While in the military service he was injured and had therefore retired prematurely. He received quite a good pension from the military. His bungalow was worth one hundred thousand rupees and about two hundred thousand rupees were in his bank account. But his total intake of food was just tea and *papad*! He survived on just that much.

One day, he had a heart attack and fell ill; he couldn't speak. He didn't have anyone to take care of him. He had rented out half his house and so the tenant came to me and said the doctor was not able to speak and was in great danger. I went along with him. I asked the doctor: "Shall I call the physician?" Gesturing, he asked who would pay the fees. I said he need not worry about it.

The physician was brought. He said that the condition was very critical and the man had to be taken to the hospital immediately. So an ambulance was called. Before entering the ambulance he asked me to lock the house and give him the keys. So, with his own eyes he made sure the house was locked – he couldn't speak – and an hour later he died! But he had made sure that he had the keys. When he died, five thousand rupees were found in his pocket. Even though he was unable to speak he was asking *me* who would pay the physician's fees!

This is how the hedge becomes the field.

Mind is useful; if you understand it well, the mind is very useful. Mind is like radar. Just as when you travel in an airplane it has radar equipment that keeps feeding information from a distance of up to two hundred miles. It takes photographs. The plane flies with such speed that if the pilot doesn't know what is happening two hundred miles ahead, a collision can happen. So the radar screen shows if there are clouds, another plane, or a bird two hundred miles ahead. The pilot has to start taking preventive measures a hundred miles in advance because the speed is so high that unless he is prepared two hundred miles ahead, he might run into all kinds of danger.

Mind is like radar, it gives you glimpses from all around. It is very useful in the hands of a wise person; it is dangerous in the hands of a foolish one. Actually, the foolish person is never able to make use of the mind; the mind makes use of him. The slave becomes the master and the master becomes the slave. This is *your* situation.

I define the worldly person as one whose field has been eaten up by the hedge. And for me, a sannyasin is one for whom the field is a field and the hedge is a hedge. Neither does the field eat up the hedge, nor does the hedge devour the field – because both are needed. The hedge is needed because the field needs protection.

So like a hedge, the mind is very useful. It is very much needed in life. But you should have the sense to know where you have to stop using it. There is certainly a need for money, but it is insanity to simply keep on accumulating it. A house is necessary, but then just to go on building it and not have a chance to live in it, not have any time to stay in it and thus waste your whole life is crazy. Everyone needs clothes, but what would you say if a person just got lost in collecting them?

If man can live with proper judgment, then there is no more effective instrument than the mind. Scientists have yet to create an instrument, which can match the mind. It can see afar, it can see up close; it can figure out the situation well; it can discover means of protection; it can create a number of devices for safeguarding life.

All of this is necessary, but this is not what life is all about. You may place a guard at the door; that is necessary. But if you were to become a guard yourself, then that would be foolish – then whom are you guarding?

Often people waste their lives making plans for living. In doing so, they never even get a chance to actually live. Every day you postpone living until the next day; first you want to make all possible arrangements. Your arrangements and plans will never be completed, so how will you ever live?

Remember, those who really want to live will have to discover the art of living even if the plans are incomplete. Otherwise your plans will never come to any completion because the mind will keep on pointing out: "This is missing, that is missing; do this, do that." The mind will go on advising you that it is not yet time to rest; how can you rest when the Taj Mahal is not yet built? If you continue to follow what the mind says, you will never get a chance to live life.

Life is short. There is no end to mind's desires. Needs are limited, everyone can fulfill them.

Now a very interesting thing happens here: man turns his needs into desires – they become endless. And when he gets into trouble because of them, he starts cutting his needs too – that also becomes something endless.

The world is made up of two types of insane people. One type is of those who have lost everything in chasing their needs. When these insane people get into trouble because of this, the other type of insane people emerges – they are actually those who reflect the inverted position of the first kind. The second kind gets into cutting back their needs. Instead of eating food, such a man will go on a fast. So either you will keep on eating or you will go on fasting. Isn't there any way for you to stop somewhere in the middle? Is it really impossible to find a balance?

Mullah Nasruddin fell ill with asthma. He went to see the doctor.

The doctor said, "You are not ill; but your mouth, your clothes stink of smoke. How many cigarettes do you smoke a day?"

Mullah replied, "Not too many, just about ten or twelve."

The doctor said, "You aren't ill, but the nicotine from the cigarettes is accumulating in your lungs; it has to be reduced. There is no need for any treatment, cut down on your cigarette smoking. Just do one thing, smoke only one cigarette after lunch. Come back to me after one month and we shall see what more can be done, step by step."

When Nasruddin returned after one month the doctor couldn't even recognize him. It looked like his whole body had swollen. The doctor became a little apprehensive.

He said, "Has this condition happened to you due to cutting down on smoking? I hardly recognize you!"

Nasruddin replied, "Certainly, this problem is because of cigarettes."

The doctor asked, "Did you follow exactly what I told you?"

Mullah said, "I got into this trouble because I followed what you said. Now I have to take my food ten to twelve times a day!"

Either you go crazy after food or, if you save yourself from this madness, another kind of madness is already waiting. The madman also has his own logic. He is very consistent in his reasoning. And once you start following the logic given by the mind the kind of craziness will keep changing – one kind of craziness leading to the next kind; but the logic will remain the same. What is mind's reasoning? Mind's reasoning is: if it gives so much pleasure eating once, eating twenty times will give twenty times more pleasure. The arithmetic is clear. But if life were arithmetic then everything would have worked out fine. Life is not like arithmetic. Eating once is good; eating twenty times is not twenty times more beneficial. But if you persist in eating twenty times more, then sooner or later you are bound to get into trouble. You will get sick, you will fall ill; your whole body will revolt and will want to throw up your food. When you get tired of eating, you will feel that if eating gives so much trouble then it is better to go on a fast, to just stop eating. Again the arithmetic is clear: if food is causing so much trouble and difficulty, then, clearly, the food is at the root of all misery. That's why so many sects around the world advocate fasting: "Stop eating!" Now you are moving to the other extreme, but you will be miserable there as well.

The technique of freeing yourself from the mind is to stop in the middle. The mind exists in extremes. It functions like a pendulum – it moves from one side to the other, not stopping in the middle. If the pendulum stops in the middle, then the clock stops. The day you stop in the middle, the mind-clock will also stop. That's the day when maya comes to a halt and its whole agony disappears within you. And that disappearance gives birth to a vast beauty – buddhahood is born. It gives birth to Kabir, Krishna, and Christ.

*You fenced the farm, but it devoured the farm itself. The entire world is puzzled; how shall I explain it?* The mind is indeed useful – if you use it. It becomes dangerous if you allow it to become a master. Don't listen to the mind. Don't ever follow the mind's advice. Listen to what the mind says, but use your own sense. The mind will say: "Listen to me!" but you should figure it out for yourself. Don't allow the mind to decide, make the decision for yourself. And if you develop the capacity to make your own decisions, then the mind won't be able to harm you. Then you will neither eat too much nor fast too much. Then you will settle down to having a balanced intake of food. And having a balanced intake of food is a wonderful thing – the body is neither hungry nor overstuffed. Then your whole of life will gain an equilibrium all over.

Wherever you achieve a certain steadiness, whenever you achieve balance – stopping in the middle – equanimity will appear. What generally happens is that either you go on chattering day and night or else you say you would rather be in silence. Is it really impossible to be in the middle? Either you want to live in the world or you wish to go away to the Himalayas! Is it really not possible to live in the world in such a way that the world remains outside and not within you? That is when equanimity appears. Certainly, you will have to pass through the world, but pass through in a way that not a mark shows up on you.

Kabir has said, he has worn the cloak of this samsara with great care. He says, "I have worn the mantle of this world with awareness, and then returned it the way I found it." He says, he returned the cloak of samsara exactly as he received it – neither did he go this way nor that way; neither did he made it dirty nor did he clean it. He just placed it back as it was after wearing it with great care. Taking care is what it is all about. Here, *taking care* means being conscious, alert, and aware; paying attention, understanding, being in balance.

So, Kabir says: *To whom shall I go and explain it?* There is no one ready to listen.

This is my experience too. You are willing to listen if I tell you to be extreme. If I tell you to go on a fast, you follow what I am saying, but if I tell you to take a balanced meal, you don't get it. If I tell you to leave your home, that this world is nothing but misery, you follow what I am saying. Before that happens, you are already living at one extreme – indulging in the world, finding it a place to just enjoy. But now you are through with that extreme. You have suffered enough living at that extreme. Now you are almost ready. Someone just has to tell you to leave everything, to escape – "This is all meaningless, futile" – and you will simple run away. That is the reason why there are so many clans of escapists. They exist because of you. When you get tired of one extreme you want to go to the other extreme; that is why there are so many types of escapists.

Your so-called monks and mendicants are simply escapists. They are your mirror images. If you are a pendulum of the clock going to the left, they are the pendulum going to the right. You are chasing women; they are escaping from women. You are accumulating wealth, they are afraid of touching wealth.

Wealth is neither worth loving nor worth being afraid of; neither does it make sense to accumulate wealth nor does it make sense to be fearful of it. Wealth is meant to be used and one who knows how to make proper use of it will neither collect it nor run away from it. Wealth is essentially a means and it can be used in a balanced way.

This is my experience too; my whole effort is to stop you in the middle. But you don't get it. You look for extremes. You have indulged in one extreme, now you are ready to go to the other extreme. And I am saying: stop in the middle! But you don't know how to stop, you know only running. Whatever the direction may be, you are simply ready to run and pursue it. And what I am saying is: Sit down, don't run!

That is why Kabir says: *The entire world is puzzled; how shall I explain it?* Kabir is absolutely a follower of the middle path. Kabir is even-minded; his equanimity is worth understanding. Every day he would go to the market, every day he would weave cloth, and every day he would sell it. But at the end of the day whatever of his earnings was left he would give away. He never left the samsara, the mundane world, but then he never held on to it either.

This is the art. He never leaves the world because he weaves cloth, goes to his shop, sells the cloth, makes some money and brings it home. The household needs are taken care of and by the evening whatever is left he gives away. He is a householder during the day and a sannyasin, a monk, at night. Your monks are monks during the day and householders at night. On the surface, outwardly, they are monks, inwardly they are householders. Kabir is outwardly a householder, but within, he is a sannyasin.

Life moves in extremes, and the mind follows extremes greedily. Balance, equanimity, is death for the mind.

Kabir says:

> ***The mind knows everything, and yet still it does the wrong thing.***
> ***What kind of cleverness is it,***
> ***that though holding a lamp you fall into a well?***

These are very sweet words, very significant. You should not only memorize them but even learn them by heart: *The mind knows everything, and yet still it does the wrong thing.*

Knowledge is of no use because the mind knows everything. But despite knowing, it ends up doing the wrong thing. You know very well that getting angry is wrong, and yet you end up getting angry. You are well aware that it is a sin to hate, and yet you still end up hating. You know very well that man gets entrapped and chained in greed – it becomes a prison – and yet you end up being greedy.

The mind knows everything, and yet still it does the wrong thing. What kind of cleverness is it… Indeed, what kind of cleverness is it…? That though holding a lamp you fall into a well? You were holding a lamp in your hand and yet you fell into a well! The lamp must have been a fake one. The well is real, fake lamps won't be of any use. That's why Kabir says: What kind of cleverness is it?

Look at your pundits. Their lives are the same as those who are ignorant and without any knowledge – there is not an iota of difference. The only difference may be that the ignorant are not as skilled in hiding their ignorance as the pundits are. But their lives are the same. The same anger, the same delusion, the same attachment and greed – no difference at all! Their knowledge is stale and borrowed; otherwise, knowledge works like a fire. Just as when you place gold in fire it comes out clean and pure, similarly, knowledge works like fire. Anyone who places his mind in it, that mind can come out clean and pure. But knowledge can also be stale and borrowed. In that case knowledge is not fire, then it is just ashes. At some point in time it was fire, but now it is nothing but ash.

What I am saying to you now is fire; after my death it will become ash. But you won't listen to me now. After my death you will ponder over it, but then it will just be ash. You can go ahead and smear your body with that ash and sit like an *avadhoot*, but that will not transform your life.

Have you seen the monks who have smeared their bodies with ash? Remember, it is fire that transforms, not ash. Ashes lie where once a fire was burning. But revolutions don't take place by looking for help from the past, they happen in the present moment – now. You can smear yourself to your heart's content with Mahavira's ashes, but your mind will not become afire, it will not transform. You may carry a great load of Buddha's ashes – urns containing these ashes are indeed very precious – but they don't create revolutions. You need to look for a living master, only then is there an alive, burning fire.

If you have fire within, then it is impossible to go against what you know. Then you actually know and that knowing is your living. Then your actions show your knowing. Once you have known that anger is meaningless, how will you be able to get angry? But this you have not known, this has simply been told to you by others – Buddha, Mahavira, Krishna say anger is harmful: this you have heard. Your eyes have not experienced it; it is just what your ears have accumulated. And this is the only difference between knowledge and knowing. Knowledge is what comes through the ears, through hearing; and then there is knowing which comes through the eyes, through seeing.

The distance between maya and *brahman* is that of four fingers – the distance between the ears and eyes. What comes through the ears is hollow, zero; what comes through one's experience, that alone is the real. In a way you know all this. Kabir says, "*The mind knows everything*..." There is nothing more that needs to be told to the mind. The mind says, "I know everything, what more can you explain to me? Do I still need to understand any further? I have read it all." Says Kabir, "*The mind knows everything, and yet still it does the wrong thing.*"

And yet your action, the way you behave in life, remains the same – the same as that of an ignorant person. Such a life does not have the fragrance of knowing, it only releases the smell of unconsciousness. But the mind stays filled with knowledge, information. This is the difference between a pundit, a scholar, and an enlightened one. In a scholar you will find nothing but a foul smell, you won't find anything but mere words. An enlightened one carries a certain fragrance; because whatever he says, he has *known* it.

Remember, truth can only be self-realized, not borrowed. There is no way you can take the truth from someone else and carry its weight. Neither can you steal the truth, nor can you buy it in the marketplace, nor can it be received in charity. Truth has to be earned by the self alone. That which you find for yourself will transform your life.

*The mind knows everything, and still it does the wrong thing. What kind of cleverness is it…* What do scholarship, knowledge, mental understanding really mean when one continues to do wrong deeds? What would you do with such expertise? Such cleverness can never work as a lamp – what kind of lamp, what sort of cleverness would it be? *…though holding a lamp you fall into a well!* You were holding a lamp in your hand, and you fell into a well!

Ramakrishna used to say: a hawk may be flying high up in the sky, but don't be under any false impression – its eyes remain fixed on the dead rat lying on a heap of garbage. The hawk flies high above in the sky but that does not mean it is higher than you. The issue is not that of flying high above; the issue is what her eyes are fixed on! Her eyes are riveted on the dead rat lying on the heap of garbage and she is waiting while circling in the sky. She is biding her time for the right moment when the road will be deserted and she can swoop down and snatch the dead rat in her mouth.

The pundit also flies in the sky, but his mind remains fixed on the dead rat lying on the ground below. The one who knows, the *gyani*, flies in the expanse above but stays there. And that is the difference. Your knowing should become your being. Regardless of how great a pundit you may become, if your knowing and your being are not the same, then Kabir says: *What kind of cleverness is it, that though holding a lamp you fall into a well?*

> ***The mind is the ocean, and the mind is the wave as well.***
> ***Many unconscious thoughts are drowned in the waves.***

When the mind is in a healthy state it is like the ocean. The same mind, when in a disturbed state, is a wave. When you become agitated, the mind is full of waves; when you become quiet and silent the same mind turns into an ocean – silent, peaceful.

Why have the enlightened beings identified anger, hatred, attachment, greed as sins? The reason is: when you get angry the mind is filled with waves, you become unhealthy, agitated. Whatever causes agitation and excitement is sin, and whatever makes you silent and peaceful is virtue. Just remember this definition.

Sin and virtue have nothing to do with another person. Ordinarily people think anger is a sin because it hurts the other. No, the other is not necessarily hurt; because if the other is a buddha, then no matter how much you may get angry, he will not be hurt. So will the anger remain a sin regardless of whether a buddha is hurt or not? No, not at all; anger is a sin because it hurts *you*: the other getting hurt is just a consequence. The person can get hurt, but that is not important. The important thing is that you get hurt; you get agitated inside, you fall apart. You lose your inner peace, the inner mirror gets clouded.

If you continue to remain in the state of anger, greed, attachment, your inner lake never gets the chance to calm down – it constantly remains in a turmoil. Then, by and by, you forget there is an ocean hidden beneath these waves because you never get a chance to have a look at it. When all the waves calm down, when there is not a single wave left, that is when you will come to experience the ocean within.

So, this is the difference between *brahman* and maya: when *brahman* is agitated, excited, it is maya; when *brahman* is calm and silent, it is *brahman*. Or you can say when maya becomes calm, then it is *brahman*. Maya is the agitated state of *brahman*; it is a sick state, an unhealthy state; it is a perverted state.

*The mind is the ocean, and the mind is the wave as well.* Who knows how many are drowned in these waves? These are not tiny little waves. One thing is certain: whosoever is unconscious is sure to drown. Kabir says many unconscious people drown. Anyone who is living unconsciously, sleepily, anyone who is not living with awareness is bound to drown. Only the boat of consciousness can save you from drowning.

> **Many unconscious thoughts are drowned in the waves.**
> **Only those who have a discerning heart can understand this, says Kabir.**

There can be two or three meanings to this statement and since all three meanings are useful it is essential to follow them. *Many unconscious thoughts are drowned in the waves. Only those who have a discerning heart can understand this, says Kabir.* Only they can understand this, says Kabir, *who have a discerning heart* – not otherwise. A discerning heart! Intellectual skill will be of no use. Regardless of how logical they may be, how well-versed in the scriptures, how expert in doctrines – no, nothing of the sort will be of any use. *Only those who have a discerning heart* will be able to understand this.

What does having a discerning heart mean? Ordinarily, we think the ability to discern, the ability to discriminate, is part of the intellect, while the heart is the domain of love. This is our common conceptual understanding. And poets have greatly popularized the concept that discretion is of the mind and love is of the heart. But this concept is misleading.

There is a discernment of the heart too. And what you call "love" is another name for your blindness. And until discernment – the perception of the heart – has emerged, the kind of love that flowers in the life of Krishna and Christ will never appear.

What is this discernment, this discrimination, which belongs to the heart? And how will you find it? Remember, the intellect carries no discernment; it carries only thoughts. The mind can only think; it cannot have any perception. The mind can think: what is right, what is wrong. The mind can gather arguments in favor or against; it can then figure out which side has more arguments and then it will see that side as right. This is not discernment; this is just cool calculation.

For example, you come across some problem in life and begin to think what can be done. The mind gives lots of options and then it gives arguments in favor and against each option. You look at all the arguments, reflect on them, and follow the one which carries more weight, which is more advantageous. This is thinking, not discernment.

So then, what is discernment? Discernment is a state of awareness where you don't have to think – you begin to see. It is a state where your eyes are open and where you don't have options whether to do this or that. Your eyes are so wide open and the perception is so profound you see only that which is right – you don't have to think.

Let us say there is a blind man here and he wants to go out. He will ask for the way out – is it to the left or to the right? Where are the stairs? He will grope with his stick and then make a move. But someone who has eyes to see never asks where the door is; he wants to get out so, without even thinking about the door, he just gets up and goes out. Any thought regarding the door never even crosses his mind. When you have eyes, what is the need to think about the door? You get up and leave, as if the door doesn't even exist. Those who don't have eyes to see are forced to think about which is the way out – to the left or to the right? They have to grope, only then can they get out.

Thinking shows a lack of perception. Thinking is a substitute for discernment, the same as a blind man's asking and groping is a substitute for eyes. One who has *vivek*, discernment, is able to see; then he follows what he sees – he doesn't think whether to go or not to go. There is no duality, no conflict, in the state of discernment. Thinking has duality, it carries conflict. Thinking contains alternatives; perception has no alternatives. Discernment is without alternatives – one simply sees and starts moving.

So you need to keep a very strange thing in mind, that no matter what you do out of thinking, you will always repent; because whenever the mind tells you to do something, the other alternative is also always present. Let us say, you are in love with two women, and you wish to marry both, but you are unable to decide whom to marry. One woman is wealthy but not good-looking; you are interested in her wealth. The other woman is poor but good-looking; you are interested in beauty too. Now what to do?

Somebody asked Mulla Nasruddin, "What shall I do? Two women – one is rich but ugly looking; the other is poor but very beautiful. What shall I do?"

Nasruddin said, "Do one thing: marry the rich one and love the poor one."

So, either the mind will try to find a compromise between the two – which is dangerous – or else the mind will decide to marry one of the two, but will repent for doing so. Should the man decide to marry the rich woman, he will have to see her face on waking up in the morning. No matter how much you may want to escape from your wife, where will you go? Ultimately you will have to come back home. Whenever he will look at her face he will repent not having married the other one, the beautiful one.

But don't let this give you the idea that marrying the beautiful woman would have solved the matter. In that case, within a few days the beauty will begin to fade, you will get used to looking at the same face – and what will you do just looking at that pretty face? Every day you will be short of money. The roof is leaking, you cannot buy tiles; your stomach is empty, and there will be no bread – daily it will hurt. And then the mind will say, "Marrying the rich one would have been better!"

Whatsoever the mind chooses, it will always regret it. Regretting and lamenting are the ultimate outcomes of what the mind does because the alternative was always there. Whatever we may do through discernment we will never regret, simply because there was never any alternative. What is there to regret?

That is why a discerning person never regrets anything. He has no regrets whatever about what may have happened in the past. He never even looks back because there was no option, no alternative – whatever was to happen, happened. And whatever is to happen, that alone will happen. So a discerning individual will always be calm, peaceful, and the thinking person will be disturbed, agitated.

So then, how to awaken this discernment, this perception of the heart? Meditation is the process for awakening discernment. A university is a training center for activating intellectual thinking. It takes about twenty or twenty-five years for a young person to train his intellectual mind. People come to me saying that they have been meditating for the last five or seven days and nothing has happened yet! Remember, intellect is the periphery; the heart is the center. You can spend twenty-five years on the intellect and even then you may perhaps earn a third-class degree when you come out of university. But for the cause of the heart, you are not ready to give even three days! And the fact is, even twenty-five lives are not enough to spare for the heart because the heart is the center.

All meditation techniques are essentially for awakening the heart center. In the past, only in India were there universities where both experiments were made, but they have been lost. Nowhere in the world were such experiments done as were done in the universities of Nalanda and Takshashila, where we worked on training the intellect and awakening a discerning heart as well.

It didn't succeed. Many obstacles came in the way. The biggest obstacle to this experiment was that once a discerning heart is awakened, the individual can no longer remain worldly. So the world is against such an experiment. A father would be afraid of sending his son to such a place where a perceptive heart is awakened, because a discerning heart is incompatible with attachment. If attachment is broken, then ties with the father will also be automatically broken. A wife will be afraid of sending her husband to a place where a discerning heart can be awakened, because discernment means freedom from passion. Once a discerning heart is awakened, desires and passion are bound to disappear.

Everyone is afraid of an awakened, discerning heart. So although the experiment was made, it failed. Indeed it was the greatest experiment in the world of human consciousness.

In Nalanda, we took care that meditation should also grow in the same proportion as knowledge, thus a balance would always be maintained. But then a person graduating from Nalanda emerged more as a sannyasin, a non-worldly person.

How long could such an experiment have survived? How long would the mundane world allow it to function?

So we uprooted Nalanda and tossed it away. So the masses destroyed Nalanda and abandoned it. They chased the Buddhists engaged in such a great experiment out of the country. Buddhism was overthrown in India because the Buddhists tried to raise discernment so much, that whoever was able to achieve it was of not much use for this world. Although they certainly turned out to be of immense use for an immeasurable world, for the world of our petty desires they proved useless.

Obviously, if a son's discerning heart is awakened, his father can never force him to make money. The son will say: okay, he will work for whatever is necessary. But the real drive is for the unnecessary; what is the point of working just for the necessary? We know that someone is wealthy only when he has earned so much that he has no more use for wealth.

Man remains poor just working for the necessary. If he earns only as much as is needed, then he is poor. Luxury and enjoyment are seen only when the need for the unnecessary arises. A discerning person, a meditative person, will stay away from the unnecessary. So it became very difficult.

Kabir says, *Only those who have a discerning heart can understand this.* Here, too, only those who have a perceptive heart can understand what I am saying, only those who have entered into meditation. Why? Because a meditator instantly sees: the mind is the wave and the same mind is the ocean. A meditator comes across many moments when the waves stop and only the ocean remains. This very experience will be helpful in following Kabir's words; without this experience you won't be able to understand what he is saying.

People who have written dissertations on Kabir come to me. Universities have honored them, granted degrees to them. But I don't see that they understand Kabir; simply because they don't have a discerning, a perceptive heart.

There is yet another meaning to Kabir's words. Kabir says: *Only those who have a discerning heart can understand this, says Kabir.* He is saying, only those who have a discerning heart are educated enough, learned enough.

The mind knows everything, and yet it does the wrong thing. What kind of cleverness is it, that though holding a lamp you fall into a well? Only those who have a perceptive heart are truly educated – everyone else is illiterate. Those who have a discerning heart are the ones who are really well-read – it is not about reading a book, rather it is a matter of reading the heart. The question is that of reading oneself. Only those who have a discerning heart… only they who have a discerning heart are well-read, only they are educated.

**You have lost it through the mind.**
**Now you can only find it through the mind.**
**Mind cannot exist without the mind.**
**A mind, when it becomes a no-mind,**
**is like an egg in which the whole brahman is hidden.**

*You have lost it through the mind* – you have lost it through the mind, now you can only find it through the mind. You have gone astray because of the mind, now mind alone will bring you home. You became a pauper because of the mind, now mind alone will make you an emperor. It is the mind which has become sick; the moment it becomes healthy, that which is lost will be found.

*You have lost it through the mind. Now you can only find it through the mind. Mind cannot exist without the mind.* It is all a mind game. The energy within you that turns into thoughts, the whole game is of that energy. That energy can be in two forms: either it turns into thoughts, in which case it is a wave; or it turns into meditation, and becomes an ocean. That is why thoughtlessness, or a state of no-thought, is the essence of all religions. The moment you enter into this state, the energy which was tied up in thoughts is released, and dissolves in the infinite. Then the river will not end up in a desert. Instead, the entire energy starts falling inside you – and then you are not losing anything. All the leaks are closed.

At present you are like a bucket with a thousand holes. As the bucket enters the well, it makes a lot of noise. While submerged in the water it feels as if it is full. The moment it is lifted up from the water, it begins to drain. You get tired pulling the bucket up, but by the time you get hold of it, you will find it is empty. This is exactly the experience of millions of people. They spend their whole lives pulling up the bucket. Many times they feel the bucket is heavy. As it rises up from the well it makes such a rattling sound that it feels as if it is coming up filled with water. But by the time they catch the bucket, it is totally empty. At the time of death everyone finds that the bucket is empty; so many holes in it.

Every thought is a hole through which you lose your energy. The moment you become thought-less, the passage through which you lose energy closes. Then the energy falls back again within yourself. You are the ocean, you are the *brahman*, you are the ultimate. You *are* the divine presence in this world. But the holes, the leakages drain you.

You have lost it through the mind. Now you can only find it through the mind. Mind cannot exist without the mind. A mind, when it becomes a no-mind, is like an egg in which the whole brahman is hidden. It is like the brahman, the infinite space is hidden in everything – whether it is visible or not. How can one see the brahman, the space? Every little bit of air contains brahman. Brahman is in every spark of fire. Neither the fire can burn brahman nor the wind can blow away the brahman.

Just as *brahman*, the infinite, is hidden in each and everything, similarly the divine presence is hidden in everybody; it is hidden in you too. The name Kabir has given to that divine presence is very significant. It is the same one as the Zen mystics have given it in Japan. Zen mystics call it a state of no-mind. Kabir calls the same state *unmani* – a state of consciousness where the mind is no more.

What does it mean: "mind is no more"? It simply means a state where all thoughts have disappeared, all waves have calmed down. The mind is no-mind. Kabir has said somewhere: "The mind has disappeared, the whole sky is roaring, the elixir is showering." The mind has ceased to be – it has become no-mind. The entire sky, the whole of space is roaring and an elixir is showering. The sky roars even when the waves of mind with its perversions are occupying your being; but then not elixir but poison showers. The sky continues to roar around you too, but what is showering is nothing but poison.

"The mind has disappeared, the whole sky is roaring, the elixir is showering." The cessation of mind, no-mind, means where mind contains no thoughts. When it becomes a no-mind, *mind...is like an egg in which the whole brahman is hidden.* The divine is hidden in no-mind the same as the *brahman* is hidden in every atom, as the sky is hidden in every mote.

***The mind is Gorakh and the mind is Govind too.***
***And the same mind is like the Aughad mendicant.***
***One who guards the mind with awareness, and is watchful,***
***automatically becomes the creator.***

One who understands what it means to guard the mind, himself becomes the *brahman*, himself becomes the very prime mover of the universe.

*One who guards the mind*… This word *jatan*, guarding, is worth remembering. What does *guarding* mean?

Let us say you find a diamond lying in the street: how will you keep it? You will keep it with care, watchfully. You will hide it quickly. You won't even take a proper look at the diamond – who knows, someone else may come to know about it. Without even really looking at it, you will immediately hide it under your clothes because you are on the street, in the middle of a marketplace, people are moving around and your home is still far away. You will first want to reach home, shut the door, turn on the light and then take a look at it. But even before reaching home, you will check your pocket several times, won't you? That is exactly what *jatan* means. One needs to keep checking many times.

Pickpockets know very well who has money in his pocket. The person keeps checking again and again. Otherwise, how would a pickpocket know? Obviously, the pickpocket doesn't have any telepathy to figure out if you are carrying banknotes. But you keep touching your pocket and are not even aware that you are doing it again and again. This gives the pickpocket a clue that there is something there.

So *jatan* means guarding something with great awareness. Somewhere Kabir gives an example of women returning from the well or a river with vessels filled with water on top of their heads. They chitchat with each other, sing songs and keep walking without even touching the pots overhead. How do they manage it? How do they hold the pots? With watchful guarding! Of course, this is how it was in the past with women returning from the well or river. Now you don't see such women because now they meet at a water outlet where there is nothing but trouble!

In the times of Kabir, women would return from water sources and there was a certain poetry in their returning from such places. They would continue to walk and chitchat while carrying the filled vessels on their heads without holding them with their hands. How were they managing to keep them steady? Inside, within, there was a watchful caring – though it was a very subtle guarding. The vessel didn't fall, it didn't break and the gossip went on, the watchfulness continued.

So Kabir says, live in this world just as women returning from the water source guarding their vessels with care and watchfulness. Attend your shop but also watch your consciousness. Be in the marketplace but don't get lost – guard yourself. Have wealth, have a wife – but also keep guarding yourself.

*Jatan* means inner remembrance. Gurdjieff has used the words *self-remembering*. Do whatever you may; just be aware of your self – that is *jatan*, guarding one's self. Buddha calls it *right mindfulness*. Whatever you may do, simply remember "I am."

Buddha used the word *smriti*, which was then corrupted. What Kabir and Nanak call *surati* is actually the word *smriti* applied by Buddha. In folk language the word gradually ended up as *surati*. But *surati* is a much sweeter word. And *smriti* also gives the connotation of memory. *Surati* acquired a totally different meaning – it came to mean self-knowledge, self-awareness.

The word *jatan* is also derived from *yatna* – but its meaning is not the same as what is meant by *yatna*. The actual meaning is: a constant inner awareness – something that is within should not be lost. Just as one finds a diamond and holds onto it tightly, similarly a constant awareness, a constant remembrance should be maintained. Whatsoever you may do, while doing it just remember that you need to guard yourself, watch yourself.

What is the purpose of guarding, of watching yourself? The purpose is that no waves should appear in your mind. The waves are certain to appear if you don't guard yourself; the ocean will disappear, the mirror will be gone. When you guard yourself a little, fewer waves will appear; if you guard to your utmost, no waves will appear. If you guard yourself totally, all waves will calm down completely. And when not one wave exists in the mind, the mind turns into a mirror. Whatever is seen in that mirror, that alone is truth.

> ***The mind is Gorakh and the mind is Govind too.***
> ***And the same mind is like the Aughad mendicant.***
> ***One who guards the mind with awareness, and is watchful,***
> ***automatically becomes the creator.***
> ***Body yoga is done by one and all, but no one does mind yoga.***
> ***Once the mind becomes yoga, all else is easily attainable.***

It is not a question of doing something through the body. The whole issue is of doing something in the inner world of awareness. So, regardless of how much you may do *shirshasana*, *siddhasana*, *sarvangasana*, or regardless of how many ways you succeed in controlling, making your body go through different kinds of contortions – all that is not very significant. The significant thing is the growing consciousness within – growing an inner light of consciousness.

*Body yoga is done by one and all, but no one does mind yoga.* That is why you may come across yogis who have attained great bodily achievements. But if you looked into them, you would find them even worse than you are.

For example, a yogi can stay buried underground for thirty days. Obviously, he has achieved a great deal because to remain in a covered ditch for thirty days without oxygen…even three seconds is difficult. When you pull him out after thirty days, he is still alive. Naturally, you will be amazed. But look into his eyes and you won't find the same radiance as is seen in the eyes of Kabir, Buddha or Gorakh. Instead, you will find a kind of melancholy, a kind of sleepiness. You won't find any spark in his life – which you would hope to see in a yogi.

If indeed *brahman* is realized within a person, then there is bound to be a certain fragrance, a certain luminosity spread all around him – you won't find any of this around this man. The interesting thing is: he remained buried for thirty days because he was going to be rewarded with five hundred rupees for doing it. Would you be able to make an enlightened buddha agree to remain underground for five hundred rupees? Certainly, this so-called yogi mastered his body, but he doesn't have a clue about how to master the mind.

There are, of course, yogis who can, on their own volition, stop the pulse of their hand or stop their heartbeat. But they do it all just to earn money. In fact, their real place is in a circus, nowhere near truth. They are useful to a circus, but what do they have to do with truth? You are running a shop, and so are they. The only difference is: your shop is at a little distance from you, while their shop is attached to their body. But the fact remains that their entire spirituality has turned into exhibitionism.

There are yogis who pull their eyes out and keep them hanging out. The first time Dr. Paul Brunton saw a yogi do this, he was astounded because he was himself a physician. It was hard to believe; it was not possible to pull one's eyes out and keep them hanging loose four inches outside. The yogi was still able to see through the eyes even though all his eye muscles were pulled out and the blood was oozing! After a while he pushed his eyes back in and fitted them into his eye sockets. Then he said his fee was two rupees for doing that. Such a miracle, but the objective was greed.

So Kabir says:

***Body yoga is done by one and all, but no one does mind yoga.***
***Once the mind becomes yoga, all else is easily attainable.***
***The mind has become as clean and pure as the water of Ganges.***
***Now the Lord follows you, calling, "Kabir, Kabir!"***

And when does the mind become yoga? What is the yoga of the mind? *Yoga* means joining, meeting, union, intercourse. *Yoga* means two becoming one. So what does *mind yoga* mean? It means where the waves of mind and the ocean of mind have become one; where the chasing mind and the still mind have become one; where mind merges in the mind. It is a moment of ultimate intercourse where mind is immersed, drowned in the mind itself. That is samadhi.

*Once the mind becomes yoga, all else is easily attainable.* Whoever attains the knack of mind meeting mind, for him everything else becomes easy. *All else is easily attainable* – he achieves everything effortlessly. He doesn't have to do anything for achieving.

*The mind has become as clean and pure…* And in this state of samadhi, in this state where mind is immersed in the mind, the mind becomes so clean and pure. Let these words continue to echo in your mind – they will be of immense help to you.

*The mind has become as clean and pure as the water of Ganges. Now the Lord follows you, calling "Kabir, Kabir!"* There is a time when the seeker seeks the divine, when he shouts the names of Ram and Rahim. But then there also comes a time when the divine follows you, calling "Kabir, Kabir!" When does that time arrive, when the divine looks for you, calls for you?

Indeed, there was a time when you used to call but nothing was heard in reply. That was the time when your mind was overflowing with waves. That time your voice was not worth listening to – it certainly was not worthy of receiving an answer. So you may go on shouting in temples and mosques. Kabir in fact asks: Is your *khuda*, your God, deaf that you are reciting the prayer so early in the morning, reciting your *namaz*, your prayer, so loudly? Has your God gone deaf? Why are you shouting so loudly?

You may go on shouting in your temples, mosques and gurdwaras but nothing will happen. Nothing will happen only by your shouting because, after all, this shouting is nothing more than your inner chattering. Just be silent. Talking is not prayer; prayer is becoming silent. Prayer is not for saying something to the divine. Prayer is actually not talking to the divine but rather prayer is a way of listening to the divine. Be silent – listen!

When the mind is immersed in mind and is silent, not a wave of thought appears – *the mind has become as clean and pure*... Then there is transparency, everything becomes pure, all perversions vanish, and all sicknesses disappear. Then the mind becomes like a clear mirror. *The mind has become so clean and pure like the water of Ganges*. Just like Ganges water.

*Now the Lord follows you, calling "Kabir, Kabir!"* Now the whole thing has become the opposite. Now the divine follows the seeker, searches for him. Then you are truly worthy; the divine comes and knocks on your door. Regardless of how many temples, mosques, and gurdwaras you may knock on, it will not be heard by the divine.

So the real issue is that of your becoming clean and pure. And, for Kabir, purity means mind merging in the mind – mind lost in the mind. Meditation means mind immersed in the mind: no wave survives – only the ocean is, not the wave. But it is very difficult.

*The entire world is confused; to whom shall I go and explain it?* Whom to explain it to? Everyone seems to have already understood it, says Kabir. They have already become wise. Borrowed knowledge has made them all wise. And that's the reason why there is no way to remove their ignorance. The first and the foremost thing to realize is to know: "I am ignorant." Only then will I be able to make you understand.

Enough for today.

# 3
# Cutting the Chains

***You have yourself forgotten the self.***
***Like a deluded dog, trapped in a palace of mirrors,***
***ends his life barking at his own image.***
***Or like a lion, seeing his reflection in the well,***
***takes a jump and falls into it.***
***Or when an elephant, seeing himself mirrored in a crystal rock,***
***breaks his tusks as he bangs against it.***
***Or when a monkey, having grabbed some sweets in his fist from***
***a jar with a narrow opening,***
***fails to retrieve his fist – and runs from door to door screaming.***

Kabir says: ***O parrot hanging upside down,***
***who is holding you?***

Before we enter this sutra, it is important that we understand a few fundamental things.

There was a Sufi mystic named Bayjid. Once, as he was relaxing outside his hut, a seeker approached and asked him: "What is religion? What is spiritual discipline? What is the path?"

Bayjid asked, "Why do you want to know?"

The young man said. "I want to be free from bondage."

Bayjid laughed. He laughed uproariously, just as a mad person does. And he said, "First make sure to find out what it is that has tied you and what you wish to be free from. Until you come back absolutely certain about this I won't give you any answer."

The story goes that the young man left and returned after many years – but now he also had that same kind of madman's laughter.

Bayjid asked, "Did you find it?"

The young man said, "Now I have nothing to ask; I am back just to reply to your laughter. I was the one who had tied himself, and I was also the one playing the trick of seeking freedom from bondage. That was nothing but a way of keeping myself from seeking truth. I used to ask: how shall I become free? Seeking the path was also a way of postponing – that I will reach once the path is found; that once I find the path, the fetters will be cut. But not knowing the way, without any technique, how can we be free from our moorings?

"It was good that you did not answer me and instead gave me that uproarious laugh of a madman. That laughter hit me; it created a deep wound within me. I searched a lot; but the more I kept searching, the more it became clear that I had tied myself – no one else had bound me. And since I am the one who is tying myself up, then where is the need for freedom? Don't tie yourself up and you are free!"

This is the first thing that needs to be understood. Seeking moksha, liberation, is also a trick; it is one way of keeping yourself away from it. When did you become unfree? Who has tied you? You are not even sick and yet you are looking for medicine. When you don't find the medicine you feel "What can I do?" You look for a master, you look for God. And the fact is you have never lost the divine, which is hidden within you. It is there even while you go on a search.

And you have experienced a faint glimpse of it too – it is not that you have completely forgotten it. No one has tied you. You have some sense of it because it is such a vast truth that it cannot be forgotten completely.

You have put the chains on yourself although you are not wearing them as chains – you are wearing them as ornaments. You have set jewels and diamonds in these chains. In fact, you have turned them into golden chains – they are not chains of iron. You have taken a great interest in these chains. Now you are afraid of getting rid of them because you don't see them as chains anymore. You have decorated your prison with great care and made it into your home. Now you ask: "How do I become free from this prison?" But you know very well that you don't want to be free; otherwise, who is stopping you?

If your house is on fire, you immediately jump up and get out of there. Then you don't ask where to find a guru, whom to ask to show you the way. Then you don't ask what the technique is to get out; then you don't start a profound study of the scriptures. At that moment, simply knowing that the house is on fire, you find your way out on your own.

But when it comes down to finding a way out of this samsara, you ask: "Where is the way out?" The fact is, you don't want to get out and the fire doesn't seem to be an enemy to you; it seems to be a friend. Then why do you ask? If indeed you don't want to get out, if it is true that you are more interested in turning the prison into your home, then go ahead and do it. Why do you ask for the way out?

Mind is cunning. While asking for the path you convince yourself on two counts that "I am not an ordinary worldly person, I am a spiritual person. Yes, I am stuck in bondage but

I want to get out of it. Yes, I do get angry; but my intention is to attain the state of no anger. Yes, I am deeply involved in sex but my focus is on attaining celibacy." This way you hide your garbage under high ideals – you place flowers on top of your wounds. Neither do you want to heal your wounds nor do you want to even have a look at them. That's why you go on asking, "Where is the path? What is the technique? Who is a guru? How can I be free?"

Who can pull you out of this duplicity of yours? You will have to take a look at this dishonesty with wide-open eyes. It is painful. Looking at the dishonesty of others is very pleasant, looking at one's own dishonesty is very painful because in doing so you become aware of your image of yourself. And certainly you have created grand images of yourself!

Even the most evil man believes, "As a person I am a good man. Even though, once in a while, I do bad things, that is a different matter. My act is bad, but as a person, I am a good man. I do bad things because of the circumstances, because of some compulsion, or because of my bad luck – but I never want to do anything wrong. And the day things go well, I won't do anything wrong, even by mistake. What can I do? I am helpless: I have a wife, children, a family to look after. So I commit a little theft, cheat a little, say something untruthful – but actually, I am not a bad person."

Even the most evil person carries a beautiful image of himself. That beautiful image is helpful for doing evil things because it prevents you from seeing the ill in evil acts. It is because of this beautiful image that you are unable to feel how tightly evil has a hold on you, and how its poison has entered into every cell of your being. That's why you go on asking for a path, a method, or a technique.

So the first thing that needs to be understood is that you are tied because you want to be tied. No matter how painful this recognition may be, let it be clear to you that the chains are in your hands – you yourself, and nobody else, has put them on.

It is easy to put the blame on someone else. The husband thinks the wife has tied him down – what stupidity! The wife thinks the husband has put a harness on her – what madness! How can someone else harness you? Can anyone prevent you if you don't wish to be tied? Can your wife prevent you? Can your husband prevent you? Can your children prevent you? Who can really prevent you? No power on earth can put you in chains. Your freedom is invincible; no one can vanquish it. If you have become a submissive slave, then you alone are responsible. No one is tying anyone down – how can they? At least there is one thing no one has any control over – your ultimate inner freedom.

Dostoevsky – a great Russian author, a great psychologist and a great philosopher – was put into prison. In one of his letters written from the prison, he says: "Only when I was imprisoned did I come to know that the world can only chain my body, not me. I am as free in the prison as I was outside – nothing can hinder my freedom."

Who can hinder your inner space? But you think your wife has tied you.

Once it happened, Sheikh Farid was passing through a village. A few of his disciples were accompanying him. Suddenly, he stopped in the middle of the market and said, "Look!" He then asked a great question. He said, "I am asking you a very basic question, answer me after pondering over it. A man ties up a cow and is leading her." Farid continued, "My question is: is the cow tied to the man or is the man tied to the cow?"

The disciples said, "What is the big deal? What kind of a basic question is this? And it doesn't look good for a person like you to be joking like this. It is clear: the cow is tied to the man because the rope is in the man's hand and is tied around the cow's neck."

So Farid said, "The next question: if we cut this rope in half, will the cow follow the man or will the man follow the cow?"

Now the disciples got a little worried. They said, "Well, obviously, this is not a joke. It needs some thinking about, because if the rope is cut, the cow will escape and the man will run after her."

Then Farid said, "What I am saying to you is that the rope is not in the man's hand but rather around his neck. To all appearances, it looks as though the cow is tied to the man, but if you look a little more deeply you will find actually the man is tied to the cow."

Now, how can a wife keep her husband hooked? How can a husband keep his wife in fetters? The fact is, you want to be tied but you are not willing to take the responsibility for it – that you dump on someone else. This makes it easier to remain chained. Then you can say: "What else can I do? People have tied us up from all sides, where can we go even if we wish to? What can we do? How can we attain freedom? It is such a vast universe and it has kept us chained."

The shopkeeper thinks a customer has tied him. The greedy person thinks money has a hold on him. A lustful person thinks it is a woman who has chained him. A worldly person thinks the world has kept him in bondage. No, no one has chained you. But you are cunning, and your cunningness is very deep-rooted. You are actually deceiving yourself, but it is being done very skillfully: "The other has tied me down, what can I do?" This makes it easier to remain chained.

We always put the blame on others. Someone uses foul language and you say, "That man made me angry." How can anyone make you angry? You are talking about something impossible. It has never happened.

Certainly, if you want to be angry, then foul language can mean something. If you don't want to be angry, then the abuse becomes meaningless. Let us say, a beautiful woman passes by and you get attracted to her. Is it the beautiful woman who is attracting you? You actually want to be attracted. You see a diamond lying in the street. You immediately grab it. Did the diamond invite you, or was it because you were already filled with a desire, which instantly grabbed the diamond?

Stop blaming others, otherwise you will never be free – because if indeed someone else has tied you, then how can you become free unless the other frees you? And there is an infinite number of others, so freedom will be impossible. And if indeed what you say is true – that someone else has kept you fettered – then there will be no possibility of moksha, freedom. In that case, you will never be free. Then there will be an infinite number of bondages because there is an infinite number of others. And as far as you are concerned: if your wife leaves you, there are plenty of other women and one of them would tie you. What would you do then? You are powerless, absolutely helpless. No matter where you go, someone will put a noose around you; someone's leash will be around your neck. So, if it is the other who chains you, then moksha is impossible.

That is why the enlightened ones such as Kabir, Nanak and Farid point to this truth as the first step. They say, the fact that you have chained yourself should be very clear to you, otherwise the journey itself will be impossible. If this is clear, then the possibility of freedom exists because then you can break the chains yourself. You have tied yourself; you alone can free yourself. Neither does anyone else put you in chains nor *can* anyone actually put you in chains.

Then there is one more thing that you need to understand, which is quite profound. Mahavira has said: There is no one who can make you free. Regardless of how much you may pray, worship or read scriptures, nobody can set you free, because if someone can set you free then someone can also bind you. But if the other has not tied you then no one else can make you free either. That is why Mahavira says: Don't be under the illusion that someone will bring you freedom. Even the greatest guru cannot set you free because the possibility of somebody setting you free exists only if someone else has tied you down.

That is why Buddha says he can only point to where the bondage lies; he cannot set you free. You are the one who has tied yourself, now you are the one who will free yourself. Mahavira can show you what the bondage is and how you can cut through it. But Mahavira himself cannot cut your fetters. And it is good that no one else can remove your chains; otherwise on one side Mahavira would cut your ropes while someone else would put them back on you. If the ropes can be cut, they can be tied as well. But if it is impossible for the other to tie you, then it is equally impossible for anyone to cut you free.

That's why masters can show you the way, but ultimately *you* will need to walk on it. Masters can give you techniques, but you are the one who will need to use them. Masters can point things out to you, but you need to live what they are pointing at. A master can be a catalytic agent, you can awaken in his presence; but, ultimately, it is you who needs to awaken. But the big problem is, as Kabir has mentioned somewhere, it is easy to wake up someone who is asleep, but it is impossible to wake up someone who is lying down but still awake! And *that* is the state you are in.

Secondly, if you were just fast asleep, someone could shake your body and wake you up. But actually you are pretending to be asleep. You have pulled the blanket up and are lying down with closed eyes. You are showing, in every possible way, that you are in a deep sleep; and the fact is, you are awake. Now how to wake you up? If someone is really asleep, it is possible to pull him out of it; but how do you do this if the person is pretending to be asleep? You are deceiving yourself – self-deception has become almost your second nature.

Let us now try to follow Kabir's sutras while keeping all these things in mind. Kabir is a rustic villager. He doesn't use highly philosophical terms. But he has a fresh and profound experience of a simple villager. The metaphors he uses are spontaneous, emerging from a village life, but they touch very deeply. The more a word becomes cultured and polished, the more dead it is. As a language gets spruced up and refined – the more it is adorned – the more it loses life. The language that a villager speaks is as alive as the person living in the village is. Kabir's language is very alive and his metaphors and symbols are straightforward. In India, Kabir is the only one who is parallel to Jesus.

Mahavira, Buddha, Krishna, Rama – they come from a highly cultured world. They belong to a highly noble and sophisticated tradition. Kabir is a simple villager – exactly like Jesus. Jesus is the son of a carpenter, while Kabir is a weaver. Jesus also uses everyday language. And you may be surprised to know that the reason half of this huge world is impacted by Jesus is because of the aliveness in his language.

The language of Mahavira and Buddha seems like paper flowers. Indeed, we find profound doctrines being discussed through it, but it doesn't touch the heart; it touches the intellect and then falls apart. The language used by Kabir and Jesus is simple, straightforward; it is based on experience, not on the scriptures. So all these metaphors are coming out of experience.

Kabir says:

***You have yourself forgotten the self.***

You have forgotten yourself, your own self, and are now blaming others for it. You got tied on your own and are now making others responsible for it.

***You have yourself forgotten the self.***
***Like a deluded dog, trapped in a palace of mirrors,***
***ends his life barking at his own image.***

The story is that an emperor once built a temple out of mirrors. It was a huge temple, which had thousands of mirrors built into it. Accidentally, a dog slipped in. The guard closed the door at night and the dog was trapped in the temple.

He was obviously in great trouble. As he looked around, he saw millions of dogs, because each mirror was reflecting a dog. The dog, surrounded by enemies, had never seen anything like this before. If there had been just one dog, he would not have minded fighting it out and winning. But there were so many of them; he could see them – above, below and all around. The dog became scared; then he thought he could scare those dogs by barking at them.

Remember, whenever you feel scared, you want to scare others – simply out of fear. You are scared already, otherwise why would you want to scare others? A fearful person tries to create fear in others. If the other becomes fearful, his fear is relieved.

So always remember: someone who is fearless will never create fear in others, but someone who is fearful himself will also scare others. Subtle methods can be applied to make others fearful. While one person may scare you by pointing a sword at your body, another may scare you by describing the whole system in hell – that there will be a raging fire, there will be huge cauldrons with boiling oil in which you will be fried! The soldier scares you with his sword, while the monk scares you with the name of hell. Indeed they use subtle means; but the fact remains that your monk is afraid and so is your soldier. Why would someone who has no fear create fear in others?

We make the other fearful in our own self-defense. So the dog also applied the same obvious method that humans do. He started barking in the hope that he could create fear. But he got himself into great trouble because when he barked, he found those millions of dogs also barked. It was actually his own voice which echoed within that deserted temple. He must have been scared to death. There was no way to escape and no place to go. Where could he have gone? He was surrounded – from above and below, all around. Perhaps you may not be able to empathize with the dog's pain, but if you take a look at your own life, you will see that it is the same suffering.

*Like a deluded dog, trapped in a palace of mirrors, ends his life barking at his own image.* When the doors were opened in the morning, the dog was found dead. No one had killed the dog; there was no one there to kill him. The temple was empty. But the dog's entire body was full of bloody wounds. Blood was splashed all over the temple. What had happened? Well, the dog went on barking, jumping, and hitting against the wall – the dog died by his own actions.

*You have yourself forgotten the self.* And this is life's story – yours too. Who are you angry with? Who do you lust after? Whom do you hate? Has it ever occurred to you that all your relationships are like mirrors? All relationships are like mirrors because you will see your own image reflected in them. The relationships that you create all around you show you photographs. You see yourself in them – no one else. Where you feel your photograph to be good, there is a friend; where you feel it to be not likeable, there is an enemy. Yours, not yours…! But regardless: all your relationships are like mirrors which reflect no one else but yourself.

Realize this, an angry person will always feel people are insulting him. If someone laughs, he will think he is being laughed at. If people are whispering on the street, he will think they are talking about him. If no one says a word, if people remain silent, he will feel it is all because of his presence. No matter what people may do, he will see his own image in it.

A friend of mine has only one son. His son once told me: "I am in great difficulty, there seems to be no way out. Please do something. Please make my father understand. If I wear fashionable clothes, he says, 'So, go ahead and show off your fancy clothes if that's what you want! You will come to realize what you are doing later, when I am dead.' If I don't dress properly, he says, 'I am not dead yet; at least wear proper clothes now. I know this is what you will end up wearing after I am gone.'"

The young man said he didn't know what to do. He said he had tried everything, but his father always came to his own conclusions. And, in a way, what his father concludes is quite logical: you cannot find fault with it.

An angry person invites anger from all around in every possible situation. A greedy person thinks people around him are ready to rob him. Friends, sons, husband or wife – all are bent upon robbing him. Relatives – all these people are focused on only one thing: how to plunder his wealth. A greedy person finds the whole world is after his money. This is the way greed is reflected in the mirror. A lustful person feels the whole world has overwhelmed him with passion. The ascetic finds the whole world is leading him into renouncing; he feels the entire world is pointing at only one thing – drop, escape.

You hear an echo of yourself – whatever you are. And the whole world is what Kabir calls a temple of mirrors: *Like a deluded dog, trapped in a palace of mirrors, ends his life barking at his own image.*

Finally, when you are dead and gone – and you go on dying every day – you will find yourself thinking that all these people were responsible for finishing you, killing you.

In the past – and even now in aboriginal tribes – if someone becomes sick, they try to find out who cast a spell on him and caused the sickness. The person gets sick but goes to the witch doctor to find out who must have made him sick. The logic is precisely the same – if a sickness has taken root, it must have been sent by somebody. If I am miserable, then somebody must be causing it. If I am stressed, then someone must be bothering me. The calculation seems clear and simple: how can you be stressed unless someone is filling you with stress? But you don't know how the human mind works. Even if you were to be left alone, and all your needs taken care of, even then you would be in the same condition.

Of the many experiments that have taken place in the West, one of them, known as sensory deprivation, is very significant. Several psychologists have worked on it. They have created artificial wombs where all kinds of conveniences are available. Food automatically reaches the bloodstream through tubes – one doesn't have to make any effort. When thirsty, water automatically reaches the body in the same way as with food. There is pitch darkness. No sound is audible.

The same combination of chemical substances that are present for a child in the womb have been recreated. They have created tubes that contain exactly the same chemical substances as in a mother's womb. The person floats in it, sleeps in it. The tub is placed in complete darkness. He has no worries about food and water, nor is he in any trouble – all comforts are provided for, everything is fine. But within fifteen minutes the person becomes uncomfortable. He keeps sending messages: "Take me out of here, get me out."

Extended experiments were done. Some people dared to participate in the experiment for twenty-one days. They were asked to send messages during those twenty-one days – various buttons were provided. If they felt angry, they had to push the red button and the psychologist upstairs would note down that the person was angry. If they felt scared, they had to push the green button, or a different button if they were filled with jealousy. In this way various buttons were placed for different feelings. And the strangest thing is, there was nobody to bother them. But at some point in time the person got angry for no reason at all. The person himself would feel uneasy as to why he was angry – but angry he certainly was.

Anger, greed, attachment, these are all your inner states. They have nothing to do with people around you. They are just like the pegs you hang your clothes on. When you hang your anger on people, they are just like pegs; you hang your greed, your lust, on a peg. Actually, it all comes from within you. And when you are filled with disappointment and dejection about life, when all is lost and death is approaching, you will perhaps say that you have complaints against the whole world; that people have ruined you. You were here to be somebody, but the world didn't allow you to become that person. You would have displayed such light and radiance, but people just nullified everything. Is this world an enemy of yours?

There seems to be no reason though why the world should be so hostile to you. Why would anyone be interested in ruining you? Clearly, everyone wants to fulfill himself but everyone believes that the rest of the world is trying to destroy them. After all, who else would you really want to end up becoming? You want to fulfill yourself while others wish to fulfill themselves. But as far as relationships are concerned, they are nothing more than mirrors in which you see your own image.

I have heard...

Once there was an exhibition of modern paintings. Modern paintings are basically nonrational, it is difficult to find meaning in them. And if painters, such as Picasso, say that these paintings have no meaning, how will you find any?

Someone asked Picasso, "What do your paintings mean?"

He replied: "The trees standing out there, what do they mean? Those flowers, what meaning do they have? The sound of that stream out there, what meaning does it convey? If they carry no meaning as such, then why do you make things difficult for me? If God is without any meaning, then why do you make things difficult for a poor person like me by asking such questions? I am also without any meaning!"

So modern painting is absolutely meaningless – just like nature is. You can feel delighted looking at it, you can feel sad, you can feel miserable or you can feel happy looking at it. But it has no meaning as such.

Once Mulla Nasruddin visited an exhibition of modern painting. While looking at the paintings he felt so troubled – nothing was making sense to him. He could not make head nor tail out of them. He couldn't even figure out whether the paintings were hanging the right way up or upside down. Finally, he stood in front of a painting and said, "This is too much! Now what is the meaning of this painting?"

The painter said, "Sir, you are standing in front of a mirror! This is not a painting."

You stand before a mirror your whole life. Therefore, conduct your relationships in the same way as you treat a mirror. Relationships are just as fragile as a mirror – just a little fall and it will break into pieces. And once a relationship breaks, it is as difficult to put it together again as is in the case with a broken mirror. Even if you succeed in putting it together again, the lines where it was broken remain. Similarly, once love is broken, no matter how much effort you put into reassembling the pieces – and you may even succeed in doing so – it will never be the same again.

A relationship is exactly like a mirror – just as fragile, and reflecting your image. In every relationship, the image reflected is always yours. Don't ever blame others. If you find your life wasted, then know you alone have done it. And the sooner you realize no one else has any hand in ruining you, the sooner a process of creativity will begin in your life.

Like a deluded dog, trapped in a palace of mirrors, ends his life barking at his own image. "You have yourself forgotten the self!" Such is your situation.

***Or like a lion, seeing his reflection in the well,***
***takes a jump and falls into it.***

And like the lion who saw his image reflected in the well, and jumped onto it – it is difficult to tolerate an enemy – the lion died. Before you jump on someone, take a little pause. Think for a moment: is there really somebody else there for you to jump on or are you pouncing on your own image? If someone vilifies you, you instantly jump on that person.

Have you ever paid attention to the fact that we get hurt when we are criticized or condemned because there is some truth in it; otherwise there is no reason to be hurt. If someone was telling utter lies about you, you would be able to laugh at it. But if a person is saying something which is true, something which you have been hiding all along but which is now getting exposed, then you will certainly jump on him. Criticism hurts because the truths you are hiding begin to unravel right in front of you.

If you think closely about the person who is calling you names, nine out of ten times you will find he is right. And there is a reason for it. The reason he is right is that it is always easy to watch the other objectively. Watching oneself objectively is very difficult: it needs a certain distance. You are not able to see yourself the way others are able to see you. You never know how others look at you.

Psychologists say: if people were really to become truthful the way religious priests ask them to be, and if people were to speak nothing but the truth, this world wouldn't last very long. If people spoke truthfully about how they think about you, everyone would turn into an enemy.

As it is, it is difficult to find a friend; and a friend appears to be friend only because he does not say what he really thinks about you. Or, even if he says something, it is behind your back. The other is able to watch you closely because there is a certain neutrality. You may also have observed one thing: if someone comes to you with a problem, you are able to give him very clear advice. But if the same problem occurred in your life, you would never apply your own advice in order to deal with it. Why?

It is easy to advise others because there is a distance in between. Even the most successful surgeon would not be able to operate on his wife, his hands might tremble; there is less distance. He has no difficulty operating on someone else's wife. What does he have to do with the other's wife? He operates on her as if he were conducting a postmortem – it makes no difference if she lives or dies. But he is attached to his own wife – there are children, a family involved; if he commits a mistake, she will die. So he is afraid, there is a shiver in his body. Even a great surgeon invites another one when his wife needs an operation. And a well-known doctor has to get his own illness diagnosed by another doctor.

It is so strange! Why would a doctor, who knows everything, want someone else to make his diagnosis? He can do it himself. But now the distance is even less; in the case of his wife, at least there was some distance. And maybe there is some unconscious desire that she will die; after all, who doesn't want to rid himself of his wife? Maybe the reason behind his fear could be the thought that he might actually kill her, he might make some mistake and finish her. It is difficult to find a husband who, in his unconscious mind, has not thought at least a few times that his wife should be dead. Similarly, it is difficult to find a wife who may not have thought at least a few times how the husband could die so she could be finished with all the trouble. Of course, after his demise, there will be a lot of wailing and crying. And the reason for this is also worth knowing.

For example, when someone dies, when people cry there is a feeling of guilt behind it because they wanted the person to die – and now he is dead. They think that they are partly responsible for it. If someone does not want to kill anyone, then he will take the death of such a person rather lightly. He will not repent much because there will be no guilty feeling. Repentance is always in proportion to the feeling of guilt.

A father dies and the son weeps a lot because while the father was alive he never touched his feet; while the father was alive the son never sat by his side and talked lovingly. Now there is no chance; now the feeling of guilt will last forever. Now there is no way of resolving this situation. On the other hand, if a son has served his father, has massaged his feet when needed, if he has paid attention to what his father said and looked after him, loved him, he will have no reason to go crazy. When the father dies he will realize, "Everyone dies, death is natural. I too will die."

But if you have done something that you shouldn't have done with your father, then you are bound to repent heavily. This is the situation in reverse; a son who cries and weeps loudly gives the impression to society that he is in great distress, whereas if a son takes the pain quietly, people will think he is dishonorable. His father is dead and he is sitting quietly.

But the reality is that someone who is sitting quietly has no guilt or repentance; someone who is weeping and yelling is merely finding a substitute. He could instead have used that same energy in massaging his father's feet or in stroking his head. Now this crying and weeping is meaningless.

It may be an unconscious fear of the doctor that he might kill his wife and so his hand will tremble. But in terms of oneself even that much distance is not possible. If he is sick, then he cannot make the diagnosis himself because now the fear is even greater that he might commit a mistake.

Mulla Nasruddin went to see his doctor. The doctor said, "Don't be worried, I am here to fix your illness. And just to reassure you, may I say that I have been through this illness myself. So don't worry."

Nasruddin said, "I can't get over my fear because, though you may have been through this illness, another doctor must have treated you."

That is why, Kabir says, What kind of cleverness or expertise is that? Holding a lamp in your hand you fell into the well! The lamp was for others; he who uses the lamp for himself becomes enlightened; he who applies the wisdom to himself becomes luminous within. Then there is no end to his mastery. But although we hold a lamp for others, we are simply blind where we ourselves are concerned. So it is possible that someone who slanders you may be saying something about you which is more true than what you can say about yourself. Kabir is right when he says: Keep your critic near you, pay attention to what he says. And you will be amazed to learn that the very thing he says which is true, hurts you the most. Truth bothers. Truth pinches. It never bothers you if someone is telling lies about you.

I have heard...

One of the great writers of the West, Oscar Wilde, wrote a very slanderous article about some other author. The author came to visit him and said, "What kind of enmity are you carrying against me? Why do you write such lies about me?"

Oscar Wilde replied, "Enough! If I were to write the real truth about you, you would be ruined!"

And it is said that the man left quietly and never complained again.

You easily tolerate lies told against you, but the truth hurts. Whatever hurts you, know that some mirror has shown you your face. At that point you feel like breaking the mirror.

I have heard...

An ugly-looking woman was against mirrors; wherever she saw a mirror she would immediately break it. This was her mania. She was brought to a psychiatrist for treatment.

The woman said, "No matter what I do I cannot stand mirrors. I look ugly because of those mirrors: *they* make me look ugly. I am beautiful without any mirrors around; but when there are mirrors I turn ugly-looking."

Now why would a mirror care to make you look ugly? What has the mirror to do with you? What vested interest does a mirror have in you? But the fact is that a mirror shows exactly who you are.

All relationships are mirrors.

In matters of relationship, people act exactly the way that woman was doing. People break relationships. The person who renounces, abandons his wife saying he cannot stand her anymore. But his wife was just a mirror. She reflected his lust; she showed his passionate desire. What can be achieved by breaking the mirror? The man is as crazy as that woman was. What will he achieve by escaping to the Himalayas? The mirror may be left behind but the lust will accompany him. In the Himalayas the danger is much greater because without the mirror being around, he will imagine and believe himself to be good-looking. But if he returned from the Himalayas after thirty years, or after thirty lives, the moment he saw himself in the mirror he would see himself as ugly, even though he had been ugly-looking all the time.

That is why the real sannyasin never runs away from relationships; rather he wakes up in relationships. He looks into the mirror attentively. A true sannyasin feels gratitude toward his relationships for showing him things, for waking him up, for making him aware who he really is. A pseudo sannyasin escapes; a genuine sannyasin awakens.

That is why I always say: don't escape – wake up! Take it as your commandment, your indicator. Don't run away from any relationship because all relationships wake you up. So awaken and transform yourself. What is the point of breaking the mirror? The day you wake up that same mirror will show you something else about yourself. As you become more good-looking, the mirror will tell you how good-looking you are. The mirror is completely neutral.

***Or like a lion, seeing his reflection in the well,***
***takes a jump and falls into it.***
***Or when an elephant, seeing himself mirrored in a crystal rock,***
***breaks his tusks as he bangs against it.***

The elephant, too, seeing his own image, hits the crystal rock and breaks his tusks.

***Or when a monkey, having grabbed some sweets in his fist from***
***a jar with a narrow opening,***
***fails to retrieve his fist – and runs from door to door screaming.***

Kabir's metaphors are very simple and straightforward. It often happens that a monkey puts his hand into a round pot to take out whatever is in it – some food or nuts. And then he closes his fist. Naturally, he grabs and closes his fist as large as he possibly can. We also do the same thing.

There is certainly a relationship between monkeys and man. Darwin can't be wrong. When there is a chance to hold something in his fist, which of them would want to have a small fist! We may call that monkey stupid. An intelligent monkey or a baby monkey may perhaps only succeed in taking out a little. He may be naïve, not experienced. But an experienced monkey will grab as much as he can in his fist. Now, as the fist becomes larger, the monkey is unable to pull his hand out of the pot's narrow opening. So the monkey jumps and runs around from door to door in agony with the pot hanging from his hand, but never opens his fist. He yells and screams – obviously he is in pain. And he may be thinking there is some trick to the jar – that is why he is caught – but he never opens his fist.

You are in the same situation. Your fist is large, which is why you never open it, and you go on banging your head on each door saying: "I want peace, I want joy, I want life!" And the fact is you are caught in a jar; and that is why there is so much trouble.

The monkey catchers take advantage of their stupidity. They bury pots in the ground; neither the monkey can escape nor can he open his fist. You don't open your fist, so how could the monkey? Do you think the monkey is less intelligent than you? He keeps trying to pull his closed fist out of the pot. That is exactly what you are doing.

People come to me and say: "We want things to keep on going the way they are, and at the same time we want to have peace of mind." What they are saying is: "Show us the way for the fist to remain closed and the mind to become peaceful. Let everything remain the way it is, let nothing be disturbed and yet let us attain mental peace." But the fact is that the mind has no peace because you have kept your fist closed inside the pot, and that is where it is hurting. That is where the pain is.

A rich man used to visit me. He would say: "Yes, one day I will renounce everything but until that happens please give me some technique. I will drop everything some day, everything, but till then...please don't let me suffer because of a lack of peace!"

As if I were responsible for his lack of peace!

He said: "Show me some technique in the meantime so that I can have peace of mind."

I said to him, "Supposing that, in the meantime, a technique for attaining peace was found. Do you really think you would drop everything when you have peace of mind if you are unable to do so now, when you are not at peace? When you are at peace you may say, 'Now there is no need to drop anything.'"

If the monkey could pull his fist out of the pot while keeping it closed, if by doing this he could be free of the pot and its trouble, then do you think the monkey would ever be so stupid as to open his fist once it is out of the pot? He didn't do it even when he was in such torture. Even you don't open your fist when you are in such misery, so do you suppose you will open it in happy times?

Have you ever heard of anyone renouncing the world because of happiness? They don't leave the world even when they are in pain, even when they are suffering, they don't leave even under the most miserable conditions, so do you think anyone would leave because he is happy? That is impossible. Even now, when life is a hell, people are unable to drop the world, so how will it be possible when all is going well?

The man said, "Whatever you say is right; but I'm not in a position to renounce right now. Will I continue to be restless like this?"

The reason was that he could not sleep at night. I used to be a guest in his house but he wouldn't let me sleep at night. He would just sit; remain seated, during the night. Out of courtesy, I would strike up some conversation with him. Finally, one day his wife told me this wouldn't work. She said, "I have made the same mistake before. Please go to bed! He is unable to sleep at night because his mind is preoccupied with large sums of money. Where finances are concerned, his mind is only interested in big numbers."

Once I was a guest at their house. He looked very sad as he drove me home from the airport. On the way he said, "This time I have incurred a big loss. I have lost half a million rupees over these last few days." He was involved in the stock market.

His wife was also with us, I was seated between the two. The wife pressed my hand and said, "Don't listen to him."

After reaching home I inquired what the matter was. His wife said, "He has incurred no loss at all. In fact, he has made half a million, although he was trying to make a million. So he goes around saying that he has lost half a million."

Now look at the monkey's fist; now he wants peace. What he had imagined the gain would be like didn't come true and that for him is a loss. As you come close to death, at the end of your life, you too will count everything which you thought would happen, but didn't, as a loss. You didn't get what you deserved, what you were worthy of, or what your birthright was.

You will have to loosen your fist. Being like a monkey won't do! And sannyas simply means being free from this monkey-like behavior. Such stupidity clearly indicates that you are troubled by excessive greed. You are troubled by much anger. You are always in trouble because you have collected so many desires, which you are completely unable to keep tightly held in your fist. Your fist is small and you have gathered so much. The fist is useful as long as it holds your needs; but the moment needs become desires, your fist seems too small. And then the larger you make your fist, the more you get trapped in the pot of this world, in samsara.

Kabir says: A monkey, having grabbed some sweets in his fist from a jar with a narrow opening, fails to retrieve his fist – and runs from door to door screaming. The monkey keeps screaming and running from door to door, crying, but keeps the pot hanging from his hand. The pain is great but then the greed is great too. Remember, greed seems more vital than the pain it causes.

Your hope of attaining pleasure and gratification from the situation you are in is greater than the misery you are going through because of it. There is no happiness, only the hope for it. Man is attached to hope. Sooner or later some plan may work, some method may succeed, some miracle may happen, someone's blessings may bring fruit – it will all work out fine, so hope! Don't let go of the pot because once you have taken your fist out then who knows whether you will get another chance to put your hand in again or not. One doesn't find a pot every day. And the fact is, there are more monkeys than there are pots!

Everyone is carrying his own pot. Who knows, the moment you get rid of the pot some other monkey may put his hand in it. You may get out of the misery but someone else may begin to suffer from it – then what will you do? So it is better to be stuck with the pot, keep it hanging, suffer; it doesn't matter if you are unable to sleep. Life may become agony and hell, it doesn't matter, but keep hope alive: sometime, someday, some plan will work out. Pray, go on worshipping, go to the temple, but keep the pot with you!

Go and listen to what people are praying for in the temple. What are they saying? They are praying for their fist to come out of the pot while still closed. Kahlil Gibran has written somewhere: "I have heard the prayers of thousands of people and I have found that their prayer means only one thing – let two plus two not become four, rather something incredible should happen. Just these are their prayers."

Kabir says: **O parrot hanging upside down,**
**who is holding you?**

The hunters who capture parrots make use of a simple technique. They first tie a rope between two trees. Along the rope they fix small sticks. As the parrots land on these sticks, the stick turns upside down because of their weight. The parrots hang in that upside-down position. The hanging parrot thinks he is caught and is afraid to let go of the stick, fearing he may fall down and die. He tries in some way to sit up straight on the stick but because the rope is thin he cannot sit up. He is comparatively heavy in weight and that is why he is bound to fall if he lets go of the stick. The more he agonizes, the more he remains suspended. And in all this fear and frustration he completely forgets that he has wings, that he can fly, that there is no question of falling down. But because of that headstand he remains caught. So beware of headstands! First people stand upside down and then they feel scared.

Kabir says: *O parrot hanging upside down, who is holding you?* O, fool, who is holding you? Just drop it; you are the one who is holding onto the rope. The moment you release it you are free!

No one is binding you; you are clinging. Moksha is not freedom from bondage, rather it is freedom from clinging. The bondage is external, but the clinging is internal. Anyone can bind you from the outside but *you* are clinging, no one else is doing it.

Whatever your clinging may be, you are caught in it. And now you are afraid. You have also forgotten about your wings, that you too can fly and there is no need to fear that you may fall down. But you have been caught for so long, you have been in bondage for so long, that you have completely forgotten that you were once free; that once upon a time you used to fly in the sky.

Parrots are unable to fly if they remain in a cage for too long. They forget that they have wings. Their capacity to fly weakens if their wings are not used for many days. That is exactly what has happened in this case.

And Kabir is being profoundly satirical when he says, *O parrot hanging upside down, who is holding you?* Who is holding you? No one is restraining you. It is you who is clinging to wrong things and suffering.

The essence of religion is: drop your clinging. Don't hold on to anything. Live whatever is, but don't cling to anything. Whether at home, or in the shop, or in the marketplace – don't cling to anything; keep your fist open. Live and enjoy the whole world, as it is meant to be. Living it, you will attain maturity. Living it, your understanding will grow. The experience will bring intelligence. So live, but live with awareness; don't cling to anything. Live in total freedom.

Pass through this world. Not a single experience is there that you should avoid or ignore. All experiences are worth going through because the potential of enlightenment within you will only awaken when you pass through these experiences. All experiences – good or bad – are worth going through. But go through them with awareness so that no experience becomes a prison and you get locked up in it.

This is what has happened. Once you experience something you get caught in it; then you would like to go through it again and again. Clinging happens. Whichever experience gives you pleasure, even just a glimpse of it, and you close your fist. You have lived with such distrust your whole life. You don't realize that life which has given you one experience can give even greater experiences than that – what is the hurry to tie yourself down? The life that has brought you here can take you to even wider shores. What is the hurry to make your home just here? You have hardly taken a step and you make it your final destination. Wait! Stop! Nothing is wrong in resting for the night; but when the dawn appears, get going.

The sages in the Vedas have said: Keep going! Keep going! Take a break, but never stop. Buddha used to tell his disciples: *Charaiveti, charaiveti* – keep walking, keep walking. Pause to rest, but don't build a house. The moment you cling to something, it immediately becomes a dwelling place for you. And once the dwelling place is built, soon it turns into a prison.

There is an old story among the Buddhists...

A man became a monk. He took initiation from a master. At the time of his initiation he asked his master, "Could you please give me a teaching to remember the rest of my life?"

The master said, "Just be aware of one thing: never own a cat."

The young initiate became a little puzzled and thought, "This man seems crazy. Here I am in search of moksha, nirvana, God, but it seems as though I've got myself trapped taking initiation from this man. And what kind of teaching is he imparting? – never own a cat!"

Then the master died.

The disciple never really understood what he had meant. He thought the master had been talking nonsense, that he had lost his mind, that he had gone senile. He was over the age of sixty. And two types of people are not worthy of trust. In the old days, those who had gone beyond sixty were not thought to be trustworthy and, in modern times, those who have become bedridden, those who are stuck in their chairs, who have become senile – now what they say is all meaningless.

So, the old man died. The disciple possessed nothing but a loincloth. When he used to take it off, mice would nibble at it. He asked the village people what he should do. They said, "Better you take a cat as a pet."

He completely forgot that the master had told him not to own a cat. The master had said it based on his own experience, because this same story had happened to him as well. The story always remains the same, just the characters change. So the disciple saw no problem and he found a cat. And that started the trouble because now he had to find food for her. The cat needed milk. True, the cat finished the mice, but now she was there!

He again asked the village people what to do. They said, "There is no problem; we will give you a cow."

So now, on the heels of the cat, the cow arrived. But for how long could the village people provide fodder for the cow? So they said, "Look there is some vacant land around your temple, why not start farming a bit?" He started farming but sometimes he would fall ill and then there was no one to water the land. It was also time-consuming; he had to cook for himself too.

The village people advised him to get married. There was already a girl in the village, ready for marriage. They got him married. Then he had children. He completely forgot everything else – the initiation, becoming a monk; it was all finished. Now he had to raise children, provide them with an education and so on. His farm grew; the business expanded.

As he was close to dying, he suddenly remembered, as if he was jolted out of sleep. He thought, "My God, this is too much. The old man was right when he said, 'Never own a cat.'"

Once you have a cat, all the rest follows. Once you have taken the first step, then it all becomes difficult.

Once I was staying somewhere as a guest and I heard two boys chit-chatting on the steps. They were from that family – the elder one was about four years old and the younger one about two-and-a-half years old. The elder one was advising the younger fellow. The younger one, who was about to start school, asked his brother, "What should I stay away from?"

The elder one replied, "Just remember one thing: if you can save yourself from it then you are really saved."

The younger one said, "Please tell me."

The bigger boy said, "C-*a*-t – cat. If you are taught this, then don't ever learn it because once you have learned it then you have to learn other things too. Just remain stuck on this one. Bigger words keep following it and then there is no end in sight. I myself got trapped in this situation. So beware!"

While I was listening to their conversation, – c-*a*-t for cat – I remembered this story and that those who succeed in saving themselves from the cat are safe from everything else. Once you cling to one thing, the clinging continues. You cling to the second and the third – it is a continuum. One after the other, it becomes a chain.

Live, go through every experience, but never cling to any experience. And if the possibility of an experience is always there; then what is the hurry to cling to any particular one? Also, never wish for a repetition of the same experience. Never ask again for the experience you have gone through once, because asking for it again means you have stopped so that you can get hooked. It means that again and again you have lost trust in life. There was so much more to come. If you keep going, this life can take you all the way to God. When you stop, you generally stop at a puny, meaningless place; you make your home on a garbage dump.

So Kabir says: *O parrot hanging upside down, who is holding you?* No one is holding you; it is *you* who owns the cat. You can be free if you want to. To be free you just need an earnest desire.

And what is this clinging? You need to make an effort to understand it. You need intense longing if you want to be free. Following such longing naturally develops the understanding of "Why am I tied?"

The enlightened beings say: you are not bound, rather you have tied yourself. If you wish to be free, you can be free this very instant. No need to waste a single moment. Like a burning flame, the profoundness, the intensity, the velocity can turn the whole past into ashes. You can be free this very moment.

Enough for today.

# 4
# Wordless Silence

*Consider those who take a master to be like a human being, to be blind.*
*They will certainly be very miserable in this world,*
*and they will continue to die and be reborn again and again.*

*In this whole universe there is no one greater than the master.*
*A master can do whatsoever he wishes,*
*even when God may not succeed in doing so.*
*There is no giver like a master and no beggar like a disciple.*
*A master bestows the wealth of all the three worlds.*

*A master is like a potter and the disciple is like a pot. Like a potter,*
*the master works on the disciple by removing all that is useless.*
*Like making a pot, with one hand the master holds a disciple from within*
*and with the other hand he hits him from without.*

*Keep a master on the highest pedestal and follow what he says.*
*Then, says Kabir, there is nothing for a devotee to fear*
*in this whole universe.*

***When both the master and God are standing before me,***
***whose feet should I touch first?***
***My gratitude to you, O master, for showing me God!***
***If the Lord is displeased with me, then the master is my only refuge.***
***But there is no refuge if the master is displeased.***

In the East consciousness has discovered the guru, the master. There is no word for guru in the languages of the West. We find words such as: *teacher*, *professor*, *mentor*, but no word similar to *master*. Let us first understand the word because it contains very subtle meanings.

A teacher is someone who gives knowledge, someone from whom we learn something which adds to our memory, to our information. A master is not a teacher – he doesn't give you knowledge to add to your existing information. A master is just the opposite of a teacher – he takes away all your knowledge. He shows you ways to drop all that you may have stored in your memory. The first thing he does is to make you totally ignorant, because the moment you experience the state of ultimate ignorance the doors to the divine open up. These doors open only for those who know nothing. The doors open for those who know that they don't know anything. For those who think they know, the doors are shut forever – not because of the divine but because of the person's own misconception that he knows.

There is no greater ego than to claim that one knows. What do you really know? Whatever you think you know is all garbage. And that garbage, too, is not really your creation; it is all borrowed. It is something you have learned from others. We call this load of garbage "erudition." We continue to carry this load and it keeps growing and makes us feel as if we are carrying a rock. This load will never grow wings so that someday you may soar into the sky of the divine. It has nothing to do with moksha or liberation either, because in order to attain moksha one must essentially be free from any weight. Your wings can soar freely, high into the sky, only when all weight is dropped. And there is no heavier weight than the weight of knowledge.

Claiming that you know is the very problem; that is your very bondage. The ego readily believes that it knows, because for the ego to acknowledge it does not know is very painful. That is why Socrates says that when someone becomes truly knowing the first thing he knows is that he knows nothing. Then the doors open – but these are not the doors of knowledge, they are the doors of experience.

Only when someone comes to experience that which he does not know is he then capable of becoming a disciple. If you have come to me with even the slightest knowledge, you will return without having learned anything. Your very knowledge will become the barrier. You won't give me a chance to reach your inner self because your knowledge will prevent me from entering. It is essential that your knowledge and understanding get out of the way.

You have to set your so-called knowledge aside because one thing is certain: through your so-called knowledge you have neither attained truth nor have you found any life or seen any light...

What have you really achieved from what you claim to know or understand? Except for earning an ego you have achieved nothing. By claiming to know, you gained the arrogance of "I know." But this haughtiness is simply hollow. Such arrogance looks just like the twists still visible in a burned-out rope.

There is no energy or power in such arrogance because what you seem to know brings no depth, no profundity to life. This knowledge takes you nowhere; on the contrary, it leads you astray. When someone admits he doesn't know, he will pause and take a rest; he won't keep walking. He will say, "I don't know where to go. Which way should I go? I don't know what my destination is. I don't know… So until I come to know, it is better to rest." At least those who don't know will not get lost!

One who says he knows – who has maps, information – such a person sets out on long journeys. But the longer the journey you choose, the farther away you will be from yourself. The person who says he is ignorant will just sit down; and just by sitting he will understand – because the one you are looking for is hiding within you. Had he been going on an outward journey, some maps could have been given to him, some scriptures could have been useful. No scripture will be of any use when going within.

A teacher merely passes on scriptures. Whatsoever information society has collected, centuries after centuries, the teacher hands it over to the next generation. A teacher is a link between two generations. A master is not a teacher. Whatever society may have given you, a master takes it away from you and makes you free from society. A master makes you free from knowledge – the knowledge you are filled with. A master makes you lighter.

So one doesn't have to go to a master for the purpose of learning, rather one needs to go to a master for unlearning.

Once someone asked Shree Raman "Please teach me, give me some instructions."

Raman replied, "For that, you will have to go somewhere else; only come here if you want to unlearn all that you have learned before. Here, we erase everything, we wipe it all out. Here, we don't wish to write anything on the sky of your consciousness. Much has already been written on it; we wish to remove it. Here we will make you empty, not fill you with anything."

You are already filled enough, and that is your problem. But you take on these problems and troubles as if they were your riches. You are eager to fill yourself even more. You think you have gone astray because you are not full enough. You think you are wandering because you lack some information, some knowledge; that if you get a little more you are sure to reach. No, you won't reach.

It is this information, this knowledge of yours that Kabir identifies saying: "What kind of cleverness is it, that though holding a lamp you fall in a well?" What kind of cleverness is this? What kind of knowledge is this? Falling into a well while holding a lamp in your hand! If you were really holding the lamp in your hand, then how in the world did you fall into the well? And if you are now in the well, then it means you must be carrying an extinguished lamp. Even when it has been extinguished, we still call it a lamp. Similarly, even though what we have may be useless, we call it knowledge.

There is one type of knowledge that Kabir has – it is a burning lamp. And there is another kind of knowledge – that of a pundit – which is an extinguished lamp. Yet we call both lamps. One shouldn't call an extinguished lamp a "lamp" – it is a linguistic fallacy. Similarly, one shouldn't call borrowed knowledge, or secondhand knowledge, "knowledge." It is misusing language. But only one among millions attains to knowing. Besides this one individual, what will happen to the rest? The rest also want to believe that they know. Such belief brings them great satisfaction. Actually, by believing it to be true, you don't really achieve anything; you just get a feeling of satisfaction that "I also know."

You won't find anyone more confused than the pundit. That is why I keep saying, a sinner may attain liberation, but not the pundit. It has never been heard that a pundit has attained moksha. A few sinners certainly have but not a pundit, because the very pundit-ness, the very scholarship is in itself the greatest sin ever; all other sins look petty in comparison with it. Why?

Let us say that there is a thief, and he has robbed someone – this is a sin. But this is not much of a sin because money, after all, is nothing but dust, trash. So this is not such a great sin; how much money would the thief have stolen, really? It is not such a big sin because the robber always has the feeling that he has done something wrong. His ego doesn't really grow doing it; rather whatever he has done pinches his ego like a thorn.

Then there is the person who has stolen knowledge – a pundit means one who has stolen knowledge. A pundit is a thief. But he acts with such flair, as if he were some big banker. And, in fact, what he has stolen is more subtle and crafty. At no time does he feel any thorn pinching him to tell him that he has stolen something. A thief feels the pinch and that can bring him to moksha. No such thorn pinches a pundit. He rides on a flower, and that very flower will cause his downfall – it is disastrous.

So the first thing is that a master doesn't give you any knowledge; rather he takes away your knowledge. He doesn't fill you; rather he actually makes you empty of all you have known. A master leads you into *shunya*, no-mind, because the whole can descend only in no-mind. A master makes you empty so that there can be room for the divine to descend. Hence there is a fundamental difference between the master and a teacher.

The second thing is that a teacher will use words because that is the only medium for him. Whatsoever he may have to say, whatsoever he may have to give, whichever knowledge he may be imparting, words are the only means. A master will also use words, knowing well that they are only an opening, a prelude. Truth can never be transferred through them.

A teacher finishes with words while a master ends in wordless silence. A master also begins with words; hence the concern that people may get confused and see a teacher as a master and a master as a teacher. After all, he has to begin with words because the journey can only start from where you are. If you are ill, then he has to begin with medicine. But medicine is not the end – health is. And being healthy means when medicine is no longer needed.

You are unwell – ailing with words. So a master will have to begin with words, but the aim will be to reach the wordless state. A teacher also begins with words, aiming at nothing but words. A master begins with words, but words are not his aim – silence or wordlessness is. A master uses words to negate your words. For example, if a thorn pierces the body, we use another thorn to pull it out. A master uses words in a similar way. You are pierced with words; a master uses his words to pull them out. But he never puts the very thorn – the word he has used to pull out the word in your body – back in your wound, in appreciation of how kind the thorn was, doing you a favor by pulling your old thorn out. The teacher, on the contrary, keeps on piercing you with thorns, with words.

The more knowledgeable you become, the more difficult it becomes to know. The more you are able to comprehend, the more difficult it becomes to understand. A master pulls one thorn out with another and then asks you to throw them both away; he asks you to become totally weightless, absolutely devoid of thorns. The ultimate aim is wordlessness, *shunya*.

A relationship is developed with the teacher; it is a relationship through the intellect. It is a connection between two heads not between two hearts. A teacher has nothing to do with the heart. The relationship with a master is not that of two intellects but of two hearts. This is why people in the West fail to understand the importance of trust, devotion toward the master. They see the master as a technician, an informed person, so they will say, "Go ahead and learn what you have to and be finished with it! Where does the question of having trust come in?"

If the relationship with the master were only of the intellect, then what the West is saying would be right. You learn, you say thank you, you pay the fees and the matter is over. It is just like when you are asking someone on the road for directions to reach the railway station – would it require any trust? The person will show you the way to the station, you will thank him and the matter will be finished. You will go your way and the person will go his way. Neither does he expect you to surrender to him and have trust in him nor will you ever think that you need trust and surrender when you are asking such a simple thing.

You asked, "Where is God?" and the master explained. You asked, "How to meditate?" and the master told you. You thanked him, you gave him presents and went home; the matter ended there.

The relationship between a teacher and a student is businesslike; there trust is not required. That is why if university teachers expect trust, respect, from their students, they are mistaken. It is simply not possible. But they carry this erroneous feeling because of the tradition that exists in the East. In the East a master is regarded with great respect and trust. These teachers think they are also masters; that they should also be given the same respect and trust. But no, they are not masters. The students are not disciples; the teacher is not a master. A student is paying fees. At the most, he will thank them – the matter will come to an end. There exists no heart to heart connection with the teacher – it is just not possible.

But in India, the feeling of deep respect for the master has existed for so long that even a university teacher thinks he is a master, without any concern whether he carries any of the qualities of a master, without realizing that not just anyone can manage to be a master. Only he who has achieved the greatness of a master can be a master. Only one who has attained the ultimate grandeur, one who has known the ultimate truth, can really be a master. Only such a person for whom there is nothing left to know is a master; one whose very being is the ultimate happening there can ever be; one who has attained samadhi. A master is one for whom the divine has become transparent; who has become one with existence; where there is not an iota of difference between him and existence – he indeed is a master.

The difference between a teacher and a student is quantitative and not qualitative. Do you think a master knows a little more than the disciple does? Not really; the difference between a master and a disciple is not, in fact, that of knowing more or less. The difference between a master and disciple is not quantitative; the difference is qualitative. A master is at one level while the disciple is at a different level. They dwell in two different worlds. They live in two different dimensions. They exist differently.

The difference between a university professor and his student is that of quantity. The professor knows a little more, the student knows a little less. If he is a little smarter, it is not too difficult for a student to know more than the professor does. It is not difficult at all; it is just a matter of degrees, quantity. Hence, a very talented student often gains more knowledge than the professor himself. It is simply a matter of some intelligence and a little more effort. And if he does not know today, he will certainly know more tomorrow. A professor may already have an M.A. degree; soon the student will earn his M.A. degree. So the difference is merely that of quantity, not of quality. As far as being is concerned, both are the same; but as far as intellectual capacity is concerned, they are different – one has more, the other has less. But what about quality? Where is the essence of a master here?

So, the distance between master and disciple is qualitative – the master is at one level and the disciple is at another. This is not a quantitative difference. The difference, the distance between the two, will disappear only when the disciple is totally transformed.

This difference will not go away by learning; a disciple may go on learning for lives and yet the difference will still remain. And it is also possible that in the world of knowledge the disciple may know more than the master does; but even then the difference between the two will remain the same as ever. Where is the problem with this? Anyone can have more knowledge than Buddha had. The fact is that today a university student knows more than Buddha did.

How much do you think Kabir knew? Anyone knows more than Kabir did. Kabir knew nothing about Einstein or about Heisenberg. He knew nothing about the atom bombs that fell on Hiroshima and Nagasaki. What did Kabir really know? As far as knowledge is concerned, if you were to put Kabir in for a matriculation exam, do you think he would pass it just like that? You may have to get a tutor for him and spend years of effort; only then would he be able to pass the exam. And that, too, is not really certain.

So it is not a question of knowing or being informed. You may go to school for lives, keep writing, earn and collect degrees – scores of them; universities may honor you with a D.Litt., and yet you will not attain even a grain of what Kabir has. Leaving you aside, even Einstein can never attain an iota of what Kabir has.

Even Einstein died with the anguish that he was dying without knowing anything, that the mystery of this universe remained out of his reach. Einstein possessed such knowledge! As far as knowledge or information is concerned, the psychologists say that perhaps no one in the history of mankind knew as much as he did. Einstein himself was amazed at how he was able to retain so much information. That is why at the time of his death, he left a will saying his brain should be scientifically investigated. His brain has been preserved in a laboratory and the investigations are still going on. His brain is incredible; it contains so much information. But what about his soul, his spirit or his being? It is exactly where yours is – there is no difference.

So keep two things in mind: the first is the quantitative spread of information; the other is the qualitative spread of being. Kabir doesn't have more things than you have. Your house is larger than Kabir's, your shop is bigger than Kabir's, your memory is greater than Kabir's, and your experience too exceeds Kabir's. And yet, Kabir is greater than you are. You may continue to be on the journey you are on now for lives together, and even then you will be nowhere near where Kabir is, what he has attained. How to explain this?

Kabir dwells in a totally different dimension – the dimension of being. Remember these two dimensions: the dimension of knowing, information, and the dimension of being. We look upon people like Kabir, Buddha, Christ and Krishna with such high esteem and reverence not because of how much they know, but rather for the purity of their being. Their being is of a different nature; it is totally different from ours. Even while living among us they are not part of us – they are from some other planet. That is why we call such people avatars. *Avatar* means that although they are among us they are not born of us. *Avatar* means they are with us but they have arrived from some other world.

For example, a ray of sun comes through a tiny hole in the roof into a dark room – that is descending, that is what an avatar is like. The ray and the darkness of the room are both present in that dark room. Apparently, on the surface, the nature of their being is the same, and yet their inner being is so vastly different. On the one hand the darkness and on the other the ray of sun – so totally opposite. The ray arrives from the world of the sun – that is descending.

The darkness belongs to Planet Earth. It never comes from anywhere else; it is always here. When a ray of light arrives, it tears the darkness apart and then leaves again. The darkness once again takes its place; it never comes from somewhere else or goes anywhere else. There is no movement in darkness. There is no growth in darkness. There is no transformation in darkness. It continues to remain as it is.

You will not find anything more dead than darkness. Even rocks move a little here and there. Mountains crawl, continents also shift. Mountains also grow or decrease in height. They all have movement and they carry life. In this world, darkness signifies the most horrific death. That's why all over the world we picture death as darkness. Be they messengers of death or the God of Death, we paint them black. The reason behind this is that there is nothing as devoid of life as darkness is. It neither moves here and there, nor does it grow or decrease. It just remains as it is, wherever it is. Rays appear, penetrate it, and then leave. Darkness once again becomes dense in its own space.

One who is sitting next to you and yet is not near you, this is what the phenomenon of descending, of avatar, is. Kabir may be sitting next to you and yet not with you – he is one with existence, far away from you. This state of oneness with the divine is what his greatness is all about.

So the difference between a master and disciple is qualitative, while between a teacher and a student it is quantitative. No kind of trust is expected between a teacher and a student. But on the other hand, nothing will happen between a master and disciple without trust because essentially a master and disciple are connected through the heart. The heart means love, and the ultimate form of love is called trust. The purest form of love is trust. The lowest form of love is sex.

So, love has three dimensions. One is sex, which is the lowest. Where love is only nominal: it is one percent love and ninety-nine percent passionate desire. Then there is the middle ground, where it is fifty-fifty, where love and lust are equal. It would be a great happening if we came to experience this second dimension of love in our life. Then there is the third happening where passionate desire remains one percent and love is ninety-nine percent – this state is known as trust, *shraddha*.

Which one percent of passionate desire remains in trust? The passionate desire to be free – that's all. Where there is ninety-nine percent passionate desire and one percent love – what kind of love is that? It is the love of bondage, a desire to be tied to someone. So bondage carries one percent of love.

You are afraid to be alone; you desire to be tied to someone, you need company. In the first dimension, ninety-nine percent is just exploitation – there is only one percent of love when you want to be tied to somebody. A bondage! That is why we are right when we call marriage a nuptial knot. Only that much love exists as is needed to tie a rope; the remaining ninety-nine percent is mutual exploitation.

In trust, exploitation disappears completely. What remains is just one percent of passionate desire, and that desire is such that you remain tied only until the moment you have found the way to freedom. As soon as you find the way to freedom, the moment you attain freedom, that one percent of bondage snaps. That very moment the disciple becomes a guru, a master.

Trust means infinite love. Now this needs to be understood a little. Wherever there is passionate desire you find a reason for it. We love for some reason. For example, you see a beautiful woman. You resonate with her personality: you like her eyes, her voice is sweet – there is a reason. Such love cannot last forever because the reasons may soon disappear. The woman will get old, her voice will become hoarse and rasping, her face will become pale, her skin will wrinkle, and her beauty will disappear. When that happens, how can love last? It was there for a reason, but the reasons are no longer there.

That is why although love is there at the beginning, it never lasts. Then we just drag it out; we simply pretend – the real love was lost a long time ago. But it hurts to realize that there is no love anymore. So we manage it carefully; we deceive each other. That's why there is so much deception in our lives. When even love is just a deception, what can there be which is not deceptive?

Trust is without any reason. In love, there is reason because ninety-nine percent is passionate desire. Trust will be totally without any reason or cause because passionate desire is only one percent in it – the desire to be free, to be liberated. So the question is: how can trust arise? And, trust without any reason means it will be beyond logic. That is why you can never give any satisfactory answer to questions about trust.

For example, if someone has trust in me and if you ask him why, he won't be able to give you any convincing answer. You may be able to persuade him that his trust is wrong. You may be able to give many reasons and destroy his trust, but he won't be able to give a single reason in support of his trust. And, if he has really understood the essence of trust, he won't as much as even try to give you any logical reason. If he has really had a taste of trust, he will laugh at your reasoning. So you may find his behavior unreasonable, illogical. You may be giving him so many arguments to destroy his trust, but none of your arguments will make any impression on him – your arguments, as it were, die as they land on him.

Trust is beyond logic, beyond reason. You either have it, or you do not have it; you cannot get it by making an effort. So how will you choose a master? Can trust really arise in you by you making a great deal of effort?

That is why there is only one way to choose a master – and that is when a master chooses you. How can you really choose a master? What you may end up doing is creating hindrances for the master choosing you. There is only one skill a person can apply in becoming a disciple, and that is to be available. He can never choose because there is no particular reason, no logic he can apply for choosing a master. If you apply any logic in choosing a master, then know well that it is not trust – it will just be a mind game.

You may say, "What this man is saying is right; I will make him my master." In that case, you have not really chosen a master. You are still searching for a teacher. You found the man's conduct acceptable. Who are you to judge his conduct? How will you determine whether his conduct is right or wrong? If you knew what is right and what is wrong, then you would yourself be a master. Then there would be no need for you to search. How will you determine if the man's conduct is right?

Whatever society has taught you about what is right and what is wrong, what is ethical and what is unethical – is that the learning you will apply in choosing your master? In that case you will be choosing a master through the medium of knowledge and not through trust. Then you will choose that very person whom you *think* should be your master. If you are born into a Jain family, your considerations will be, for example, whether the person fasts, eats one meal a day, does not take food at night, does not touch water at night, drinks only warm water – and that's how you will make your choice. In this way the work of choosing your master is done! If only the test could be so cheap – that just on the basis of water you come to know, and if the man drinks cold water then the matter is closed. Digambara Jain monks never take a bath, so if the person you want as a master takes a bath, then for you the matter is over.

Once I was a guest in a family. I take a bath twice a day. The host asked me, "What are you doing? Even though you are an enlightened person, you take a bath twice a day?" His concern was that water carries bacteria and you can get killed.

Jain monks, particularly Digambara Jain monks, never take a bath. Their bodies stink.

So if your society has taught you cleanliness, you will not accept a Digambara Jain monk as your master. "What kind of a master is he?" you might say. His mouth stinks because he cannot use any means to clean his teeth and mouth. If he absolutely has to, then he needs to do it surreptitiously.

If you chose according to your *own* concepts and ideas, then you would not have really chosen a master. It would actually mean you were a master yourself because you carried a concept of your own, which you then used as a criterion.

Trust means I drop all my ideas and concepts. Trust means I will set aside all my views and look straight at the person. It means I won't think – I will see. I won't think – rather I will experience the fragrance of the person. I will not bring in my beliefs as I look at the person, I will not draw any screen between us – I will look straight into that person's eyes.

Trust arises only when you keep the intellect aside. Anyone who is willing to do this will find a master. A master is always available; the moment someone is ready, a master becomes available. What is lacking is just the being ready. Even if a person goes from one master to another, he will go with an open mind. Then wherever the meeting with *your* master happens, you will stop there. It is indeed a happening of its own; you cannot make it happen. Hence I said you should just be available.

There have been many masters. In every era many people attain enlightenment. Just approach them in an open and available state, that's all. Somewhere your heart will fall in tune with the master's. And when hearts meet…in fact, such falling in tune cannot happen forcibly. Just as love is a happening, so is trust. Can you give any logical reason why you are in love with a certain woman? All your reasoning will be false, because first you will fall in love, then you will look for the reason; then you will find ways to explain why it happened.

Love is a happening. That is why people say that love is blind. They are right. But at the same time having eyes is meaningless without love. What will you do just having eyes? Even blind love is worth choosing because even blind love has a certain capacity to see what your physical eyes can't. Trust is also blind – that is the meaning of its being beyond logic. If trust is there, it is there; if not, then it is not. Nothing will happen by you doing something about it.

You just need to be available, open. Be in the company of masters; be present at their communion, sit near them, and somewhere it will happen. And when it happens you will be unable to utter a single word. You won't be able to give any logical reason because so many arguments can be made to destroy your reasoning. For example, if you say that Kabir is your master, then a Jain person may say, "How can he be your master? He has a wife, he has a son – he is not celibate. He has not renounced his wife and children yet. How could he be your master? He continues to weave clothes and sell them. No, he can never be a master." So even if a Jain person stays close to Kabir, he will never have any connection with him.

There are Sufi mystics. If you tell them, "Here is Mahavira who is enlightened, and he is my master," the Sufi followers will not accept him as a master. They may say, "A master always hides himself. Here, Mahavira is wandering naked – making himself visible. A master camouflages himself in such a way that one can hardly ever find him. A master never reveals himself because a master is not a worldly phenomenon. A master is only meant for those who are in search of the divine. And one who is in search of the divine, regardless of where the master may be hiding, he will find him."

Hindus have never even mentioned Mahavira's name in their scriptures; as if he never existed. Why would they mention him? He never looked like a master to them. They have their beliefs – and then difficulties arise.

Once I was having a conversation with a devotee. He was a pundit, quite knowledgeable. The topic turned to Jesus and he said, "Whatever else he may be, I cannot accept Jesus as an avatar because avatars don't die on the cross." Certainly, neither Rama died on the cross nor did Buddha. But Jesus did. And then he said, "We must also remember man has to pay for his karma." – The doctrine of karma! – "Jesus must have committed some sins in the past, that's why he suffered hanging on the cross."

In India, no one would be willing to accept Jesus as master – a master and hanging on a cross?

According to the Jains, when Mahavira walked the thorns on the path would immediately turn upside down because Mahavira's karma was so pure, how could a thorn pierce his body? Suffering is caused because of one's karma, they say. So, seeing Mahavira approaching, the thorn would instantly turn upside down so as not to pierce Mahavira. So the matter of hanging on the cross… Can you ever imagine Mahavira on the cross? Impossible! How could he be crucified?

But if you talk to a Christian, he would say, "Your Mahavira, your Buddha, your Rama and Krishna – they are nothing compared to Jesus. There is no contest. Jesus suffered hanging on the cross because he sacrificed his life to make people free, to make the whole world free of sin. Your Mahaviras and Buddhas are all selfish, busy in their own meditation – they care little about the world. Their concern is how *their* soul can be liberated, while Jesus' concern was how everyone could be liberated. This is what an avatar is – the son of God! The rest are all minor, selfish people."

How can one determine who is a master? There is no way except by just being available. If you are available, suddenly one day, when you are close to someone, you will find trust arising; a flower blossoming within you, which is beyond logic, which you won't be able to justify. You will end up a loser even if you do justify; you would be in trouble if you were to explain it to someone. It can be refuted by anyone.

Finding a master cannot happen without trust because it is only through the eyes of trust that you can see him. The relationship between master and disciple is not cerebral; it is that of trust, it is based on love. It is a very intimate relationship; there is no relationship more intimate than this in the whole wide world. Even a husband-wife relationship is not as intimate; nor does such a relationship exist between father and son or between brothers. They are distant in nature because these are body-related. Why is your father your father? It is because you are born out of his body; otherwise how else are you related to him? Why is your mother your mother? It is because you are born out of her body. These are all relationships of the body. Where is the soul, the being, related in all of these?

You are connected with your brother or your sister because you are an offspring of the same body. But this relationship is of the body. There is only one relationship in the world, which is not of the body – that is the relationship between a master and disciple. It has nothing to do with the body; it is a relationship of the being. And only when you are in a relationship of the being with someone that person can help you attain the divine.

Now let us enter this sutra. The sutra is very significant. Make sure you understand, pay attention to each word carefully. Keep every word deeply embedded in your memory.

***Consider those who take a master to be like a human being, to be blind.***

**They will certainly be very miserable in this world,**
**and they will continue to die and be reborn again and again.**

Know that those who see a master as a human being are blind, because you can only connect with him when you see him as divine. If you take him as being human, then you will have a bodily relationship with him. You may hold him in high regard but it will have a reason, it won't be beyond reasoning. You won't have any trust in him. This is the difference between regard and trust. Regard for someone is based on reason. It could be because the person knows more, or the person is ethical, or he has renounced the world – he is this or he is that. The respect is for a reason. Trust, on the other hand, is without any reason.

That is why one can be disrespectful, but one can never be distrusting. For example, if you come to know the person is not so ethical, your regard will crumble – but the trust will not; because the trust was not on account of any ethical behavior anyway. So what bearing can ethical behavior have? You may find the person is not as knowledgeable as you had thought him to be; even then the trust will continue, but the respect you had given will fall away.

So Kabir says: *Consider those who take a master to be like a human being, to be blind.* They are blind, they don't have eyes. Of course, a master is also a human being. He has a body just as we do; he gets hungry and thirsty just as we do. He also perspires under the sun – of course, he is a human.

A good many stories were invented just to convince such blind people…

The Jains say Mahavira never perspired. This is to make the blind, the ignorant, see the greatness of Mahavira. Of course Mahavira perspired – unless he was made of plastic. It is natural to perspire. But then why was this story concocted? Because otherwise the devotee would say, "Oh, he is nothing but a human being like we are." It is said that Mahavira never went to the toilet. If that were the case, no one in the world would have ever suffered so much from constipation! But to explain to a devotee that Mahavira went to the toilet would mean he would think Mahavira was just like the rest of us. Then where would the difference be? So all this was to show how different Mahavira was from us.

But does this difference matter? At the most, you may feel great regard for him, but not trust. Trust will only arise when Mahavira also perspires, feels hungry, falls sick. And still you see the divine in him – only then trust arises.

The body is like a dwelling place. And Mahavira's body is exactly like yours. Otherwise how could Mahavira have died? How could he have been born?

So his body is exactly like yours, but the difference is that while you have believed yourself to be nothing but a body, Mahavira has known he is higher than the body. You are attached to your body, you are identified with the body; Mahavira has transcended it. He is in the body, but he is not just the body. A lamp is made of earth, but the flame is not of earth. If you have seen just the earthen lamp, then you are indeed blind. Kabir says: See the flame!

That flame certainly never perspires, never stinks; that flame never gets hungry or thirsty. But the lamp will get thirsty, it will require oil, it will get tired, it will break; it will certainly die. *Consider those who take a master to be like a human being, to be blind*. Those who see a master as just another human being are blind – blind because then you won't establish any contact with him. You need to raise your eyes, your vision.

Mansoor was hanged. He was laughing while he was being hanged. Someone from the crowd asked, "Why are you laughing? Is it something to be happy about?"

Mansoor replied, "At least you have raised your eyes while looking at me." While he was being hanged, people had to raise their eyes to see him. So Mansoor said, "I am happy that at least you have raised your eyes a little."

What Mansoor is saying is very symbolic; the crowd may not have understood him. A crowd can never understand. Those who were hanging him may not have understood a thing that Mansoor was saying. What Mansoor was saying is: "Even while I am being hanged, it is enough if you can simply look up a little; it is enough, you will benefit from doing so. It is not a question of my getting hanged; just let your eyes look up a little."

Look at a master – certainly he is in a body, but he is not just the body. You will be able to see him only through the eyes of trust. Whenever you look at someone through trust, the body disappears. Whenever you look at someone through intense love, you don't see the body. You begin to see and realize the individuality, the soul, the very existential being instead. Whenever you love someone, the person is never there – the divine is. In ordinary life, too, when you fall in love with someone, the person you are in love with doesn't appear to be ordinary; suddenly, loving eyes reveal the extraordinary in that person.

Majnu was crazy about Laila. The king of his town called him and said: "You are crazy. This Laila is just an ordinary girl, not good-looking. Why are you unnecessarily being so miserable? I feel pity for you."

He would weep and cry; wandering from one town to another repeating "Laila, Laila" – that was his mantra. People wept for him and the king also felt pity for him.

The king said, "There are beautiful girls in my palace, I will invite them here and you can choose the most beautiful one.

He placed a dozen beautiful girls before Majnu, but the king saw tears rolling from his eyes. Majnu would look at each girl closely and then say, "No, this is not Laila."

He said to the king, "Please forgive me, there is a difference between the way you and I see. You see Laila as an ordinary girl. And here I am; I don't see anyone but her; something is wrong. Maybe the fault lies in me. But certainly I see something in Laila that you don't. And I can live only through my eyes; how can I live through your eyes?"

Ordinarily, when a person falls in love – where love is one percent and passionate desire is ninety-nine percent – even then he begins to feel something unearthly in the other, something supernatural. But when trust arises, where ninety-nine percent is love and only one percent passionate desire remains, instantly he experiences the presence of the divine. Hence, in this country we have called the master *divine*, we have placed him even higher than the divine. There are reasons for it.

Consider those who take a master to be like a human being, to be blind. They will certainly be very miserable in this world, and they will continue to die and be reborn again and again. Kabir says such people will certainly remain unhappy in this world because there is no joy possible without trust. It is not possible to experience the being without trust. It is not possible to realize the presence of the divine without trust. And if you cannot recognize the presence of the divine in a master, how can you recognize it in trees, in rocks and in the mountains? If you didn't see it in a master, how will you see the divine in the statue of a temple? If the recognition didn't happen in the living being, how will it be possible in the lifeless?

It is so strange: in a temple you bow down before an image made of stone and chant, "Bhagwan…Bhagwan," but you find great difficulty saying it when you face a master. Have you ever wondered whether you would have found the same difficulty if the person carved in the image had been alive? You would certainly have faced the same difficulty. It is very easy to say "Bhagwan" standing in front of Mahavira's statue because obviously this statue, made of marble, never perspires, it never feels hungry. The statue is always in the state of fasting – there is no question of eating food. The marble statue never gets thirsty, never gets sick, it won't die either. We have created statues made of stone with a great deal of thought behind them – with the very idea that they must not show anything that is seen in a living human being.

There are many marble statues…

Once it happened that I was visiting a town for a few days. One of the neighbors was thought to be a little eccentric. He was retired. He had once been a professor of logic at some university. So, as such logicians become somewhat crazy, and then, on top, retired…! I thought maybe someday I would see him, but even I grew doubtful.

One day, as I was passing his house, I saw him watering flowers in a flowerpot with a watering can. But, strangely, no water was coming out of the can and he was just standing there like a statue. I looked a little more closely and found that the watering can didn't even have a base. So I said to him, "Hello, maybe you are lost in thought so you didn't notice, but the can doesn't have a base."

He replied, "Don't worry. Who said these flowers are real? They are made of plastic."

But there is one special characteristic of a plastic flower: it neither wilts nor dies. It looks everlasting – just like a traditional orthodox Hindu. A real flower blooms in the morning and it wilts by the evening. An artificial flower looks the same – morning, evening and night.

The original Mahavira is like a real flower – he will bloom in the morning and wilt by the evening. But then you will feel he is just like all of us. Then you will ask what the difference is between him and us. Seeing him as just another human being, it will be difficult to worship him. A marble statue neither wilts nor is born nor dies – it is eternal. You can easily kneel before it. You are so false yourself that you are able to worship only the false. It is difficult for you to worship the true, the real.

You are so lifeless yourself that it is only possible for you to worship the dead. You are unable to connect with the living. A master is a living phenomenon. Nothing will happen for you by making his statue. You will certainly make his statue, but after his death – and then nothing will be solved, it won't help you in any way.

And remember, the ego never gets hurt bowing down before a statue. There is no one there; you have yourself purchased the statue from the market. You are its owner. If you wish, you can throw it out any time; the statue won't be able to do anything. When you offer food, then that is the mealtime for it. You ask the god to sleep – the god has to sleep. When you want to shut the temple doors, the doors are shut. You are the master. This deity is just like a toy for you. Your ego is never hurt before it. But when you bow down before a living person then that creates a difficulty for you. It is only your ego that is the obstacle for trust to arise.

Remember, your reasoning is not the obstacle – your ego is. Reasoning is only a trick to hide the ego when you say, "How can I bow down? Until I find a person worthy enough, how can I bow down?" You will never find such a person because you will find some reason not to.

Mulla Nasruddin remained unmarried for a long time.

I asked him: "Why, what is the reason? Now it is long overdue. You should find someone, time is running out."

He replied: "I am already searching. But I want a woman who is perfect in every sense. I have come across hundreds of women but none was a perfect woman. Until I meet a perfect woman I won't fall in love."

So I asked, "You couldn't find a single woman, searching your whole life?"

He said, "Well, I did find one or two but they were also in search of a perfect husband."

So even if you find a perfect master, remember, he is in search of a perfect disciple too. You won't find such a master; the whole exercise is simply to save yourself from actually having a master.

Consider those who take a master to be like a human being, to be blind. They will certainly be very miserable in this world, and they will continue to die and be reborn again and again. Such people are bound to be miserable in this world. Misery shows you are wrong. Happiness shows you are right. Consider this as a criterion: if your life is miserable, then know that you are wrong, know that whatever you are doing is all a mistake. Something is fundamentally wrong because the flowers of happiness bloom only when you are fundamentally right. And remember, if someone is indeed happy, then don't try to destroy it by giving arguments against it; because being happy alone is the only criterion that the person is right.

People come to see me…

A couple of days ago, a friend said: "You are driving people crazy; I can't see that God exists anywhere or that God can be found. You are driving people nuts."

I replied, "It is a matter between people and me, don't come into the picture. You are healthy, you are happy – that's good."

He said, "But that is the problem; I am neither healthy nor am I happy."

So I said, "Just take care that you are healthy and happy; sooner or later you will come closer to God. Don't worry if God exists or not because God is not a matter of a logical conclusion. God is a feeling of gratitude emerging from the deepest experience of happiness."

When you are happy, you cannot believe there is no God – otherwise how could you be happy? When you are happy, when your heart is overwhelmed and there is song in every cell of your being, you can never accept that existence could be devoid of consciousness. The reason is that you will see in existence only that which is happening within you. If you are unhappy, life is hell, devoid of God. If you are happy, life – existence – is heaven; every particle is saturated with, filled with God. It is not a question of arriving at a conclusion, thinking whether God exists or not. It is not a matter of going through philosophies, studying scriptures, gathering arguments – that's all foolishness. If you are happy, God is there – instantly. If you are miserable, God disappears!

So I told him to leave my crazy people alone. If they are happy, then what difference does it make whether God exists or not? And, if you are unhappy, then also what does it matter whether God exists or not? In the final analysis what will matter is: are you happy or are you miserable? The final conclusion will be – does the flower of joy and happiness bloom in a person's life or not? That is the determining factor; so pay attention to it.

If, when being close to some individual, a flower of joy blossoms in your life, drop your reasoning and set aside your intellect; at that point just open your heart. That is where trust will manifest. That is where the master will appear. A master is not an external, outer phenomenon – he is an experience seen through the eyes of trust. It is like when you open your eyes, you see the sunshine and when you close your eyes it is all dark. Similarly, when you open up, as you show trust, you see the master; when you close down, shut out the trust, the master disappears.

A master is an experience that comes out of your trust. Intellect will always see a trusting eye as blind. But for those who have gained trust there is no greater blindness than that which is seen through the intellect. But one thing is certain…

Let us say, there is a small boy. Whatsoever he says is obviously not based on experience. Then a young man says something. It shows some experience, he has seen both childhood and youth. Then there is an old man. What he says carries even more experience; he has seen childhood and youth as well as old age. So when a young man and an old man are in conversation there won't be any meeting point because the young man has seen only two aspects of life, he hasn't seen the third one yet. Whatever the old man might say about youth, it is worth considering because he has seen youth, has seen it decline and is now experiencing the opposite of youth.

Now the old person is standing at the peak of life. That's why, in the East, we give so much respect to an elderly person because he has seen it all. We don't pay such respect to a young person because he has yet to see. In the West, the young person is given respect – which is a mistake. Only the views of someone who has seen it all can have some meaning, some value. Someone who has gone into logic and reasoning, someone who has raised doubt and then has realized trust, what he says has a value; it is meaningful because he has been through both – doubt and trust.

An atheist is like a child, while a theist – a self-realized person – is like an old man. Everyone has to pass through the atheist state, but not all are able to become theists as many children die in childhood. A theist has experienced both dimensions of life. Through denial, he has found that the more you deny the more you shrink: the more you say: no, no, no, the smaller you become. He has gone through the other experience too; the more you say yes, the more you accept, the more you become infinite. If you say no, only you are left – shrunk, stinking! When you say yes, you disappear as a person. What remains is infinity – only the divine remains. When you say no, you become like an insignificant dust particle – just nothing. When you say yes, you become as vast, as infinite as consciousness is, as the sky is.

*They will certainly be very miserable in this world, and will also continue to die and be reborn again and again.* Such people will certainly stay miserable in the world; and they will die and be reborn again and again. Again and again Yama, the Lord of Death, will come and take them away. Because of them, poor Yama will have to go through a lot of trouble. These people will keep being born and then dying again and again; they will go through misery and death over and over.

A person who is awakened is free from both birth and death. The person who becomes one with the divine has neither to appear in the world nor to leave it. This is what the East calls freedom from transmigration, freedom from birth and death. His journey comes to an end; he has arrived at the destination.

***In this whole universe there is no one greater than the master.***
***A master can do whatsoever he wishes,***
***even when God may not succeed in doing so.***

These words are difficult to follow unless one has profound trust. Even a theist, a believer, can get a little alarmed that maybe Kabir is going a little beyond limits. A believer may say: having trust in the master is fine; but now Kabir is saying: in the whole universe there is no one greater than the master. But the fact is: in the entire universe there is no one greater than the master. That is why he is known as a master. A master means there is nothing weightier than he is.

*...God may not succeed in doing so.* Even God – if he wishes to do anything – would not be able to do what a master can do; a master can do whatever he wishes. What is the meaning of placing a master above God?

You can accept, up to a point, placing a master on the same level as God, and, as you have no idea of trust, you may also think that it's possible that a master is divine. But placing a master above the divine! It seems like Kabir is exaggerating. Not at all! What Kabir is saying is: the means are greater than the end.

You cannot reach the goal without the means. The path is greater than the goal because without the path you will never make it to the destination. And so, if you can't reach the goal without the path then imagine which is greater? If the path is indispensable, if you cannot move an inch toward the goal without being on the path, then that would mean the goal is nothing but the end of the path. If you cannot climb on the roof without the ladder, then that makes the ladder greater than the roof.

*A master can do whatsoever he wishes, even when God may not succeed in doing so.* Even God will be unable to do what he wishes but a master can do whatever he wishes. Why is it so? There are many reasons behind it. Try to understand.

At the initial state man is in darkness, ignorance; he has gone astray. The state of the divine is supreme knowledge, he has arrived. The master is in between – half man, half divine – a bridge between the divine and man. The divine can hardly understand your problem. Regardless of how much you may cry and wail, the divine's ears will not be able to hear your voice because it does not have ears – it is the ultimate state, nothing coming out of misery can ever reach there. It is a state of supreme void, no-mind – *shunya*. You may go on screaming, it will reverberate in the open sky and disappear – you won't get any answer from the divine. It is the ultimate state. You cannot make any contact with it.

But the master is in the middle. He is half like you and half like the divine – it is a meeting point of both, where two borders meet. A master is a point where your presence ends and the presence of the divine begins. At that meeting point on the periphery of both something can be said. You can say something to a master; he will understand because he has passed through the same situation that you have gone through. He has lived through the same hardships, anxieties, and miseries that you are going through now. What you are living in the present he has lived in the past. That which will be your future is his present moment.

A master is at the point where both you and the divine are in contact – right in the middle. If you say something, and if the master hears it, then consider God has heard it through him. When you make a statement, the master will be able to understand because he has been speaking the same language that you speak. The divine can never follow your language. Which language can it follow? How will it follow it?

It happened during the Second World War that a German and a British soldier were having a conversation; they were on the battlefield. The British soldier said, "Our victory is certain, you can cease trying."

The German asked, "Why are you so certain about your victory?"

The Britisher said, "We pray every day; God is with us."

The German said, "We also pray, and God is with us."

The British soldier laughed. He said, "You are crazy; have you ever heard that God understands German? God knows only English."

You laugh at this, but actually all people make similar claims. You may go and ask Indian pundits and they will say Sanskrit is God's language. What does that mean? It means God understands the Sanskrit language. If you are speaking Hindi, it is useless; Sanskrit is needed. And that too absolutely perfect because God is very particular about grammar!

This is the reason why the pundits of Kashi in Varanasi never cared for Kabir; they accused him of speaking a nonsensical language. They gave a particular name to Kabir's language, they called it *sadhukkadi*, a language that uneducated seekers unaware of the scriptures would use; a language not of the common man but of the uneducated sadhus who are unpredictable and say whatever comes into their heads. For example, Kabir also uses Persian and Sanskrit, and he uses Pali as well – he mixes them all together. Even God must be finding it difficult; he must have hired ten to fifteen interpreters asking them to figure out what nonsense Kabir is talking!

No matter what language you speak, God won't be able to follow it – whether it is Sanskrit or English or whatever. How can God follow man's language? Only man can understand man's language. If that is the case, then how can God be of any help?

A master is a person who, on the one hand, understands your language and, on the other hand, whose life – whose being – is totally absorbed in the divine. His one hand is in your hand and his other one in God's hand. Thus whatever you say, he will be able to follow. He will do whatever you ask him to do. He will see whether what you are asking for is appropriate, then something can be done about it because his other hand is that of the divine. A master is both. What Kabir is saying is right; I agree with him. What he is saying is not an exaggeration – it is absolutely correct.

***A master can do whatsoever he wishes,***
***even when God may not succeed in doing so.***
***There is no giver like a master and no beggar like a disciple.***
***A master bestows the wealth of all the three worlds.***

There is no other giver greater than a master. A master means one who goes on giving. But what he gives is very subtle. If you approach him to ask for petty things, you will return empty-handed. However, if you approach him to ask for the infinite, you will get it. *There is no giver like a master...* But it is possible for him to give only if the disciple approaches him as a beggar. If you come to him with arrogance, with an attitude that you deserve it or that you are entitled to it, then you will miss: ... *no beggar like a disciple.*

A disciple is one who is the ultimate beggar! A disciple should be one whose heart is nothing but a begging bowl – he is the supreme beggar! It is only then that a tuning happens with the master because, after all, only a supreme beggar can have a meeting with the supreme giver. If he keeps giving and you remain like an upside-down pot, then all will go to waste. A beggar means one whose pot is the right way up.

It happened...

In China, there lived a great wise man called Lei Tzu who was one of the disciples from Lao Tzu's tradition. A disciple once approached him and asked him something. Lei Tzu said, "I will answer you when the time is right; you need to be prepared for it. You have asked me, but are you courageous enough to take my answer? I will certainly give it to you, but are you sure you will not be crushed under it? Do you know what you are asking for?"

The disciple became a little scared. He remained quiet for a whole year and when he got no answer from Lei Tzu he left.

He went to another master and told him that he come after spending a year with Lei Tzu but had got nothing from him. The master said, "You had better leave from here because you don't have a vessel at all. If Lei Tzu could not fill it, what can a poor person like me give you? You fool! You came empty-handed from Lei Tzu! Well, then I have nothing for you. You'd better leave from here – you had better escape otherwise people might say you stayed with me for a year for nothing."

Having heard this the man went back to Lei Tzu. He said, "It is so strange, now what shall I do? I went to other people but they said if you went to Lei Tzu and came here thirsty after visiting that infinite lake, we won't be of any use to you, we are just small ponds. So I have come back."

Lei Tzu said, "Listen: when I came to my master, for three years he never even looked at me. There was no question of asking anything. He would look at all the others, but would ignore me and never look at me. And he would ignore me in a way as if that seat was empty.

"I understood; he was hinting at the fact that I should become like an empty space. It is for this reason he did not look at me. Had you been in my place, you would have run away. Your ego would have been hurt because you had come and you were not even being looked at. I continued sitting and slowly accepted it, saying let it be as he wishes. Suddenly, one day he looked at me – it was like bliss showering on me. I was as thrilled as I had never been before in my life.

"For three years I sat quietly as if I didn't exist…! He would not even look at me. He would talk to others, chitchat with them, make inquiries, but would not throw even a glance at me. And it was not a matter of just one or two days – it was a three-year long period! But I felt quite contented; I was overflowing.

"After that, I was never concerned about whether he looked at me or not. Three more years passed. First he indicated to me that I should become a nothingness, *shunya*. And then, when he looked at me, I understood what he was hinting at – that now I should become as one who sees, a watcher. In the same way as he looked at me, now I should look at myself. For the next three years I watched myself. And then, one day, he glanced at me and for the first time he smiled. I felt blessed, I was overwhelmed. Now I fully understood what he meant: be a *shunya*, a no-mind; be a watcher, be blissful.

"I then began smiling for no reason, I began laughing for no reason, for no reason I began to celebrate, for no reason I remained happy. People thought I had gone mad. Again after another three years he came to me, placed his hand on my head, and said, "Your *sadhana*, your spiritual work is now over. Now there is no distinction between you and me. Now go and wake others up. You have got it, now share it with others."

Lei Tzu said, "And here you are; you stayed here for a year but never for a moment did you become silent. The same question kept resounding in your mind: when will you get the answer… As if getting the answer was more important than the master!"

It is because of the ego that you find your questions to be very important. You want an answer and that too is a demand of the ego. But unless you actually see the person from whom you are seeking the answer, no answer will be possible. That is exactly what *satsang*, communion with a master, means.

Sit near the master silently. Whenever he wishes it, when you are ready, he will fulfill you. Just leave yourself in his hands.

> ***There is no giver like a master and no beggar like a disciple.***
> ***A master bestows the wealth of all the three worlds.***
>
> ***A master is like a potter and the disciple is like a pot. Like a potter,***
> ***the master works on the disciple by removing all that is useless.***
> ***Like making a pot, with one hand the master holds a disciple from within***
> ***and with the other hand he hits him from without.***

These are very lovely words. Have you ever seen a potter? He creates a pot. *A master is like a potter and the disciple is like a pot* – he is getting a disciple ready. The disciple is like a pot. The master is the potter. And why is he making you like a pot? He is doing it so that you can be filled. A pot is nothing but emptiness. A pot is not just the walls it is made of – a pot is actually emptiness. The empty space inside, the *shunya*, is what a pot really is. The master builds a thin wall around you while creating an empty space inside.

A master is like a potter and the disciple is like a pot. Like a potter, the master works on the disciple by removing all that is useless. The master works on what is lacking in you and what is needed – whatever has to be removed and whatever has to be added. ...with one hand the master holds a disciple from within...

It is worth watching a potter at work. With one hand he supports the pot from inside – he handles the clay – while with the other hand he hits the pot from the outside. That is the whole process a master is engaged in. He hits you from the outside while supporting you from within.

If you see only the outer hits, you will certainly escape. But if you see the support given from within, the outer hits will become very precious to you. You will feel blessed that the hits were given from the outside because they are both necessary. The support from inside the pot builds the outer wall; without it, it would fall apart. Hitting from the outside makes the wall stronger because otherwise when filling the pot with water for the first time, it would break. It is necessary to hit from the outside to make it strong.

A master will give all kinds of hits. If the disciple receives such hits later in life, they may break the pot, so the master gives them now. And that is where the difficulty lies: the moment a disciple receives such a hit he escapes. When he gets the hit, he thinks, "The master did not look at me, didn't ask me to come and sit with him, didn't give me any respect. Or the master said something that was insulting. Or he answered me in such a way that it hit me, hurt me."

A hit from the outside is necessary; otherwise you won't get stronger, and then, when the whole showers on you, you will fall apart. The support from the inside... A master uses both hands. He will give support from inside with one hand so that you don't break right now; with the other hand he will hit you from the outside so that you may never break.

***A master is like a potter and the disciple is like a pot. Like a potter, the master works on the disciple by removing all that is useless. Like making a pot, with one hand the master holds a disciple from within and with the other hand he hits him from without.***

***Keep a master on the highest pedestal and follow what he says.***
***Then, says Kabir, there is nothing for a devotee to fear***
***in this whole universe.***

What does this mean? It is easy to place a master on the highest pedestal, but it is difficult to follow what he says. But, in fact, following his command, his directions, in itself means placing him on the highest pedestal. It is very easy to place your head at the feet of the master. But it will make no difference. Outwardly you may bow down; inwardly you never bend. Inside you remain stubbornly upright.

I was once a guest of a family. The housewife was scolding her son because he was making a lot of noise and causing trouble. The lady said, "Now enough is enough. Go and sit on that chair at once!"

Children know very well where the limits are, so he sat on the chair. From there he kept staring at his mother as if telling her, "Alright, outwardly I am seated here, but inside I am still standing as before."

It is very easy to bend from the outside; it is very easy to show respect outwardly. Following a command is very difficult because it means bending oneself from the inside. Following a command means that whatever the master may say you don't bring in your reasoning, your arguments.

If you start thinking, applying your logic and then following, that would mean you were following your own commands and not the master's. Then you will do whatever agrees with your intellect. But even if your intellect tells you what the master is saying is not right, even then you must follow what the master says. Only then will the intellect lose its power. As long as you go on following your intellect, you won't drop down from the head; your roots won't reach your heart. Many a times, the master will ask you to do things that even he knows are unreasonable, which he also knows the intellect won't agree with. He knows very well that even an ordinary man would say, "This is crazy!"

Gurdjieff used to give such commands to his disciples – ones which were totally against the intellect.

Once, a man came to him. He had never drunk any alcohol before. He was a vegetarian and of good character. Gurdjieff asked him to eat meat and drink alcohol. Now, obviously, you would say he was absolutely mad. The man must have been shocked. He said, "What are you talking about?" He ran away.

One of Gurdjieff's disciples asked him why he said such a thing. Gurdjieff replied, "The purpose was very clear. The man was against eating meat. He was against drinking alcohol. And because of his not eating meat and not drinking, he was carrying a great ego: 'I am pious; I am ethical; I am religious; I am vegetarian!' It was necessary to shatter this arrogance."

When a vegetarian approached him, Gurdjieff would say: "Eat this meat!" Naturally, the intellect said, "This is the way to corrupt me. Can he be called a master?" But some stayed, and since the master had asked them to they would eat the meat. Once the master asked, the matter was over. But then he wouldn't ask them to eat it again. Sometimes it happened that as the disciple went ahead and chose meat, he would stop him – that was it; the matter was finished. There was no point in eating the meat anymore.

Women used to come to Gurdjieff. He would say "First take all your jewelry off and give it to me." Once a woman came to him – she was a great musician. She was very rich; she had expensive jewelry. When she came to the master, in the same way as when one visits a temple, she came wearing all her jewelry – obviously she expected many people would be watching. But she had no idea what was going to happen.

Gurdjieff said: "We shall talk about other matters later. First here is a handkerchief, place all your jewelry on it." The woman took off all her jewelry and placed it on the handkerchief. Gurdjieff tied the handkerchief and put it in his jacket pocket. After some conversation the lady left. That night, Gurdjieff returned the handkerchief. The lady was surprised because there was more jewelry in it than she had left behind; Gurdjieff had added some more.

Two weeks later another woman came to his ashram. She asked the woman who had gone before, "I have often heard that Gurdjieff asks for the jewelry. Did he ask for yours too?"

The woman replied, "Yes he did, but returned it later that night."

The newcomer said, "Then there is nothing to be afraid of." So she went to see Gurdjieff. The moment Gurdjieff asked for her jewelry she took it all off. Since she had learned that Gurdjieff returned jewelry, even adding some more, she had brought whatever jewelry she had. Gurdjieff seized it all. He never returned it.

You will not be able to deceive a master – that is impossible. He has to break you; he has to destroy you the way you are so that you can be made anew. Your pot has to be recreated again. Your intellect will not be of any use. Having trust in a master means: "I am not, only you are." Having trust in the master means: "Now I will fulfill whatever you ask." Many times strange events have taken place.

Marpa, a Tibetan monk, once went to his master. He was a very simple man. But he was so simple and innocent that other disciples became suspicious that one day he might become the master's heir. He was a true successor – and he did become the successor.

The disciples began causing problems. One day they said to Marpa, without the master actually knowing about it, "The master has commanded that if your trust is authentic, you will jump from this mountain." Marpa jumped. The disciples ran down below to see. It was a dangerous precipice; there was no chance of survival. When they reached the bottom they found Marpa meditating under a tree. They thought, "This must be a coincidence. It can't be true; it has to be a coincidence."

Once, a house was on fire. The disciples said to Marpa, "The master has commanded you to enter the burning house." Marpa never asked the master if he had indeed sent these commands or whether it was all these people's doing. How untrusting it would be to ask such a thing! Let it be the master's wish. So he walked into the fire – and not even his clothes caught fire.

Another time, they were crossing a river. The disciples told Marpa, "Jump! You can even walk on water because it is said in the scriptures that one who has an unbreakable trust can walk on water." So Marpa walked on water. Then it became difficult to take it as a coincidence.

They went to the master and said, "Reverend one, please pardon us, but it is strange because we kept harassing Marpa in your name but the power of your name is limitless. He walked into a fire but never got burned. He jumped from the mountain but didn't die. He easily walked on water."

The master felt flattered; he was not really a self-realized person. He was a man of good character, behaved well. He had followed all kinds of yoga practices but he had not reached yet. He said to his disciples, "If Marpa could walk in my name, then I can do so myself. What is so great about it? How is Marpa so special? The secret lies in my name."

So one day, as they were taking a boat ride, the disciples asked the master to walk on water. The master said, "No problem!" He tried, fell, and nearly drowned. He was pulled out of the water with great difficulty.

Marpa did not walk on water because of the master's name; he walked on it because of his trust in the master.

If you understand it well, trust *is* the master. The master is merely an excuse for trust to arise within you. So sometimes such incredible things have happened: even though the master was not a real master, the disciple reached the ultimate state. However, it also happens daily that the master was real but the disciple never reaches. Trust is the key.

A master's command means that whatever he may say, whether it sounds relevant or irrelevant to your intellect, you don't bring your own mind into it. You just set aside your intellect and stay determined only to listen to the master. And as your capacity to listen to the master increases, so will your capacity to surrender to the master. Then the master will be on the highest pedestal. The day your intellect steps down from your head, the master will take over and become your intellect. He will work as your discerning power, your intelligence. This is the true meaning of *Keep a master on the highest pedestal and follow what he says. Then, says Kabir, there is nothing for a devotee to fear in this whole universe.*

> ***When both the master and God are standing before me,***
> ***whose feet should I touch first?***
> ***My gratitude to you, O master, for showing me God!***

This sutra can have two meanings – both are beautiful. ...*both the master and God are standing before me...* Kabir shares his experience and says: "Then came a moment when both the master and God, the Lord, were standing before me." Someday, such a moment is bound to come. The master is the door; if not today then tomorrow the divine will appear. The master is the path – sooner or later the goal will be reached. And, in the very first moment, it will happen that the master will be standing before you and so will the divine. At such a unique moment whose feet should one touch first?

So, Kabir says, "I was in great uncertainty. Both the master and God are before me, whose feet should I touch? *Whose feet should I touch first?*

The second statement can have two meanings. The first meaning: *My gratitude to you, O master, for showing me God!*

Here Kabir is saying, "I am grateful to you, my master, for when I was not certain you immediately indicated to me to go and touch the feet of God." *My gratitude to you, O master, for showing me God!* The moment I was caught in a dilemma, you signaled to me that I should go and touch God's feet. You made it clear that your role was only up to that point; that you functioned as a signpost indicating when the destination has been reached, and that now you were not needed. You indicated to me: "Now leave the master and touch God's feet."

This is the one meaning which is generally taken. The second meaning is even more significant. It is my own experience and this second meaning fits well with Kabir's earlier words.

The second meaning of: ...both the master and God are standing before me, whose feet should I touch first? My gratitude to you, O master, for showing me God. Kabir is saying, "I am in a dilemma, whose feet should I touch? Both, the master and God, are standing before me. Then I bypassed God and touched the master's feet because it was he who, through his grace, showed me God." This will be the right meaning because the previous sutras say: In this whole universe there is no one greater than the master. A master can do whatsoever he wishes, even when God may not succeed in doing so. Since Kabir has placed the master above God, then the second meaning is the right one.

And that is how it should be; because, finally, at the end of the journey, while taking leave from the master – the point from where the journey toward God began – it is appropriate that the master's feet should be touched first. This last point of the journey is the moment of saying good-bye; after this the master will not be there, only God will. From this point on the master, the connecting bridge, will no longer be there – the one who had brought you here, holding your hand all along the way, will not be with you any longer. In this moment of parting, it is certainly appropriate that Kabir must have said, "In that situation I then first touched the feet of the master because without his grace it would have been impossible to have arrived at this juncture – it was possible all because of him."

And the same feeling is reinforced further in the following sutra:

**If the Lord is displeased with me, then the master is my only refuge.**
**But there is no refuge if the master is displeased.**

The entire *sadhana*, the entire spiritual work of a disciple, is that of becoming a shadow of the master. That is what total surrender is all about. It is total self-annihilation. It is only then that the master will be able to get you ready for that ultimate happening where your being will merge with the divine.

How will the master make you ready for this? If you really understand well, then the master provides the preliminary preparation for that ultimate event – the phenomenon where the soul disappears into the divine. The preparation is that of first disappearing into the master. That is the elementary training. When it is over, that very moment, the door opens, that very instant both the master and God appear before you. It is the point from where the master departs and the journey to God begins.

So, it is like a three-way journey. One way is that which you have chosen through your intellect – it is the way of the ego. The second way is the way to the Param Brahma, the supreme being. Both go parallel; they don't meet anywhere. The third one is the middle path which joins these two parallel paths – and that is what the master is. He dissolves your ego; he takes you away from the ego and leads you to the egoless *brahman* – the supreme being.

The more you melt, the more the divine becomes crystallized. The more you erase yourself, the more the divine becomes apparent.

People ask me: where is God? They should rather ask why they are so hard and dense. Where is the space for the divine to enter? Your house is fully occupied – occupied by you. The master will make it empty. And before God can descend...God is totally unknown to you, you might get frightened. Even if the divine appeared in front of your door right now, perhaps you wouldn't even open the door. You may abandon your house and escape in such a hurry that he may not come back again.

The divine is vast. The divine is an infinite abyss, which will frighten you; you will get dizzy. By and by, the master will make you feel comfortable and at ease.

For example, you know the river falls into the ocean. You want to take your boat to the ocean. So first you sail it on the river and practice. It is possible to practice on the river because the danger is less. You cannot practice sailing on the ocean where the danger is great. If you want to learn swimming, it is better to learn it in the river which has banks, where you find people on the banks and your voice can be heard; where it is convenient and someone can save you.

A master is a flowing river – a master is the Ganges. First you need to learn swimming in this master-river and then slowly, slowly the Ganges will take you to the ocean. Once it has reached the ocean all banks will be left behind; then there won't be anyone to help. There you will be totally alone. Before arriving at that ultimate aloneness, the master's company and support is essential. Before the master enters your life you are in a crowd – a crowd means many, endless. With a master there are two, there is a duality. *Brahman* means one, the non-dual. Before you move away from the crowd, you will have to be at ease with the two. Only then will it be possible for you to move away from the two and feel comfortable with oneness.

Kabir is right:

***When both the master and God are standing before me,***
***whose feet should I touch first? My gratitude to you, O master,***
***for showing me God!***
***If the Lord is displeased with me, then the master is my only refuge.***
***But there is no refuge if the master is displeased.***

Enough for today.

# 5
# The Fabric of Life

*I have woven this very finely spun sheet of cloth.*
*I am amazed at what the warp and the woof are made of.*
*The cloth's warp is made of ingla and pingla, nerves,*
*and the woof, made of sushumna, runs through it.*
*This body has eight lotuses and ten doors;*
*it is made of five tattvas, outer realities, and five mahatattvas,*
*as well as three gunas, the basic life forces.*
*God took ten months working meticulously at weaving it.*
*The same woven cloth is worn by gods, humans, and monks*
*but all three leave it unclean.*
*Kabir, the humble slave, has worn it with awareness*
*and returned it as unblemished as it first was.*

Kabir is a simple weaver, so his metaphors are obviously those used by a weaver. And yet, through these metaphors he has said it all – something which even the Upanishads are not able to say. Though they talk about it, the Vedas fail to say it, and Buddha and Mahavira simply leave it, saying that it is indescribable.

The closer the metaphor is to life, the more capable it is of revealing the truth; the farther away it is from life, the less capable it becomes of expressing the truth. Kabir is closest to living a truly ordinary life. And remember, there is never an extraordinary life in the world – the extraordinary is hidden within the ordinary. In attempting to become extraordinary, a person will not only miss being ordinary but will also miss the extraordinary hidden within it.

The ego seeks the extraordinary. The ego wants to accomplish great things; but life is made of small, little things. Life consists of such small things as getting up, weaving cloth, selling cloth, having a meal, going to sleep, waking up again... Whosoever tries to be special will certainly be deprived of living life, while one who stays aware doing ordinary things, one who does the same ordinary things consciously, will attain the extraordinary. That is the meaning of what Kabir calls *jatan* – awareness.

*Jatan* means doing the ordinary with awareness; connecting one's consciousness even with the most ordinary. The moment consciousness joins the insignificant, the insignificant becomes vast. And when unawareness is connected with the infinite, the infinite becomes insignificant. You may go to the temple if you wish, but you won't find God there because you will go in a state of unawareness. Whatever you see there will be a reflection of your passionate desires.

If only you had awareness, then what would the need be to go to the temple? If you are indeed aware, you would find the very place where you are nothing but a temple – what else is there? Only the ignorant will travel to Kashi and Kaaba. For a wise person, wherever he is that is his Kashi; that is his Kaaba. The divine is everywhere. It is not that *brahman* is present more in one place and less in another, or that *brahman* is crystallized at one place while only partly present at another, or available at one place and unavailable at another. *Brahman* is everywhere, equally distributed.

Buddha has said that you may taste the ocean from any place and it will taste salty. Whether you taste it from this shore or that shore or from the middle; whether you taste it from its deepest point or taste a wave – you may try the ocean anywhere, but at every place the taste will be salty. The same is true with *brahman* – its taste is also the same everywhere.

The temple and the mosque are creations of the ignorant person so he builds them in his own way – and they show his reflection. Your God can never be greater than you until you yourself become as great as God. But that is where the complexity lies: if you try to become great, you will end up remaining small because the desire to be great is the desire of a petty mind. If you are at ease with small things, suddenly you will realize that there is nothing small – everything is great.

The insignificant, the petty, doesn't exist – it simply shows the limitation of your perception. For example, I open a window and see the light through it: what I actually see is the light that fits within the window frame. A whole sky is out there, but I see only that much sky as I am able to see through the window frame. And if I have never been outside, if I have never seen the wide-open sky, if I continue to look through the window frame, then naturally I will believe that the sky that fits within the window frame is the only sky.

But that is not the sky; the window frame is simply giving that shape to it. The window is giving a limited perception; the sky has no limit. Your eyes are also no better than windows, your ears are no better than windows, your hands are no better than the windows.

Our senses are like small windows through which we see *brahman*, and hence the *brahman* looks small. But if you were to see, stepping out of your senses, immediately the limitations would disappear and the insignificant would become infinite. There were never any limitations in the first place; we created them. Limitations are imaginary. So never call any work small.

This is Kabir's primary message: never see any work as small, insignificant, because the infinite is hidden in the small, in the insignificant. The moment you call it small, you will turn your back on it. And the point at which you turn your back is the very point where the divine is. So any time you turn your back, it will always be a back turned against the divine.

Where would you go in search of the "great"? What is this "great" anyway? Is serving the nation great? Is serving humanity great? Is sacrificing oneself great? Is being a martyr great?

Remember, anyone may prove capable of instantly becoming a martyr at any moment. Who would not be capable of committing suicide in an instant? Martyrdom looks difficult but it is not, because the matter is finished in an instant. You get hanged in an instant; the bullet pierces through the body in an instant.

True martyrs are those who live with awareness throughout the long span of life, because they have to carry the cross on their shoulders for their whole lives. True martyrs are those who search for the infinite in the insignificant. Their search will never be reported in the newspapers and no one will bring them flowers or put a garland round their neck. Quietly, they will be aware and experience the infinite while having a meal alone; they will realize it while weaving cloth or while taking a bath. Who would care to honor them? People would say, "Have you gone mad? We honor martyrs who are hanged. You have shown awareness while eating food – that is your business! What do we have to do with it? We are not interested in such insignificant matters," they will say.

But the fact is: the infinite is hidden within the insignificant the same as a tree is hidden within a seed. You sow a tiny seed and a huge tree comes out of it. That small, tiny, seed is the seed of *jatan* – the seed of meditation. Whatsoever you do, do it meditatively, do it with awareness.

But our state of mind is very strange. When we get bored with one kind of work we immediately choose some opposite kind of work. For example, if you get tired of the samsara, the mundane world, you turn to some religious activity, but you will remain as unconscious doing religious work as you were before in the mundane world. The act will change but you will not.

Before, while attending the shop, you were repeating the mantra "Rupee, rupee, rupee." Now you will sit in the temple and repeat the mantra "Rama, Rama, Rama." You will remain the same; you will be as unconscious saying *Rama* as you were saying *rupee*. Saying *Rama* will be as much a part of your sleep as was saying *rupee*. Before you were in the shop and even now you are still in the shop – you are the one who has turned all the temples into shops. You will obviously remain the same, no matter where you may go. How can you be different?

No one has ever changed just by changing the circumstances. It is changing the mind-set that changes you. Not the state of affairs but the state of mind has to be changed. That is the real transformation. That is why, despite being a weaver, Kabir was awakened. He has said very priceless things in this sutra. Try to understand each and every word.

***I have woven this very finely spun sheet of cloth.***

If you have ever watched a weaver weaving, or if you have ever spun on the spinning wheel, you will have noticed one thing: the finer the thread you would like to spin on the spinning wheel or on a weaving loom, the more awareness you will need. The thicker you want the thread to be, the less awareness is needed. If you would like to spin it very fine, then you will need to work with particular care, with *jatan* – greater awareness – because even with a slight unawareness the thread will break.

Kabir is saying: *I have woven this very finely spun sheet of cloth*. It means it has been woven with great *jatan*, great care. It means it has been woven with awareness. It means never for a moment did his hand tremble, his consciousness shake even one bit: "Weaving it, I was completely steady." The finer, the more subtle the work is, the more awareness will be required. Being unaware may not matter while doing any gross work but unawareness will not do when you are working on subtle things.

That is why we call the subtlest work "art" because while doing it the consciousness needs to be very alert – a little mistake and it will all be ruined. So the first thing is that the more you live with awareness, the more you will be able to experience the fineness and subtlety of life. And the more you experience the subtle, the more awake you will be. Both are connected and both are supportive of each other.

For example, you are walking along a street and so is a drunkard – on the same street. But watch his feet: he does not take one step rightly, but of course he will reach home somehow. But if on your walk you see a buddha walking, you will find that the same difference you see in your walk and that of the drunkard exists between your walk and that of the buddha. Looking at it one way, the drunkard will reach home and so will you, and the buddha will also reach home. But the nature and quality of the walk will differ. The drunkard walks totally unconsciously, a buddha is walking fully consciously, and you are somewhere in between. Once in a while you have a glimpse of awareness, but then it all becomes dark. Sometimes you are awake, at other times you are asleep. Sometimes your eyes are open, at other times your eyes are closed.

If you watch closely, you will find the more you grow in awareness the more the way you walk will show a certain elegance, a dexterity – what in the Gita Krishna calls *deftness*. The yogi becomes skillful. The yogi has to weave a very fine fabric. He has to take each step carefully; he has to take each breath with care. For him life is very fragile and very precious. He never walks like a drunkard. Kabir says that he walks the way a pregnant woman walks: paying attention, very carefully. She carries a new life within her. And the life inside her is only biological; while the life that grows inside a spiritual aspirant, inside a seeker, is a young shoot of the divine.

Imagine if the divine was going to be born through you, how carefully you would walk – just a little mistake and it could cause a miscarriage. Just a little slip, twisting your leg and falling down, and centuries of hard work could be wasted. As the goal comes closer, more and more awareness is required. There was no fear at all of going astray when you were far from the destination because where was the question of going astray? – you had already gone astray. Awareness is needed as the destination comes closer because now you can easily go astray.

Sufis say: "What fear do the worldly people have? We are the ones who really fear. What do the worldly people have to lose? We are the ones who have something to lose. The worldly person can walk anywhere he wants; he has nothing that he can lose. But we can never walk in a wayward fashion because the treasure is large and can be lost just as it is about to be gained. It can slip through our hands." The sight of the destination can be lost just as one is about to reach. And the higher up you are, the further you will fall. That is why you should keep the word *jatan* carefully in your mind.

What fear can a person who is already slipping into a ditch have of falling? But someone who is standing on the peak of the Gourishankar mountain will certainly have fear. But this is not fear in the sense of being scared; this fear is more like being cautious – the fear is because of the fact that one has something which may get lost.

Once it happened…

There was a Japanese monk Bokuju and he lived in the capital city of Tokyo. This story is about three hundred years old. As was common practice in ancient times, the emperor of Japan used to go on a horse ride incognito to see what was happening in the city. While the entire city was asleep, a monk would stay awake under a tree. Often he would be standing, but even while seated he would keep his eyes open.

The emperor could not hold back his curiosity. The whole night, no matter what time he went, he would find the monk awake. Sometimes he would find the monk strolling, sometimes seated or some other time standing – but always awake. The emperor never found him asleep.

Months passed by, the emperor's curiosity went on growing. Finally, one day, he couldn't hold himself back. He stopped by and said to the monk, "I am curious about one thing. Although I am not fit to ask nor do I have any right to ask, my curiosity is growing intensely and I cannot hold myself back from asking: why do you stay awake the whole night?"

The monk replied, "I have a treasure. To protect it, I stay awake."

The emperor was even more puzzled. He said, "I don't see any treasure; what I see are just broken pieces of earthenware, your begging bowl, these rags of yours – you call these your treasure? Are you in your right senses? And who would care to steal these?"

The monk said: "You won't be able to understand the treasure I am talking about. You can see only the broken earthen pots and these dirty rags. And what does it matter if the clothes are dirty or beautiful – after all they are all just clothes. And whether the earthenware is broken into pieces or there are vessels made of gold – they are all worthless. Who is talking about such things? There is another treasure which needs to be guarded."

The emperor said, "The treasure I have is no smaller, but I go to sleep."

The monk said: "With the kind of treasure you have, you can sleep easily. Even if you were to lose it, nothing would be really lost. If I lose the treasure I have, then everything will be lost. And I am just about to attain. It is almost in my hands, a little error and I don't know how many more lives I will need again to reach it."

Kabir is talking about the same treasure. It needs great awareness. It will require you to stay up all night and spend the day fully conscious. It will need you to take every step with care and awareness.

*Sadhu* means one who is living with *jatan*, with awareness; whatsoever he may be doing, he is doing it with self-remembrance. As your self-remembrance grows, you will see how superfine you have woven the cloth.

The fabric, the cloth of life, is very fine. And the more you are able to see how fine it is, the more you will be able to recognize the subtlety of its making, the more you will be filled with gratitude, the more you will find the treasure invaluable. Instead of rocks and pebbles you will see diamonds emerging. And the closer you feel yourself getting to the treasure, the more aware you will become. The doors of greater treasure will begin to open the more aware you become. Both are interdependent.

Where will you start? You can start from anywhere. Maybe you will begin with seeing how finely the fabric of life is woven.

That is what Kabir is explaining in this sutra.

***I am amazed at what the warp and the woof are made of.***

There is nothing more subtle in this world than the fabric of this life. This visible body of yours is hiding the invisible body. Every cell of your body that you can touch is hiding that which is impossible to touch. Behind these eyes of yours is the seer who is imperceptible. When you extend your hand and touch someone, it is not just the hand that touches; in fact, that which cannot be touched but is hidden behind, is also touched by your hand.

Although you have a gross physical body, hidden behind it is the incorporeal body. It is a warp and woof of the gross and the subtle. And the fabric, the cloth, is very fine. Also the physical human body that you see is not really as gross as you believe it to be. And as you penetrate deeper you will find that this physical body, too, is very subtle – because you have never really known your body, you have never really seen it.

Yogis say that there are millions of nerves in our bodies, and now science agrees with it. Now science also acknowledges that the yogis have the right understanding about this. Just in your brain alone there are a hundred billion nerve cells. The brain is very small – it hardly weighs one and a half kilograms – and that too Einstein's brain, not everyone's. So a one-and-a-half-kilogram brain contains a hundred billion nerve cells. There is nothing subtler and smaller than those tissues. You can't see them with the naked eye. Even your hair is thicker than those tissues. If we piled up one hundred thousand nerve cells on top of one another that would be as thick as one strand of your hair.

This is the reason why brain surgery could not develop earlier because when cutting at one point something else may have been cut – the nerves are so fine. It is dangerous even to insert an instrument into the brain because in the process of just inserting an instrument you may cut millions of tissues. This is the reason why it took so long to develop brain surgery. It was so difficult to create such subtle instruments and it was also difficult to find hands that were skillful enough. Even now, brain surgery has not become a perfect science because we don't yet have complete knowledge about the brain.

Your consciousness is hidden within this web of a hundred billion nerve cells. The web is, of course, subtle but consciousness is even more subtle than that. This web of tissues cannot be seen with the naked eye, but the consciousness cannot be seen at all. Even the largest possible microscope will not help you to see it. Each of these hundred billion nerve cells can contain ten million pieces of information. Each nerve cell can collect ten million pieces of informative knowledge.

Neurologists say that if a way could be found, all the existing libraries around the world could be contained in the brain of a single individual. One person alone can gather that much information. You don't use more than two percent of your brain. Even the greatest genius uses fifteen percent of his brain; eighty-five percent goes unused. We cannot even imagine the kind of extraordinary genius who will someday be able to use one hundred percent of his brain. People like Einstein would look like tiny glittering lamps before the brilliance of that giant sun. It is not just that the brain is subtle, the entire body is made of such a subtle warp and woof.

Those yogis put in a lot of effort, and that effort was unique. Scientists have instruments to prove things; the yogis didn't have any. Scientists have all kinds of things to help them – laboratories, means of observation, techniques to dissect the body – yet the yogis had none of these. Neither did they do any autopsies on dead bodies nor did they examine anyone. Their way of observing was exceptional. They awoke from within and observed the interior of the body from looking inside. They had no means of looking at the interior of the body from the outside.

There are two ways of looking at this house. One way is to look at it by standing outside; that will be looking at the outer appearance, the outer façade of the house. And then there is another way of looking at it, which will be seen by the person who is living inside the house. The scientist looks from the outside; it is the view of a passerby on the road. He is not resident in the house. He is not standing inside the house. Anyone looking at the house from the outside also says he appreciates its many subtleties. Now imagine those who have seen the house from the inside, those who because they are fully awake, have seen the warp and the woof from within... The day you see the hundred billion nerve cells from within is the day that you will understand what Kabir is saying: *I have woven this very finely spun sheet of cloth.*

The muslin of Dhaka is not even close to being so fine; no weaver has ever been able to weave muslin of a kind that matches the way your brain is made – no one will ever be able to because that weaving has been done by a great craftsman. Kabir is saying that even God takes ten months to weave it; God takes ten months to weave this one piece of fabric – the human body.

I have woven this very finely spun sheet of cloth. I am amazed at what the warp and the woof are made of.

Kabir is amazed; he has had a revelation, his inner world has become luminous and in that light he is seeing the warp and woof of the body. Each and every fine subtlety has become apparent to him. And, Kabir, in his amazement, is saying: ...at *what the warp and the woof are made of.* What are the threads this cloth is made of? He is in a state of awe and amazement. Whenever a yogi is awakened within he is filled with astonishment and wonder – being in a state of wonder is the first thing that happens. The yogi is astounded, becomes speechless.

The world that you see outside is nothing; there is an even larger world that you are hiding within you. You have never seen it because in order to see it you need to be settled and steady inside, you need to raise awareness within. Only when your consciousness begins to burn like a flame will the inner house become manifest. And I say with authority that in the history of humanity no one has used a better terminology than Kabir. The weaver has got it right:

**I have woven this very finely spun sheet of cloth.**
**I am amazed at what the warp and the woof are made of.**
**The cloth's warp is made of ingla and pingla, nerves,**
**and the woof, made of sushumna, runs through it.**

This is a designation used by the yogis. *Sushumna*, according to the yogis, is the spinal cord – but not just the spinal cord. The spinal cord is the external cover. Exactly through the middle of it flows a subtle stream of light, a subtle energy, like electricity. And that very thing is what supports your brain. Your brain, which consists of a hundred billion nerve cells, is at the other end of this *sushumna*, your spinal cord. Scientists say that your spinal cord developed into the brain; so your brain is nothing but the other end of the spinal cord. Try to understand this.

Your life has two ends and so does your body. One end of it is the brain and the other end is your sex center. That's why the yogis mention two centers: they call one the *muladhar*, which is your sex center, and the second they call the *sahasrar*; and you don't know anything about the *sahasrar*. So the spinal cord has two ends: one is passion for sex and the other is passion for the divine. At one end there is karma, sex, and at the other end God, the divine – and between the two is the stream of energy which is known as *sushumna*. The spinal cord is its outer sheath. Just as the tree is hidden in the seed, and the seed is the outer sheath, the same is with the spinal cord. Within this spinal cord is hidden the *sushumna* of the yogis.

As you begin to become aware, the energy begins to flow upward. The more asleep, unconscious, you are, the more it flows downward. Sleep, or unconsciousness, means you will be familiar with life only through sexuality; you won't know anything else. You will be familiar only with one end. That end is just the first door. If you got stuck there, it would be like wasting the whole of your life standing at the very steps of a palace. You would believe that it is your home and would stay there forever. Most people spend their life in the porch; they don't even reach the steps; they don't even get to knock on the door.

As you begin to be awake…and there can be two ways of awakening. One method is that of Patanjali. That method is to raise the energy hidden in the spinal cord – the energy known as *kundalini*. The *shirshasan*, or headstand, is useful for that because in that posture the energy easily begins to fall toward the head. Asanas, yogic postures, are useful because through them pressure is applied on the consciousness so that your energy may begin to rise. That's why *brahmacharya*, celibacy, is so valuable – if the energy was allowed to continue to flow downward then not much of it would be left to rise upward.

For example, we build a dam on a river and by doing that we shut off the passage where the river was flowing downward. When a dam is built on a river, a vast energy of electricity gets stored. *Brahmacharya* is similar to building a dam. As the door is blocked from one side, the energy begins to build up. When a lot of energy is accumulated, it needs a passage to move through.

The accumulated energy will begin to flow toward the head if the *shirshasan*, the headstand, is added to *brahmacharya*. These are bodily methods. Patanjali and Hatha yoga will wake you up through these physical means. As your energy begins to flow upward, you will become more and more aware.

The second way is that of Kabir, of Buddha. This second method is that as you go on becoming more aware, the energy will rise higher and higher. As you continue to use awareness in life – for example, walking with awareness, sitting with awareness, getting up with awareness, going to bed with awareness and holding on to awareness till the body goes to sleep – the moment will come when the body is drowned in sleep but the awareness will remain intact – then even in sleep awareness will continue to be there.

Hence Krishna says that even while others are asleep, the yogi never sleeps. This does not mean the yogi just remains seated, keeping his eyes open. He also sleeps – but only his body sleeps. His witnessing consciousness within remains awake. So as the witnessing consciousness grows, the energy will rise higher. They are interdependent – raise the energy upward and the witnessing consciousness will grow.

But raising the energy upward is a very difficult and troublesome path. It would require a long *sadhana*, a long spiritual discipline, and a long physical training. And it is a very long journey; it cannot be completed in one lifetime because it is like traveling in a bullock cart. That is why Hatha yoga gradually went out of practice. It was replaced by Raja yoga because Raja yoga works directly on the consciousness and the consciousness easily gains momentum; it requires no disciplining of the body.

The sadhana of consciousness is very easy. You just need to maintain your awareness. If you wish to go into the discipline of Hatha yoga, then the body needs to be totally healthy which is difficult to achieve these days. It is difficult to find a holistically healthy body today because the whole of nature has been distorted and the entire natural lifestyle has been messed up. Everything now is unnatural. The air you breathe is unnatural. Scientists have discovered that the air of Mumbai, Tokyo, and New York is filled with such poisonous gasses that they are amazed how people are staying alive in such polluted air. They should be dead! But man somehow makes adjustments. The stream of life slows down, but man adjusts himself to any given situation. The current of life slows down, but man does not die. His way of living becomes dull, it moves in an unconscious state, and yet man does not die. The air is poisoned all around. The Hatha yogis had no idea that someday cars would be on the road, trains would be running, there would be motorcycles – petrol would be burning all around and oxygen would slowly become less and less available.

Now the situation is that soon only well-to-do people will have access to oxygen. By the end of this century, everyone will have to wear oxygen masks – everybody. They have already started experimenting in Russia. Soon they are going to start in America. As the century comes to an end, oxygen will have disappeared. So you will need to carry an oxygen flask around – but only very wealthy people will be able to make use of it. The poor man will, of course, be in difficulty. Just as a poor man now has to stand in queue near a water tap because water is scarce, similarly, sooner or later, he will have to stand in queue for air as well so he can take deep breaths of oxygen that will somehow last him for twenty-four hours.

Food is poisonous. Everything is unnatural. The natural minerals people need have disappeared; man has used them up but has not replenished them. The fertilizers we are using now are all artificial; they are man-made. They are all poisoning our food. All over the world atomic tests are going on. They are poisoning the air. Everywhere radioactive elements have entered into everything. Nothing is pure anymore – it can never be. In such a condition Hatha yoga is of no use. Hatha yoga was once a part of a very natural world where everything was natural. Even in such a natural world, a Hatha yogi had to go through several lifetimes. It is a long journey because someone who is moving with the help of the gross is actually riding on a bullock cart.

Someone who is willing to use the subtle discovers faster means. That is why, gradually, Raja yoga replaced Hatha yoga altogether. It completely replaced Hatha yoga. Buddha, Kabir, Nanak, and Dadu are all Raja yogis. And all of them have opposed Hatha yoga, because now it is not possible to reach through it; now it is finished.

Kabir is saying that the more you are awake within, the more your energy will begin to flow. The passage through which energy flows is known as *sushumna*. Kabir calls it *sushumna*. And *sushumna* is the middle path; on both its sides are two other nerves which are known as the *ida* and *pingla* respectively. Both these nerves are inside the body and the life energy flows through them as well. You may not have noticed it and the present-day physiologists have also never paid attention to it, although now some scientists are beginning to take an interest in it.

When you breathe, for some time the breath flows through the left nostril, and then through the right nostril. When the breath flows through the left nostril, the state of the entire body is different, and when it flows through the right one, the body is in a different state. With *ida* and *pingala* yogis have connecting doors for both these breaths – and they are indeed connected.

When your breath moves through the left nostril, your life energy travels through one path; when it moves through the right, it travels through another path. Yogis have given several names to identify them. Some call them the *surya nadi*, sun nerve, and *chandra nadi*, moon nerve. One nostril is like the sun; when you breathe through it your whole body heats up. Your other nostril is the moon; when you breathe through it your whole body is filled with peace. Your right-side breathing is of the sun and your left-side breathing is of the moon. Watch sometimes, when you have a headache, block the right-side breathing and breathe through the left side. Soon you will find the pain has disappeared because the left-side breathing is of the moon, it gives peace. If you feel lazy, tired and fatigued, stop breathing through the left side and breathe through the right side. Soon you will find the energy has started moving, the body has become warm, it has become active – this is because of the sun breath.

Modern-day biologists have given very little attention to this matter, but a few scientists have started showing interest – there is certainly some mystery in all of this. When someone wakes up in the morning and finds his right-side breathing on he remains active the whole day; someone whose left-side breathing is active when waking up in the morning will feel sluggish and inert the whole day.

The person whose left-side breathing keeps going will feel more alive at night; he will stay up late at night. Night is like day for him. The person who has the right-side breathing on will get ready to go to bed as the evening approaches. He will effortlessly wake up very early in the morning. A day is a day for him.

Every person must find his own natural inclination otherwise great troubles may arise. Those who breathe from the sun side are more active, so naturally they condemn those who are not so active. They call them names such as lazy, idle and indolent. They tell these people: "Get up and go to work! Rise before dawn!" Generally, men are right-side breathers and women are left-side breathers – this is how it should be.

There is an ancient tradition in India where a wife is expected to sit on the left side of her husband – that symbolizes left-side breathing. She is a moonside breather; night is her day – she fully blossoms at night. Women don't like to wake up early in the morning. They have to because the husband, her lord, is asleep. But this does not fit with her natural inclination and it causes harmful effects.

My experience is that often women suffer more from headaches because of heaviness, melancholy. And one among many other reasons for this is that they get up in the morning earlier than they should. The natural thing would be for the husband to prepare the morning tea.

Now scientists have also reached the same conclusion, although they have understood it from another direction. They are saying that for two hours in twenty-four every person's body temperature falls. These two hours are really meant for having a good sleep. The person who sleeps for these two hours will feel refreshed for the rest of the day and the person who stays awake during these two hours will be troubled the following day. Not everyone has the same two hours. It would be easier if they were the same, then a law could be made that everybody must sleep between three and five o'clock at night. But the hours are not the same for everyone.

For example, for some people, these two hours are between two and four in the night and for others they are between five and seven. There are also people who have these hours between seven and nine in the morning. These two hours are different for everyone and you can work them out. You can keep a record of your body temperature for twenty-four hours and you will come to know which two hours are for you. You must sleep during these two hours whether it is *brahmamuhurta* or not.

A person who sleeps at this time will feel fresh the whole day. Then his sleep is complete. There is no need to sleep for eight hours; those two hours will be enough. If you miss those two hours, then even twelve hours of sleep will not solve anything. During the two hours when the body temperature falls the entire body is relaxed; all activity ceases. Then you become just like a corpse. You will not have any dreams; it will be a deep sleep.

Researchers also found out that for men the two hours come earlier than for women. For example, if for a man the hours are between four and six or between three and five in the morning, then for women generally the hours are between six and eight or between five and seven in the morning. In the West they have started advising that women should wake up a little later; there is no harm in their staying up late at night.

Men should wake up early. But even here there are differences. Not all men are the same, not all women are the same. In fact, many women are more mannish than men. Many men are more womanly than women.

Just yesterday, Mulla Nasruddin came to see me.

He said, "Believe it or not I made my wife crawl on her knees."

I said, "Really?"

He said, "That's the truth, not even an iota of a lie."

So I said, "Didn't she say anything?"

He said, "Of course, she did! She said, 'Just get out from under the bed and then I will show you!'"

Mulla was hiding under the bed and this is how he made his wife crawl on her knees.

There are men who are womanly and there are women who are mannish. Then the two hour sleep phenomenon will be different. Each person has to find his own time. And just as your thumbprints are different from the thumbprints of any other person, so are the other characteristics and particulars in your life – none match anyone else's.

Recently, I was reading a book on biology in which the biologist, mentioning the latest research, says not only thumbprints but even the kidney of one person is different from the kidney of another person. Each person's heart is different from the heart of another person. Every cell of one person's body is different from another person's. Every individual carries a unique template. God has not only woven some very fine fabric, each piece is also different from the next.

God's creativity is infinite – he never repeats. He never makes a second one of you; he never makes anyone like you again. In this you are blessed; and if you could understand this blessedness, a great peace and joy would arise in your life. God has never created anyone like you and will never again create anyone like you. So don't ever lose this great opportunity, which will not come back again. He is watching over you; because he has never made anyone like you before nor will you be made again as you are now. You are absolutely unique.

That is why you should never, ever, imitate anyone, not even by mistake. Never, ever, make the mistake of becoming like Rama, Buddha, or Krishna because God would like you to be totally what you are; to be honestly what you are – yourself. Blossom like the flower you are; no one else is the same flower as you are. If you try to become like Rama, that will look artificial – made out of paper, Japanese. You will be true and authentic only when you are just yourself.

I am amazed at what the warp and the woof are made of. The cloth's warp is made of ingla and pingla, nerves, and the woof, made of sushumna, runs through it.

Recently, a great experiment took place in Russia. A photographer named Kirlian has discovered a new kind of photography – it is one of the most significant discoveries of this century. He has developed such subtle films, the photography is so sensitive, that it can take films of subtle energies. Understand this a little because only then will you be able to know about *ida, pingla,* and *sushumna*. These are all energy fields. These are nothing but electromagnetic fields.

Kirlian's discovery happened accidentally. He was just a photographer but he had a passion for making sensitive films. Once, by mistake, his hand appeared in front of the camera and it was photographed. But when he saw the photograph he was quite amazed. Three fingers of his hand looked all right and the thumb was fine. But the little finger looked strange – it looked sick. All the other fingers looked fine in the picture except that one finger which looked unwell. Looking at the photograph, it appeared the finger was affected by some disease.

Six months later the little finger became diseased. And when it was photographed again and compared with the photograph taken six months before both looked identical.

It occurred to him, "Could it be that the disease enters in the electromagnetic field even before entering the body? – because the photograph of the disease appeared first and the disease followed later." Then he began doing other experiments because one door had already opened. Using very sensitive films he took photographs of buds and found pictures of full-blown flowers. The flower was expected to blossom four days later but its electric energy blossomed before that. It is due to the electric energy that the flower's petals bloom. We don't get to see that energy; we only see the flower. When he compared the photographs, he was completely amazed because they matched each other so well.

So he discovered that at first when the electric energy blossoms, the energy appears as a flower. Then, four days later, the actual flower blooms. And when he compared both pictures they appeared to be identical.

During the last thirty years Kirlian has done many experiments. And he has proved authentically that within the human body there is a deeper body, and that deeper body is made of electric energy. If we succeeded in photographing that energy, we would see that what takes six months to occur in the physical body has already happened in that body.

This is of great use. The day this Kirlian photography becomes a complete science no one in the world will ever have to fall sick. We will be able to detect sickness six months in advance and know it is approaching. Then treatment can be done there and then. Even though he is not well, the person doesn't know it as he is not actually sick yet. The sickness takes six months to move from the subtle to the gross. The ancient yogis have called the picture of your electric energy *aura*.

Kirlian also found difference in color. For example, when a person is healthy within four inches around his body there is a different kind of aura. When the person is sick, the color of the aura is different. When the person is happy the color is different, when he is unhappy it is different. The moment you become unhappy unhappiness also colors your electric energy. Until the color of this electric energy changes you can never be happy. Your gross body is just a shadow; the real body is hidden inside. It is this real body that we have called…

> **The cloth's warp is made of ingla and pingla, nerves,**
> **and the woof, made of sushumna, runs through it.**
> **This body has eight lotuses and ten doors;**
> **it is made of five tattvas, outer realities, and five mahatattvas,**
> **as well as three gunas, the basic life forces.**

This energy field inside the body has eight lotuses, eight chakras. It has ten doors, those of the sense organs. It is made of five *tattvas* and five *mahatattvas*. It is created of three *gunas*.

So Kabir is saying that the eight lotuses, which we call the chakras, if you understand rightly… And there is a reason why they are called lotuses. It is just a symbol. You may have sometimes seen water moving in a circle, a swirl. Similarly, there are circles of electricity in the body where the energy moves circularly – in a swirl. And these swirls look similar to a lotus – as if a lotus is swirling. With an ignorant person it happens as if the lotus is bent downward – the stem of the lotus facing upward and the lotus flower drooping down, wilted. As the energy begins to move upward, the stem begins to straighten up and the lotus stands erect. We have placed Buddha and Vishnu standing on the lotus – standing on a fully-blossomed lotus. That lotus symbolizes the same electric energy. It shows that the lotus of Buddha, of Vishnu, has fully blossomed and in that blossoming they have found the ultimate truth. Our lotuses droop downward until our energy starts rising up. Normally our energy flows downward.

Let us say, there are lotuses and a heavy rain falls on them; the force of the rain will naturally bend the lotuses and turn their heads to face downward. As long as you are full of lust, as long as lust is drenching you heavily from above, your energy is flowing downward – all the lotuses will be bent. The day energy begins to flow upward, when it begins to rise up – what the Vedas call *urdhvaretas* – when your energy starts moving upward, the lotuses will begin to face up and all the lotuses will begin to bloom. The last lotus, what Kabir calls the eighth lotus, is *sahasrar*.

This counting of the lotuses varies. Someone counts them as seven lotuses, another counts them as eight, while someone else counts them as nine and somebody else as eleven. Such differences in counting are possible. It all depends how you count. There are many lotuses. Every atom of your energy contains a lotus. So you can count as many of them – and according to whichever calculation – as you may wish. Then, also, each person halts at different places on a journey. For example, while going on a journey someone may take a rest every ten miles, so if it is a hundred-mile journey, he will stop every ten miles and so make ten stops. Another person may stop every fifteen miles and so would make less than ten stops. A third person may choose to walk twenty miles and then take a rest; he will have only five stops.

Buddha talks about six lotuses; he must have halted only six times. On that infinite journey he must have stopped at six places. He must have found difficulty at six places. He must have had to let flowers bloom in six places – so six lotuses. Kabir says eight lotuses. There is no conflict in this. But between pundits there is a lot of debate about who is right. Where is the problem? I can make a halt after ten miles, it is up to me; I may stop after twenty miles, that is my choice. Wherever I stop, that will be my first halt, my first lotus.

There are some who have never even talked about the lotuses. It seems that Mahavira, for example, never made any stops. Jet age! It looks like he jumped straight from the first center to the last center. This is also possible, it is indeed possible. And it is certainly possible for a person like Mahavira. That's why we have given him the name: Mahavira. This name is given because he has great energy, massive energy.

The greater the energy, the longer the jump one can take – without making any halt in between. So he has not talked about a lotus at all; he has not mentioned the in-between chakras at all. But that does not mean he has not gone through the middle chakras. For example, the train you are traveling in may not stop at the in-between stations, but it certainly passes through them. It makes no difference whether you stop between one railway junction and another, or whether you travel in a goods train. But a person who is traveling in a fast train and doesn't stop at in-between stations has no reason to talk about these stations. He is traveling junction to junction…he will talk about one junction and one other. Then there are those who travel in a slow passenger train. Nothing is wrong in traveling in a slow passenger train…

I have a friend. He is very wealthy but he always travels in a regional train. He says, "Poor people travel in an express train, they are short of time." And I can see his point.

He says, "Where is the fun in traveling by train otherwise"?

He gets down at every station, drinks water, buys refreshments – he does this and he does that. Otherwise, what fun can there be in traveling? When the train halts at the station he meets people, strikes up a conversation with them.

Once I accompanied him, so the place I could otherwise have reached in twelve hours he made me reach in three days. But he is a very loveable man. In his company the three days felt like three seconds. And I also felt that what he was saying was right. It is up to each person how he wants to move. There is no room for any dispute.

That is why, to me, it makes no difference whether one says nine lotuses, or someone else says ten or somebody says eleven lotuses – it does not matter. What Kabir is saying is absolutely right.

Eight lotuses and ten sense organs – ten spinning wheels – are moving. There are ten sense organs: five organs of action, *karmendriyas*, and five organs of sensing, *jnana indriyas*. Kabir is saying that these sense organs are spinning wheels – he is using the symbols of a weaver. There are five elements, *tattvas*. There are three *gunas* – rajas, tamas, sattva. The inner cloth is made of all these.

***God took ten months working meticulously at weaving it.***

God takes ten months to weave each piece of cloth.

***The same cloth is worn by gods, humans, and monks***
***but all three leave it unclean.***
***Kabir, the humble slave, has worn it with awareness***
***and returned it as unblemished as it first was.***

Even God needs time to create this cloth because what is being created is so precious. You never consider yourself to have any worth. God, the whole of existence, spends ten months creating you, but you never recognize you are worth anything. You live as if you are worthless. You are ready to sell yourself for peanuts. You have no idea what great fortune has been bestowed upon you. You waste it just for nothing. You are not able to make any use of it.

Here, Kabir is saying a very significant thing; it is rather subtle. Pay great attention so you can understand it. He is saying, *The same cloth is worn by gods, humans, and monks…*

He has chosen three symbols: gods, those who live in heaven, they represent nothing but pure hedonism. They simply wallow in sensual gratification. Heaven means a place of pleasure. There we have created the wish-fulfilling tree, *kalpataru*. The moment you sit under it and wish for something the wish is instantly fulfilled – there is no action involved between the desire and its fulfillment. So heaven is not a place of action, it is a place of enjoyment. This is exactly what our passionate desire is – that the moment one wishes for something it should instantly be taken care of. It should not even take the time it requires to push a button. But here, on this earth, it takes a long time.

For example, here on earth, you want to build a house, but it does not get built as instantly as you wished. It might get built after you have been through agony and agitation your whole life. Perhaps by the time it gets done you will not be in a condition to live in it. By the time it is built you may find life is over. You want to make money with much desire, with great dreams, but when you actually have the wealth you will find that you have already lost what you could have enjoyed. In time, all things get destroyed.

That is why our final dream is that of enjoyment: heaven, where your passionate desires take no time to be fulfilled. As soon as you desire something, it instantly gets fulfilled. That is why it is so enjoyable to be rich. What is the real difference between being rich and being poor? A poor man's desire cannot be fulfilled immediately, but a rich man can fulfill his immediately. The more wealth he has, the smaller the gap will be between his desires and their fulfillment. The moment he desires a big palace, a big palace will appear.

But, says Kabir, even gods make the sheets dirty. Indulging in lust makes the sheets dirty. A hedonist means one who has gone astray by identifying completely with his passionate desires. When hungry, he thinks "I am hungry." When passion arises, he thinks "I am passionate." When anger arises, he thinks "I am angry." A hedonist means one who has become so attached to his passionate desires that there is no space left in between.

Even gods will take a fall. Heaven is not the last state. India discovered a final state, which they call moksha. This needs to be understood a little because the concept of moksha exists nowhere else in the world. Hell exists, heaven exists and earth exists, but moksha is absolutely an Indian concept – purely Indian. India has put in a lot of effort into religion and that is why it reached the point of being able to search in this direction. Just as the West has made efforts with science, India has made efforts in the field of religion. We don't consider heaven as the ultimate state. You will fall from there too, because for how long can you keep chasing pleasure. Lustful indulgence creates boredom. If you ever go to heaven, you will find all the gods yawning because they are bored.

Just think, if you instantly get what you want, how long will you be able to enjoy it? Ten to twelve hours? Hardly! If you get what you want immediately, for how long will your passions last? Such enjoyment of your desires will bore you.

That is why there are stories in the Puranas where bored gods yearn to come back to the earth. There is one advantage on the earth: here, passionate cravings are not satisfied immediately – it takes time. And the real fun lies in time. So the poets say, "In waiting…in waiting is the fun." There is not much fun in having something; what will you do once you have it? The whole fun is in waiting, in longing, in hoping the goal is coming closer, and closer. The fun is in hoping. After getting what you want the fun disappears.

The gods have got it; they enjoy, but they get identified with their lustful enjoyment. These gods are not known for their awareness. You won't find anyone more asleep than Indra, the king of the gods. He is completely lost in drinking, in frolicking. The *apsaras*, the heavenly beauties, are dancing around and yet he is always worried. The stories talk of his fear of losing his throne. Why, otherwise, should he bother if a sage is sitting in meditation? But as soon as someone goes into deep spiritual practice, Indra's throne begins to shake.

These stories are very significant; they are of great value. What this means is that both – the renouncer and the hedonist – are two ends of the same continuum; the same as two pans of the scales. As you put more weight onto one pan, the other pan begins to shake. When a sage renounces too much, Indra gets alarmed. His side of the scales shakes. Why? Because both are connected with the same thing; they are two pans of the same scales. If this sage renounces too much, then he will become entitled to enjoyment; he can become Indra sometime. In that case Indra will be displaced. Indra's condition is the same as that of the politicians in Delhi. Whether it is Indra or Indira, it makes no difference; the throne keeps shaking. And whether it is Vashishtha or Vishwamitra or Jayprakash, they are two pans of the same scales. As the one pan gets heavier, the other one begins to rise.

So the story is very significant. No story is ever meaningless. This story will look significant if we see the psychology behind it. The hedonist will always be afraid of the one who has renounced the material world because, after all, why is he renouncing everything? He is making such a hue and cry about it, doing penance and mortifying himself so that he becomes entitled to fun and merriment after death.

So there is not much difference between the hedonist and the renouncer. Both are two sides of the same coin; both have the same desire. One has already achieved it, while the other is putting his heart and soul into the hope of getting it. So, in fact, the renouncer also has dreams of fun and enjoyment. He has renounced all women here, but dreams of heavenly beauties. He has given up food here; he is fasting, but also waiting to enjoy sweets in heaven. Here, he has drained and tortured his body and now he is waiting to have a shining golden body, a body of a god which never gets old, whose hair never goes gray. In heaven, people don't age; their age remains the same. At least, it is said that women remain stuck at the age of sixteen. No *apsara*, nymph, is older than sixteen. So much time has gone by, yet they are still sixteen. They never get any older. Here, too, women try hard not to age, but it doesn't work on the earth!

One day, Mulla Nasruddin told me, "Ageing all alone, all by myself; I feel bad."

I said, "Alone? But your wife is there."

He said, "For the last ten years her age has not increased. I am ageing all alone."

All husbands age alone. The wife remains where she was long ago. In heaven, age never increases, the body never deteriorates; there is no evidence of any disease. Have you ever heard of a doctor in heaven? – an allopathic or an ayurvedic doctor or a *hakim*, a Unani physician? Not one. Here on earth even Buddha needed a doctor. In heaven, there is no disease, no sickness, no old age – there is simply lustful fun and merriment. The only disease there is that one gets bored.

A rich man gets bored. A poor man will not look so bored. A wealthy man will look absolutely bored. Nothing is left in his life because the waiting is over; there is nothing to wait for, all is achieved. Now, suddenly, all has come to a full stop. The chase, the speed, all have come to a halt. Now there is nowhere to go; now he is in trouble. He is in agony to come back to earth.

Kabir says whether they are gods, humans or sages, they all make their sheets dirty. The gods make them dirty through their lust and indulgence and the sages make them dirty through their renunciation. These words of Kabir are very revolutionary. Kabir is saying that even if you renounce everything, if it is done in unawareness then it is no different from being full of lust and indulging in it – their nature is the same. There is no fundamental difference in how both see things.

The pleasure-seeker, the hedonist, is fanatically seeking wealth; the renouncer is fanatical about giving up wealth. But both have wealth as the center of their perception. The hedonist says he has a hundred million rupees; the renouncer says he has given up a hundred million rupees. But both are keeping account of a hundred million rupees. The pleasure-seeker says gold is everything; the renouncer says gold is nothing but dirt. But both talk about gold. If indeed gold is dirt, then why even talk about it? Why doesn't anyone talk about dirt? If gold is truly nothing more than dirt, then why should it be talked about?

Once, there was a mystic in Maharashtra. His name was Ranka. He was a poor man, a renunciate. He would cut wood and sell it; whatever he earned he used for buying food. In the evening he would share his leftovers with others.

Once there was untimely rain which lasted for two or three days. He had no food to eat for three days. He had a wife, her name was Banka – Ranka was the husband, Banka the wife. The rains stopped on the fourth day. They went to the forest and were on their way home. The wood was wet and there was no certainty it would sell. They were tired and hungry.

The husband, who was walking ahead of his wife, suddenly saw a bag lying on the side of the road filled with golden coins. The bag was open and had a few coins inside. He was a renouncer – one who Kabir would call a *muni*. He thought, "Why is that dirt lying there? It might tempt someone." So he threw it into a pit and covered it with earth.

By that time his wife, who had been following him, caught up. She asked, "What are you doing?"

He replied, "There was some gold lying here. And gold is, after all, nothing but dirt. So I threw it into the pit and covered it with dirt."

The wife said, "Didn't you feel ashamed, throwing dirt upon dirt? If indeed it was dirt, then why did you place dirt on top of the dirt?"

No, for the person who says gold is nothing but dirt, gold is still gold; otherwise there would be no reason to talk about it. Both the renouncer and the pleasure-seeker are tied at the same place. Their situations may be different but they have their eyes on the same thing. The renouncer is against that which the pleasure-seeker is in favor of, but both show the same unawareness. One is asleep on the left side and the other is asleep on the right side – but it makes no difference to the sleep. Both are asleep; both are dreaming. They are both asleep, back to back. Sleep is the main factor. Man is between the two states of unconsciousness.

Kabir is saying, both the renouncer and the pleasure-seeker destroy the sheet. And in between is man – a hodgepodge: a renouncer in the morning, a pleasure-seeker in the evening; a renouncer in the evening and a pleasure-seeker at night. He changes many times in twenty-four hours – in fact many times in much less than twenty-four hours.

Recently, they have made a small watch in America. There is Nixon's photo on the dial and as the seconds pass his eyes move.

It is a joke, but they have made something good. The eyes move every second. The photo actually represents man. You change every second. As you get hungry, you become a lustful pleasure-seeker; once the stomach is filled you immediately become a renouncer. After making love you turn on your side and become an absolute renouncer; you begin to think of becoming celibate. You start thinking, "This is all useless; what is the point in all of this?" You have thought this way many times. It is difficult to find a man who does not feel gloomy after making love. One loses energy making love. Tired and worn out, you don't gain anything; and you were imagining so much, you had so many dreams – that you might get this, you might get that. But you get nothing except feeling sad, gloomy.

After making love, everyone thinks of celibacy, but for how long? Due to food, air and work the energy will regenerate within twenty-four hours. Food will again create energy. After twenty-four hours passion will once again arise, thoughts of women will again cross your mind. In that moment you will completely forget that just twenty-four hours earlier you had really understood the great significance of celibacy. Now, again, women will look important. And this circle has been moving around forever; many times you have been through both things. After sex you begin to think of renouncing it. Then again you get hungry and once again you think of pleasure. Between the two extremes – the pleasure-seeker and the renouncer – stands man.

Man is nothing but a hodgepodge – confused. His timing is equally divided. For example, if you kept a diary, you would be able to write in it correctly: "Renouncer in the morning, hedonist in the afternoon; again the renouncer and again the pleasure-seeker. Then I went to the temple, then I arrived at the shop; then, at the shop, I started thinking about the temple; then again in the temple I start thinking about the shop." You will find that you are a mixture of both. If it is true that both a pure renouncer and a pure pleasure-seeker destroy the sheet once, you will destroy it twice. You will destroy the sheet with both ideas: renouncing and indulging. The renouncer is sleeping on the left side while the pleasure-seeker is sleeping on the right side. You keep on changing sides in your sleep. You will destroy the sheet totally. At least both the renouncer and the pleasure-seeker are steady in their respective directions – you keep on moving in a circle. Your state of excitement will completely destroy this subtle fabric.

That is why Kabir says, The same woven cloth is worn by gods, humans, and monks, but all three leave it unclean. Kabir, the humble slave, has worn it with awareness and returned it as unblemished as it first was.

Kabir, the humble slave, wore the cloth with great care and attention; watchfully and meditatively. *And returned it as unblemished as it first was.* He returned it exactly as the divine gave it to him. This is moksha. This is the state of a free soul. You return it purely as it was given to you, without distorting it in any way.

When a child is born it brings along a clean sheet – totally spotless, innocent. Then the distortion starts, it begins to gather. The old man dies like a wreck; all in ruins. Nothing has been achieved. In fact, he has lost even whatever he already had before. Kabir says that even a wise man dies; but when he does, he saves what was given to him. He leaves the sheet as blemish-free as it was when he received it.

How would you keep this sheet free from blemish? Kabir is a householder, he has a wife and a child; he brings his earnings home; and yet he says, *Kabir, the humble slave, has worn it with awareness*... What seems to be the art of preserving this sheet? There is an art: awareness. There is an art: discernment. There is an art: awakened consciousness. Do whatsoever you are doing, whatsoever you are supposed to do. Whatever is destined, fulfill it. There is no point in escaping. But when you do whatever you do, don't be a doer. Go to the temple, pray, but don't be the doer. Let the divine be the doer; why would you want to be bothered with doing? Let the divine handle it. Just remain a witness. See yourself just as an actor, as if you had a role to play in a drama and you have to perform it.

For example, you have been given the role of Rama in a *Ramleela* play, so you will have to weep. When Sita is abducted, you will have to ask the trees, "Where has my Sita gone?" You will have to scream and shout, you will have to do everything. But as far as your inner world is concerned, you have neither lost Sita nor is it your problem; you are just acting it out. Once behind the curtain you will again go on chitchatting, having tea with Ravana. Behind the curtain you will chitchat with him, but in front of the curtain you will be standing with your bow and arrow. Life is just a *leela*, a play. If you can move with awareness, then it is nothing other than acting.

I have a friend; he is a professor of psychology. Once I was a guest in his house. He has a son, their only son – my friend had quite recently married – but his son was refusing to eat his meal. The wife was very upset; she scolded him, tried to persuade him, but nothing worked. So the husband said, "Wait and let me apply a little psychology." After all, he was a professor of psychology. The professor was still new to being a husband and a father. So I became curious to see what kind of psychology he was planning to use.

So he told his son, "Look, just wear your jacket, put on a hat, take a walking stick in your hand, go out, and think you are our guest." The son became very happy.

Children are always very interested in acting. That is their innocence. An old man instead would have said, "Why do such acting? What is the point of it? What is the meaning of it all?" But the child became very happy. Immediately, he put on a jacket, put on a hat, took the stick in his hand, and rushed out. The father said, "Now ring the doorbell from outside, and we will open the door. You have to play the role of a guest."

Soon the sound of his little footsteps were heard on the steps. He rang the doorbell. The door was opened and he was welcomed. The father said, "Please come in; you are our guest. And you have come at the right time; the food is ready – please join us."

The boy followed him in and we all came to the dining table. The boy placed his hat and the walking stick on a chair. The father said, "You are our guest; please accept whatever humble meal we have prepared."

The boy said, "Excuse me, but I have come just after eating my meal."

Since it was acting, he did it well!

Life is nothing but a drama. If you consider it more than that then you are bound to go astray. Granted, the stage is large; agreed, there are many characters – but life as such is just acting. And never, ever, become a doer in it. If you can keep this much in your awareness, then you will also be able to say:

> ***Kabir, the humble slave, has worn it with awareness and returned it as unblemished as it first was.***

Enough for today.

# 6
# Love Is an Invitation

***The path of bhakti is very delicate.***
***Neither averse to it, nor desirous for it,***
***I am simply lost at your feet.***
***Day and night, he is drenched in the juicy stream***
***of the ways of devotion.***
***The truth of the scriptures is imbedded in the melody of bhakti,***
***just as a fish is at one with the water.***
***I offer my head in the service of my Lord without any delay.***

Kabir is a great coming together – a confluence like Prayagraj, a holy place where whatever is superior has come together. The Ganges, Yamuna and Saraswati rivers have all merged in him. *Jnana*, bhakti, and karma – all three are joined here. Karma is easily visible; it is difficult to hide bhakti, but *jnana* is a deeper stream. At the great holy place, Prayag, you can see the Ganges and Yamuna rivers, but the Saraswati is invisible. Saraswati is the goddess of *jnana*. Make sure you understand this rightly.

Obviously karma will be visible because karma means the external, the visible. It is difficult to hide bhakti, devotion; it is like trying to hide that you have fallen in love. In this world you can hide everything else, but hiding love is impossible. The way the lover walks will change, his eyes will look different – they will show a certain drunkenness, they will reflect ecstasy. The person's presence will have a melodious quality. He will walk, sit, get up as always but you will be able to see something has changed. Anyone will be able to notice it; even a blind person will recognize it. That's why lovers have never been able to hide their love. And if lovers cannot hide just an ordinary love, hiding love for the divine will be impossible. Love will shine like a lamp shines in a dark house. The light will spread far and wide.

*Jnana*, knowing, is unmanifest like the river Saraswati. Karma, action, is manifest like the Ganges. Love is between the manifest and the unmanifest; it is like the river Yamuna. The stream of *jnana* is very deep inside; it is like the river Saraswati. That is why one can only hide meditation. The truth is, it is very difficult to manifest meditation.

This is why people like the Sufis could remain hidden because they followed the path of meditation. You won't come to know if a person is a Sufi although he may be your next-door neighbor. Even a wife will not be able to know which state of meditation her husband is immersed in because the whole matter, the whole play, happens deep within. One can hide it; in fact it is difficult to manifest it.

It is difficult to hide love. It is difficult to hide it and it is also difficult to express it. It exists just in the middle of both. Action is manifest. Kabir is all the three – *jnana*, bhakti and karma: knowledge, devotion and action.

Throughout his life, Kabir never avoided action; he never stopped karma. Certainly, he is a *bhakta*, a devotee of the divine. His whole life is filled with ecstasy and singing devotional songs. From dawn to dusk he went on singing these songs. They are not ordinary songs. His songs have not just come out of his throat;

neither have they come from his intellect or thoughts. These songs have emerged from the deepest recesses of his being.

There is not much poetry in his songs and they are not composed in any particular meter. There are a great many mistakes in them. But there is heart in his songs – and when has the heart ever cared to follow the laws of meter when composing a song? The heart flows, discarding all laws. The heart is like the flooded Ganges in monsoon – it flows breaking all its banks. The intellect is simply dry; it is just like the narrower Ganges in summer, flowing bound by the banks. The heart flows, filled totally to the brim. So Kabir sang his whole life – he has not written these songs, he has sung them.

A poet composes a song, makes an effort, embellishes it; arranges the language properly – the grammar and meter following all the laws related to writing poetry. And then there is a rishi who simply sings. A rishi is also a poet but a poet is not a rishi. A rishi also sings, but his song is not some kind of intellectual effort with proper use of language, grammar or meter. His song is an expression of an overflowing heart. When he is unable to hold it within, the song begins to flow outward. His song is a manifestation of his ecstasy.

Kabir sang all his life. Bhakti, devotion, flows through his songs. He couldn't hide his devotion – no one ever can. But he could hold meditation within; that is what *jatan* is – it is an internal phenomenon. It has nothing to do with the world outside. It happens in absolute aloneness. While being in karma you are there and so is the whole samsara, the whole world. In bhakti, you are there and so is your beloved, the divine being. In meditation you are all alone; in meditation even God is not there.

Kabir has said, "While searching, O friend, Kabir got lost." Kabir is saying, "When I went on a search I myself got lost. Now I am unable to find myself. Leaving aside what I went searching for, the situation now is that I don't even know where to find who went in search in the first place."

A moment arrives in meditation when you don't find what you went looking for but instead you yourself get lost. But the moment you are lost you find the divine. Hence there is a great paradox: you won't be able to meet God because when God is there, you won't be. As long as you are there, the divine cannot be. That's the reason why a meeting never occurs between man and the divine – the meeting is always between the divine and the divine; man is lost on the way.

Man melts, dissolves completely, as he goes on the search. By the time the moment of union arrives, you will suddenly find that which you had set out to look for is left behind somewhere on the way. And you had never realized that the one who actually arrives at the destination was in fact hiding within you; that the one who has reached the destination was always within you – there was no need to go anywhere. If you had just bent your neck, you would have seen the divine right within yourself.

The destination is within us; the divine is within oneself. What is lacking is the seeker, is losing oneself. In dhyana, meditation, you are all alone. In *jnana*, knowing, you are all alone. Meditation is the way to knowing. Bhakti is the way to love. Service is the way to karma.

For Christ, serving others was the way, so service became the way Christianity worshipped. Buddha made meditation the center of spiritual work. Therefore, in Buddhism, both service and devotion disappeared, only meditation remained. Mira, Chaitanya lived solely through bhakti, devotion. Kabir is all three.

Therefore, I say, Kabir is like Prayagraj, the supreme place for a pilgrimage, the greatest among all the places of pilgrimage because all three streams meet and merge in him. Such a great synthesis as has happened in Kabir is unparalleled. That is why it is difficult to understand Kabir because it will always become awkward to figure out when three different streams come to a meeting point. Here logic will be of no use. Sometimes Kabir will seem to be saying one thing, sometimes the other. Sometimes he will say something and then contradict it because what is true about karma will not be true about bhakti. And what is true about bhakti will become a hindrance in karma. That is the reason why a great mysteriousness surrounds people like Kabir. For centuries efforts have been made to unravel the mystery, but it can never be unraveled.

The song before us today is related to bhakti. Let us first understand what bhakti is, then we shall follow the song. We know love; we have no connection with bhakti. And even as far as love is concerned, we don't know much about it – maybe just a speck of it, or just a moment of it. We have seen just a few glimpses of it in life. Only for a moment have we had the feeling of being lost in someone. Whenever you feel lost in someone, know that it is love.

If you have never experienced being lost in someone – never – then know you have remained untouched by love. And someone who has remained untouched by love will never be able to understand bhakti. If a person has never had a bath in a nearby lake, how can he ever experience what it is to be in the ocean? How can someone who has never looked through a window ever go and stand under the sky? One who has not known what ordinary love is will never come to know the extraordinariness of bhakti.

So always leave the doors of life open. Let love descend from whichever direction it may come because it is the first sounding of bhakti, it is the first ray of bhakti. If you shut down the doors of love, then regardless of how many temples you may beat your head in, regardless of how many mosques you may cry and shout in, regardless of how many churches you may sing your songs in – all your songs and cries will be wasted. It won't be heard anywhere, because your shouting and screaming will come from your head; it cannot come from your heart. The heart will remain closed. The seed has never broken open; it has never sprouted within you.

You may say: "No, I have loved – I love my wife, I love my children." But look at this closely because the very definition of love is when you melt with someone. Was there ever a moment when you dissolved yourself in your wife? No, all husbands want their wives to dissolve in them and all wives want their husbands to melt with them. And the fact is: when there is love, the lover never wants the other to melt with himself but rather he wants to dissolve himself in the other. And when someone melts with another person, it becomes, just naturally, a reason for the other to melt with him also.

What you call love is not really love. It is a form of exploitation; and it is violent. If you wish to possess your beloved, then you don't know what love is all about; then you have not known what love is. Love never wants to possess; it wants to give possession to the other. Love never wants to be the owner; it wants the other to be the owner. That's why Kabir says again and again: "*Dasa*, slave, Kabir says…" What does he mean by *slave*? It means love wants to give possession; it wants the other to be one's master. Ordinarily, your love wants to be the master of the other; hence it is fake. Just a little cunningness on your part and it all goes wrong. You want the other to be your slave, while love wants you to be the slave of the other.

Love is very humble. Love is not aggressive. Love is invitation, not aggression. Love is a call, a beckoning. Love means preparing to annihilate oneself. When you show the willingness to annihilate yourself, the other also drops the fear of annihilating himself. When you try to control the other, naturally the other also likes to have control over you. This is precisely the quarrel, the strife, between lovers.

Actually there can never be any room for quarrelling in love. But we see lovers constantly fighting with each other. The very basic cause of their fighting is that both are trying to annihilate the other. Regardless of how much the wife says that she is nothing but a slave, a servant, her whole effort is to become the master. Regardless of a father saying how much he loves his son, he is not willing to dissolve in the son. The father wants the son to toe the line he sets, to become his shadow. The father wants to annihilate the son: "It is my commandment; what I say is right for you too. What I say should be your way. What I say is the right direction for you. Follow my directions." This is what makes a father happy.

When someone follows your directions, then it means you have made him lose himself in you. This is not love. If a father truly loves his son, he will tell him: "Don't bother about following me. Become yourself. My support is all there for you, my strength is all there for you; but never be my shadow. Be yourself; be what you are, attain the fragrance of your own life. It doesn't matter if you have to disobey me by doing so, because what use are my commandments? It doesn't matter if you have to stay away from me to get to your fragrance; after all, what is the point in being with me if you don't attain to that fragrance?"

If a father really loves his son, he will dissolve himself in him. If a son really loves his father, he will dissolve himself in his father. If a wife loves, then she will melt with her husband. But we are afraid of losing ourselves. The disappearance of self feels as if we will be gone, we will be lost; no trace of us will be left behind. The ego gets hurt. The ego gets very scared of what will happen if it is no longer there. That is why the ego makes sure that love never happens.

Remember, nothing is as strongly against love as the ego. Hatred is not the opposite of love, it is absence of love. The ego is the opposite of love, because if love means melting away, then the ego is what tries to stop you from melting. It claims: "I am here to save you from disappearing." By and by, because of the ego, we shut all the doors of melting in the other.

This is precisely the reason why we have invented marriage in place of love: because love is dangerous. Marriage is convenient. Marriage is a convenience. Love is trouble. In love, there is always a fear that one will miss and fall into the ditch, which is always nearby. And the path is uneven, not clean and neat. Marriage is like a royal path – made of cement and concrete. Thousands are walking on it, there is a huge crowd all around; there is security. The police are posted everywhere. Courts are standing along the way. The magistrate is ready, wearing his regalia.

Marriage is a social institution; love is an individual jump. You are all alone in love; in marriage the whole world is with you. If something should go wrong with the marriage, you can make inquiries in the court. Attorneys can be of help. You can find solutions in the law books.

When in love, neither an attorney will be with you nor will you have any law book. No book has ever found a place in the world of love and no attorney has any place in it. In love, you are absolutely alone. And you are afraid of being alone. Then again, the very meaning of love is erasing oneself. Erasing, annihilating, yourself feels like you are going to die; be aware of this.

My experience is that people are afraid of three things. After being involved in finding solutions for hundreds of people's lives, I have deduced that there are three things that people are afraid of. First, love – and someone who is afraid of love is actually afraid of God because God is the ultimate result of love. Second, death – someone who is afraid of death is actually afraid of life because death is the last event, the peak, the concluding factor, the essence of an entire life. And the third is meditation. Meditation is like both – love and death. You have to die in it, but you also find the divine. Meditation is the most dangerous of all. Once you are afraid of love, the doors to the divine close.

If you could not merge and melt with any ordinary man or a woman, how will you be able to melt into this vast existence? You will struggle, you will fight; you will try to save yourself. And the more you try to save yourself, the more you will find yourself becoming weaker. Who are you fighting with anyway? You are a tiny part of this vastness; how will you be able to fight with it? You are born out of it. You are like a wave in the ocean; how can the wave fight with the ocean? You are like a new bud appearing on the tree; how can this bud fight with the whole tree? And, even if it fights, will it be victorious? Its defeat is certain. Whosoever fights is bound to be defeated. A person trying to save himself will not survive.

Jesus has said that the moment you save yourself you will be lost. And once you are lost, then there will be no way for you to melt. How can we fight with the whole? For example, if my hand had a fight with me, how could it win? It would mean the hand has gone crazy – it will be defeated, it will be wiped out, it will destroy itself through its very own efforts. You will have to immerse yourself in the infinite; you will have to drop all struggle; you will have to totally surrender. As Kabir says, you will have to surrender and disappear at its feet.

The very first lesson for that leap into the infinite is of love. But we have become scared of love. Instead, we have invented marriage. Marriage is good if it happens like a flowering of love; if it is a byproduct of love alone. But marriage is a misfortune if it comes out of a system, if it is planned and arranged.

It is so strange. Parents, the family, the priest, the society and mediators arrange a marriage, and they never even care to ask the people for whom they take this decision. They know it is dangerous to ask them. Why? Because these people – the parents, the family – know those concerned are not experienced yet. Remember, experience will always be against love. An experienced person means one who is an egoist. A non-experienced person means one who is egoless.

Children can fall in love easily; old people don't fall in love. They are so experienced and their experience has filled them with so much ego that now they cannot make such a mistake. What they call a mistake, they don't know if it is a mistake or not, because by missing love they have missed everything. The greatest art is that of effacing oneself, the art of melting – melting in such a way that all borders disappear; melting in such a way that you no longer know that you exist.

The first glimpses of prayer appear in love. And God is nothing but the ultimate outcome of love. Bhakti is the expansion of love. But such an expansion can happen only if the seed exists. Only if the drop is there, can the ocean be. What can you do if there is no drop?

That is why, at the moment you set out on the path of bhakti, give this some thought: has love entered in your life? If it has not, then don't ever choose the path of bhakti – even mistakenly – because all your efforts will be wasted. It is like wanting to harvest without seeds. You will keep waiting and the crop will never appear. You may scream but you will have no answer. You may go to the temple, bang your head till it breaks, but nothing will happen because there is no seed at all.

Devotion is not the path for those in whose life love has not yet arrived. Meditation, karma will be right for them, but not devotion. Meditation can be without love; you are all by yourself, no need to connect with anyone else. Bhakti, devotion, is the ultimate connection. Meditation means breaking all connections. Although they look absolutely different from each other, their result is the same.

Make sure you understand what love is. The essence of love is about drowning oneself, erasing oneself, melting, effacing oneself. And when this melting happens with the whole of existence, and not just with any one person, then it is bhakti. God is not a person. God is the whole of existence; God is the name for all that is. When your love becomes so vast that wherever you look you begin to see the divine, whether it is a rock, a tree, a human being or an animal; wherever you look you see God's presence. When your love becomes so profound that it can see a glimpse of that presence in each and every leaf, where you can hear its song echoed in each and every particle – then that is what we call bhakti.

But it is essential that you have first learned the lesson of love. As I see it, this world is nothing but a school where we prepare ourselves for the divine. This world is not against God; it is a place to prepare to receive the divine. All our contacts and relationships are preparations for that ultimate connection to take place. And this is how it should be because if the world is against the divine, or if the divine is against the world, how can the world survive? Then the very basis of the world's existence will disappear. That is why those who have taught that if you want to find God you have to be against this world have taught something which is wrong. You won't find God by going against the world; you can attain the divine only by transcending the world. And there is a huge difference between the two.

Transcendence means rising above the world; it does not mean going against the world. The more profound your experience is of this world, the more you will begin to rise above it. As you go deeper into a love of the mundane, you will find the world is disappearing and the divine is emerging. If you fell deeply, rightly, in love with just one person, then that same person would disappear in a few days and become a door, and through this door you will begin to hear the footsteps of the divine.

But the problem is: you are unable to fall in love, even with one person – you are too unkind. Your heart has completely turned to stone. You talk about love, you hum and sing poetry, but all that talk is cerebral; there is no stirring in your heart. The heart remains untouched; it is all an intellectual activity. And the fact is: until your heart is touched, until your heart has become moist, until juices have started flowing in your heart, and until you feel a new stirring, a new thrill in your heart...

Behind your actual heartbeat there is still another heartbeat that you have not heard yet. The normal heartbeat is due to the blood circulating but there is still another heartbeat which is because of love circulating. Down the ages, though complete strangers to one another, between different people, in different races of the world, in different cultures, whenever the topic of love has occurred, whenever people have talked about love, they have placed their hand on their hearts. There is no difference as far as this is concerned. This is quite strange. There are differences in every other matter, but in this matter there is no difference in the whole human race. Obviously, this placing of the hand on the heart cannot just be a cultural or social phenomenon – it must be existential; otherwise, if it had been a social phenomenon, differences would have existed.

There exist differences in everything. For example, there are races where to say "yes" the head is moved up and down and there are other races where to say "yes" the head is moved from left to right. Then there are races where to say "no" people move their heads from left to right and there are races where to say "no" they move their heads up and down. Obviously, this moving of the head is a cultural thing; it comes from social upbringing – it is not existential.

There are differences in small, little things. I have done a lot of research and found that there is one thing where differences don't exist and that is whenever talk turns to love, people place their hand on their heart. This placing of the hand on the heart is an existential thing.

On which heart do we place our hand? If you ask a biologist, he will say: "You are crazy; there is nothing like the heart you are talking about, there are lungs and a pumping station. There is a pumping station – an arrangement for pumping blood, nothing else is there. And the heartbeats are just because of the blood circulating. It is not all about this heart – that is only a pulmonary system." But hidden behind this heart is another heart. When love is flowing within you, you listen to the heartbeats of this heart. Kabir is talking about this heart. But the juice of love flows only when the rock of the ego is broken. This rock of the ego is placed on your heart. That's the reason why you cannot hear its heartbeats.

Now let us try and follow these sutras.

***The path of bhakti is very delicate.***

Kabir is saying that the path of bhakti is very delicate – it has to be. The path of karma is very gross: give bread to the hungry, care for the sick, help the poor, and serve the needy. So the path of karma is the grossest. That's why Christianity could create so much impact in the West, because the West is so involved with grossness, it is materialistic. The more materialistic a person is, the more he will find himself attracted to karma because matter is the closest thing to karma, action. Karma is like the front door of your house.

Act, but whatever you do, do it in the spirit of surrendering the act to the divine. That's why Christianity became very effective. Half the world today is Christian and the reason for this is clear: the whole mechanism of Christianity is based on karma. Other religions are compelled to compete with Christianity. That is why they also talk a little about karma, but it doesn't fit because their experiences are much deeper and more subtle, so they don't match with the Christian approach.

We could never imagine a monk, a sannyasin, massaging a poor man's feet. In fact, here in the East the poor have been massaging the monks' feet. We have been serving the monks; we never expected any monk to serve. We cannot even imagine Buddha and Mahavira serving the sick in a hospital. Even the sick won't allow them to do so. People will revolt against them; the sick will move away, run away from the hospital. "How can they serve us?" they will ask. The reason is that Buddha and Mahavira are at the deepest and the most profound point of truth, which is meditation.

Meditation is subtle, very subtle. Karma is gross, very gross. Between the two is the delicate bhakti. But even a devotee on the path of bhakti could not impress others much. A devotee sings, he dances, he is ecstatic – but what can others gain from his ecstasy? A hungry person won't get any bread, a sick person will not get treatment. Therefore both the paths – *jnana* and bhakti – slowly began to fade away. And that which was totally gross, that which was the grossest – the path of karma – has remained.

There are thousands of commentaries on the Gita. The grossest of all commentaries is one written by Lokmanya Tilak, but it proved very effective. It made a big impact on this country because Lokmanya put stress on karma. A commentary by Ramanuj is delicate; its emphasis is on the bhakti. But both Ramanuj and Shankar turned pale because Lokmanya's commentary has made the biggest impression.

India, too, has slowly drifted toward the gross. Now we also see only that which is just matter; now we don't see anything but matter. Our capacity to see the subtle has also deteriorated. We have lost our connection with the delicate. In fact, it requires a certain cultural height, a certain purity and decency, to understand and appreciate the delicate.

Once, Mulla Nasruddin invited a very famous musician of classical music. He was able to get him after much difficulty and he invited all of his neighbors. When they were all seated, and as the concert was about to begin, the musician asked Mulla, very respectfully, which raga, which melody, he would like to listen to.

Mulla replied, "Any raga will do, my purpose is to harass the neighbors!"

Classical music is a very delicate matter. But if you don't understand it, then it can be quite annoying.

If you come across a *bhakta*, a devotee, he can be annoying; you fail to understand him. If a devotee were to stand near you, you might think he is mad, that he is out of his mind. Now this is the situation: we are unable to make contact with a devotee because we are standing at such a low level. From that point we are unable to see a delicate flower; our eyes are not able to recognize it. If Chaitanya came back and passed through your village dancing, or if Meera came back and sang songs in your street, you wouldn't get much joy out of them. It is difficult; because you won't be able to figure out on what level that phenomenon is happening.

Even when Chaitanya was singing and dancing, people in Bengal called him lewd. Now, this makes things difficult. If you look at him now, you may think he is a disciple of Prabhupada; that perhaps he had joined the Krishna Consciousness movement.

In order to understand Chaitanya one needs a certain emotional state, and emotions are not thoughts; thoughts you can get from the scriptures, you can learn them in a university.

But emotion is an experience – either you have it or you don't have it. Emotion implies that you have also experienced it, that you have also had a glimpse of it, that you have also lived it – maybe not that deeply, maybe not intensely – but that you have also entered the river and made an effort to swim; that you also know what swimming is all about.

A thought can be borrowed, but an emotion can never be borrowed. Emotion is an experience; either it is or it is not. Regardless of how much someone may say what fun swimming is – what a thrill it is to swim, swimming is so mysterious – if you have never entered the river, you might say, "Maybe," or you might ask, "What will swimming do for me? What will happen just by throwing my limbs here and there in the water?" But you would have no idea, because what a swimmer experiences is not just throwing his limbs around in the water. In fact, swimming is creating a certain rhythm between him and water. And when the swimmer is truly at his peak of swimming, the swimming stops. Then the river does the rest. He just floats in the river, he doesn't swim. Then he need not make any effort; then there exists a certain harmony between him and the core of the river; then he comes to know the deity of river. Now it is as if the god of the river lifts him up and carries him. Now he is taken care of by someone. The river never drowns him; the river is not his enemy. Now there exists a deep friendship between the two.

If you have never jumped into a river, then at the most you will see a man throwing his limbs around and think, "What good is that, except as just an exercise. That one can do even at home; one can throw one's limbs around even while lying in bed. It amounts to the same kind of exercise – maybe even more. So why bother? Why take any risk?"

But you have no idea what is happening inside the swimmer. If the swimming technique is right, then thoughts disappear, a rapport is established with the running current. The river carries you along. The swimmer slowly drops his separateness and becomes part of the current – he just floats, as if he is the river. And he can neither share it nor can he tell you about the joy that he experiences from this floating. No matter how much he explains, unless you have had some experience... So, as the sages say: "It is like a person who cannot speak trying to describe the taste of molasses."

If you give some molasses to a person who cannot speak, he can taste it but he cannot describe the taste. Forget about him; you can speak, and if you are offered molasses, you will be able to taste it. You can speak – but what will you talk about? And to the one who has never known sweetness, who has never experienced sweetness, to such a person, regardless of how much you may say that it is sweet...sweet...sweet, he will hear the word but the word will be meaningless to him because meaning comes from an experience.

Sweetness is an experience. Kabir says: "Sugar in the mouth of a dumb person." In fact, all are dumb in matters of emotion. With thoughts people are vocal; in matters of emotion they are dumb. You can never know a person's emotional state. If you have experienced love even a little, you will have an idea of how delicate, how superfine and subtle, the path of bhakti is.

What does *delicate* really mean? What does it mean to be delicate? Delicate means that which needs a lot of care in handling. You must have seen musicians. Before starting the concert, they spend some time tuning their musical instruments. Those who don't follow music find all that boring. The musicians will sometimes knock their instrument with a small hammer; sometimes tighten the strings or do some other thing. But what are they actually doing? They are trying to bring the instrument to a delicate point so that the music can be played. They fix strings in such a way that the strings are neither too tight nor too loose. If the strings are too loose, you cannot play on them; if they are too tight, they will break. So the strings need to be neither loose nor tight – just in the middle. And when strings come to an even point a certain rightness, a balance, exists – and that is exactly when the music is born. Bhakti is this kind of an art of living.

Bhakti is born exactly in the middle. *Jnana* and karma too are extreme points. One who is busy in action lives at one extreme, the gross level. The one who is given to *jnana*, knowledge, lives at another extreme, the subtle. A *bhakta*, a devotee, lives in the middle. He has to work meticulously to tune the instrument – it is so delicate.

Kabir says: The path of bhakti is very delicate. I am...

***Neither averse to it, nor desirous for it.***

The strings are neither too tight nor too loose.

***Neither averse to it, nor desirous for it.***
***I am simply lost at your feet.***

Let us understand this, let us listen to it carefully. "I am neither averse, nor am I desirous..." There are two extremes. One is that of passionate desire or lust; the other is that of no passion, no desire. The one who is desirous, the one who goes on desiring this and that – who goes on asking non-stop – such a person is not difficult to understand. Our experience, too, is very similar. Similar kinds of people are all around, the crowd is made up of such people; the marketplace is theirs, the shops are theirs, the temples are theirs. They are continuously asking. They say, "We want this!" and as soon as they have received it, their demand extends further and they say, "We want that!" They remain beggars, they never become masters. They always remain beggars, they never become emperors. They never get a chance to give because they are never free from asking and begging. The question of their giving charity doesn't arise because they are hungry themselves; their own bowl is not yet filled.

It happened…

In Kabir's time there was a mystic called Farid. Once, the village people approached Farid and said: "We need a school in our village. We know Emperor Akbar respects you a lot. Visit him sometime, and ask him to build a school for us. We are sure he will listen to you. You can certainly manage it."

Akbar was a devotee of Farid. So Farid agreed to visit Akbar and went to see him. It was early in the morning when Farid arrived. He had free access so he was taken straight inside the palace. Akbar was busy praying in his private mosque. Farid stood behind him. As Akbar was about to finish his prayers, he raised his hands up like a beggar and said: "Oh God! Please increase my wealth, please expand my kingdom!"

Farid immediately turned and left. The prayer finished, Akbar heard retreating footsteps on the stairs. He looked behind him and started running; Farid was going away. He had never come before, always Akbar had gone to visit him. Farid had come because he thought that as he had to ask for something, he must go to Akbar.

Akbar fell at his feet and said: "You came and now you are going away. Have I done anything wrong? Have I committed some mistake?"

Farid replied, "I am the one who has made a mistake, not you. I came to ask you for something but found that you yourself are not free from asking. No, I won't make you any poorer. That school I came to ask for would be too costly for you.

"And then I thought: 'I can go straight and ask from the one from whom *you* are asking. Why should I place a beggar in between?' Until now I thought you were an emperor, but now I realize I was mistaken."

As long as desire exists, no one can ever be an emperor. And until you are, how will you give? And even if you were to give, you would give as part of a bargain; you would give to get something; you would give with a plan to get more in return. Your charity will be more like an investment. There will be a desire to get something.

So it is clear that a person filled with desires is really a beggar. This is the reason why those who understood this dropped desiring; they moved into no-desiring. People like Buddha or Mahavira – they dropped all desiring. They said: "We will give up desiring because only then the tendency to beg stops."

The matter is very clear, straight and logical. The path of a beggar is plain and simple. The path of a non-desiring person is also plain and simple: he has dropped all desiring, and has no craving anymore.

Thus, Mahavira and Buddha became true emperors. You cannot find any other emperors like them. Similarly, it is difficult to find such beggars as Alexander, Napoleon, and Akbar. It is difficult to find emperors like Mahavira and Buddha. They just gave up desiring. They simply closed the chapter; they shut the door. And as there was no more desiring, an empire came into being. They became complete in themselves.

But Kabir says: *The path of bhakti is very delicate.* It is indeed a very delicate matter. *Neither averse to it, nor desirous for it, I am simply lost at your feet.* One neither carries any desire nor is one non-desirous. One appears before God as if there is nothing to desire, and yet one stands before him like a beggar. One asks for nothing because the moment you ask, the connection breaks. In that case, what you ask for becomes more important and God becomes secondary. Then God becomes the means and what you desire becomes the end.

What Kabir is saying is that you stand before God as if you are a beggar and yet there is no desire at all. Then you can stand there as if you are an emperor. There is a state of no-desire because you are not asking for anything. But you are also standing like a person who has desires, because you are bowing down as if asking for the whole world. You aren't really asking for it, but you are standing like a beggar. You are there as an emperor, of course, but with a begging bowl in your hand. That's why *the path of bhakti is very delicate*.

The devotee neither asks for something nor says he has attained the state of no-desire. Neither does he say he has stopped desiring nor does he say he still has some desires.

Try to understand this.

A *bhakta* is both a beggar and an emperor at the same time – an emperor of the kind that regardless of what he is given it will make no difference to him. Not even the smallest thing will be added to him, everything will remain as it is. But he stands before God as if he is not alone. It is as if the whole world is asking from God through him; he himself has not asked for even an iota of anything. It means he is an emperor but is standing with a begging bowl.

The begging bowl is there because standing like an emperor is not the way to face God. You can only stand before him as a beggar. How can you stand before God like a proud emperor? That's why both Mahavira and Buddha denied God, said that there is no God. How can there be a God if you are standing before him like an emperor? That is why there is no place for God in the vision of Mahavira and Buddha. To them, the question of God doesn't even arise. You yourself are God – and the matter is finished.

When you go to the temple, when you go to the mosque, you go to ask for something. If you don't get what you want in a Hindu temple, and someone tells you that you will get it from such and such a Muslim saint, or at such and such a Muslim mystic's grave, you don't mind going there secretly, even if you are a Hindu. You continue to be a Hindu and yet don't hesitate to pay a visit to a Muslim mystic's tomb. How can one trust a beggar? What integrity does he have? Does a beggar ever have any integrity? He goes wherever he can get what he wants. If he gets it from one house then fine; otherwise he will go and beg at another house.

The beggar neither has any integrity nor does he care for God or have anything to do with God. If he is asking for something, and if someone tells him he can have it on the condition of becoming an atheist, that man won't mind becoming an atheist. He will say, "Forget God. What do I have to do with him. I went to the temple to ask for good health, to get rid of sickness – that's the only reason I went." God couldn't do it; now someone says he will give you medicine that will cure you, but you need to drop God from that moment on. You won't mind saying: "I am absolutely ready – in fact, I have always been ready." We go to ask for something in the hope that we will get it. We give our thanks if we get what we want; if we don't get it, then we show our displeasure. It is very difficult to find a true believer in the world. You are all atheists inside. You have become believers because you carry desires and you feel God will fulfill those desires. So maybe he is…

I have a friend – an elderly person. He has remained an atheist his whole life. He is a very famous man, a great writer and speaker. Suddenly one day his son came to me, running from his home, and said that his father was very ill and was remembering me. He had had a heart attack. He survived the attack but he was severely shaken. His limbs were shivering.

When I reached him I heard him murmuring slowly "Rama, Rama, Rama." I was very surprised because he was an atheist. I shook him and said, "What are you doing? Are you degrading and corrupting yourself like this at the time of death?"

He replied, "Leave all that aside; please don't raise the matter. Who knows, maybe God exists."

At the time of death man gets scared. He thinks, "Who knows? Maybe there is a God."

Then he said, "What's the harm? It doesn't matter if he doesn't exist, but if he does, then I have already remembered him."

So even God is part of your calculation; he too is the projection of your fear. Your God means your fear. You remember him when you are scared; when you have no fear, you completely forget him. When you are happy, you hardly ever remember him; but when you are unhappy you immediately begin to repeat "Rama, Rama..." No, you are basically an atheist; believing is part of your cleverness, your cunningness. Believing is not an extension of your heart; it is basically part of your logic. When you are in need, you become a believer; when you are carefree, you become an atheist.

Once, Mulla Nasruddin was traveling in a boat. Other people were also on board. Suddenly, a storm came up and the boat began to sink. People started shouting and screaming. Someone was shouting, "Oh, God! If you save me, I will give these many rupees to charity." Someone else was saying, "Please save me, I will give a cow." Yet another person was saying, "If you save me, I will do this and I will do that!"

As all this was going on Nasruddin shouted, "Wait, don't say anything else. The shore is close by." Hearing this, those who were promising to give to charity and such forgot all about their promises and got busy packing their luggage.

We remember God only in bad times, but as soon as the shore gets closer, then who bothers about God? God is just there to help when the boat begins to sink. Once the boat approaches the shore, then what purpose does God have? We go and knock on God's doors only when we want to ask for something. Then when Buddha and Mahavira appeared, people dropped asking. They saw that there is nothing but trouble when we ask for something.

Desire takes you nowhere; it simply creates new problems. The more you desire, the more depressed you get. There is one interesting characteristic of desires: even if they are fulfilled, you find unhappiness and also if they are not fulfilled you find unhappiness. If they are fulfilled, you suddenly find that despite your dreams, despite all the rainbows of your imagination and all the flowers that blossomed in your heart, you have found nothing. After going to all that trouble what you found was a trifle. Even having found what you were looking for you still feel you went through all that trouble for nothing. And if you hadn't got it, you would also feel unhappy because you would wonder what you might have found.

A psychologist once visited a psychiatric hospital in order to do research. The superintendent took him around. In one room a man was screaming loudly and crying while he was holding a photograph clutched to his chest. The psychologist asked what the man's problem was. The superintendent replied, "The photograph he is holding is of a woman he once loved. But he never got the woman and that turned him mad. Now he beats his chest while holding the photograph and keeps on crying and weeping."

In the next room the psychologist saw a man behind bars pulling at his hair. He was also holding a photograph in his hand – biting it, throwing it against the wall, kicking it with his feet. When asked what had happened to this man the superintendent said: "He got that woman. Both were in love with the same woman. One turned mad because he couldn't get her, this fellow went mad because he got her."

One person turns mad because his desire is fulfilled; another goes mad because it is not fulfilled! Either way desire brings unhappiness. You become sad when you get what you want because ultimately you discover that really you got nothing. You feel sad if you don't get what you want because you couldn't get it. A desiring person, a person filled with craving, is bound to become unhappy. One who has seen this, one who has tried to penetrate life even a little, one who has understood the futility of desiring, will drop desire immediately. He will attain the state of no-desire. Non-desiring will become his sutra. Both desiring and non-desiring are easy to achieve.

Kabir is saying: *The path of bhakti is very delicate.* There is nothing to ask for and yet one stands like a beggar. One becomes an emperor; nothing to ask for and yet one is bent down like a slave. *Neither averse to it, nor desirous for it, I am simply lost at your feet.* One is neither asking for anything nor has one any desire to be fulfilled – one is *simply lost at your feet*; just holding on to God's feet. You only hold someone's feet when you wish to ask for something. You would find it meaningless to hold someone's feet if you don't have to ask for anything.

That is why Kabir says that the path is delicate. There is nothing to ask for and yet you are holding onto the feet. But whosoever attains to this state – holding the feet even though there is nothing to ask for; an emperor and yet holding the begging bowl – he receives a lot. He gets it all even without asking for it. Treasures are showered all around without any asking because the person is an emperor and yet he is bowing down like a slave.

You can never make Mahavira bend down. Mahavira won't be able to pray with folded hands, bending his knees. There is no connection whatsoever between Mahavira and prayer. When there is nothing left to ask for, then what is the point of bowing down? You might ask, "Have you gone mad? Why would he bend down?" But when you understand you will see that the logic is the same. Your logical view is to bend down if you want something. Now there is nothing left to ask for, so don't bend – it is the same logic.

Kabir is beyond logic, that's why it is difficult to find a person more beyond logic than a *bhakta*. A *bhakta* is a paradox; he is a meeting point of two opposites – he is in between the two. At one end he is Mahavira – the emperor; at the other end he is an ordinary beggar. Both together.

*Neither averse to it, nor desirous for it, I am simply lost at your feet.* What does this getting lost, drowning oneself at the feet of the divine mean? Normally, when you bow down only the body bends while the ego remains erect inside. It never bends. In fact, if the ego bends then that would be truly bending. There is no point in just the body bending down. As the ego begins to bend down you begin to dissolve; you begin to experience a new ecstasy, a new colorful joy begins to emerge within. That's the reason why you will find a *jnani* very dry, without any juice. You cannot expect poetry from Mahavira nor can you hear any song from him. Mahavira won't dance either – you cannot even imagine Mahavira dancing. Chaitanya will dance; Meera will dance.

A *bhakta* will be soft and moist – will be totally absorbed. A *jnani* will be dry, like a desert without any foliage. Although he too will attain to the ultimate; *jnani* people have attained to it but that achievement will be desert-like. A *bhakta* will be like a running stream – continuously singing. A *jnani* will be quiet, silent. A *bhakta* will be full of song; even his silence will be melodious and his song will carry a silence. He is in the middle. His speech will have music; even when he is quiet you will be able to hear music. Every pore of his being will be playing a tune.

***Day and night, he is drenched in the juicy stream of the ways of devotion.***

A *bhakta* will be drenched – as if he has just emerged from taking a bath in the river. But it is not as if he is drenched in the juicy stream all the time. *Day and night I am drenched in the ways of devotion.* Here *bhakta* indicates devotion; it stands for *kirtan*, singing songs and dancing in praise of existence; it suggests continuously remembering the name of God. *Bhakta* implies being always at the feet of God. Outwardly you may be busy with other things, but inside the tune of the divine continues.

Every moment there is a feeling of gratitude. Every moment one feels that what God has given is more than one deserves, more than one may be worthy of. Then what about this asking? When without asking one is already receiving it, it would be foolish to ask. When God has already given life, he has already given a heart that beats with love, and when he has offered so many dimensions to make life blissful, what more is left to ask for? He will simply express his gratitude every moment of his life.

There was a Sufi mystic, Baijid. He was once walking down the road with his disciples. He accidentally hit a rock and his foot was injured. He sat there, bent down, blood flowing from his foot. With folded hands he looked up at the sky.

The disciples asked, "What are you doing? We thought you had bent down because you had been hurt and there was blood flowing from your foot. But it seems you are praying."

Baijid replied, "You are not aware of the secrets of existence. Possibly I would have been killed today if it had not saved me. Existence prevented me from being killed by letting the rock hit my foot. And that, too, is the graceful way of existence – reminding me of it."

A *bhakta*, a devotee, remains thankful even when he faces troubles in life. A non-devotee complains even when there is happiness in his life because regardless of how much happiness he may receive, he always thinks he could have had more – why only this much? A *bhakta*, on the other hand, always thinks he could have faced more no matter how much trouble he already has – just this much? Both are looking from a totally different angle and perspective. This difference in attitude shows that the non-*bhakta* will always remain unhappy and will live in hell while the *bhakta* will always live in heaven and remain happy. When you learn how to live happily, the happiness increases; when you learn how to live in misery, the misery increases. Heaven and hell are all a matter of habit – and habits die hard.

*Day and night I am drenched in the ways of devotion*. The truth of the scriptures is imbedded in the melody of bhakti, like a fish in water. Like a fish in water, all the scriptures and the whole truth are hidden in the melody of bhakti.

> **The truth of the scriptures is imbedded in the melody of bhakti, just as a fish is at one with the water.**

And one who has attained that melody of bhakti, one who has taken that wine and is drunk with it, will find that just as fish swim in a river, so the whole truth is hidden in that melody. Whatsoever is written in the Shrutis, in the Vedas, and whatsoever is praised by the scriptures, all of it is already hidden in the stream of devotion.

***I offer my head in the service of my Lord without any delay.***

So, only one thing needs to be done – offering oneself to the service of the divine. *I offer my head in the service of my Lord without any delay.* This last statement can have two meanings – both are significant and both need to be understood.

*I offer my head in the service of my Lord – sai. Sai* is a distorted form of the word *swami*. So, there is only one thing that needs to be done for the divine, the swami – offering one's head. Here *head* means the intellect. *Head* means thoughts. *Head* means logic. *Head* means concepts, beliefs, words. The composite of all these together is what is referred to here as "head." Just offering your head will not do – that anyone can cut off and present. But even if you cut off your head and give it as an offering, thoughts will continue to hover inside. The skull will still remain a Hindu skull, a Muslim skull, a Christian skull, a Jain skull. Not much will be achieved just by cutting off the head from the body. The issue is not of cutting off the skull. That is very easy. Many self-destructive people do this; there is not much of a problem to it.

What needs to happen is for the head to remain on the outside but disappear from the inside – so no thought arises, no reasoning arises, no concept, no bias remains anymore; you become totally empty from within. When God's wish – and God's wish alone – becomes your wish, then what is the need for this skull? It is needed only if you think you are insecure, if you think you are living in insecurity; if you think that you alone have to take care of yourself. That is the reason you think that you need it – because you feel you must think, figure it out, find a way. But if, in fact, the divine is finding a way for you, when he alone is making a way for you, when he alone is regulating your breath – then why don't you leave everything to him?

Once an emperor was passing along a road where a Sufi mystic was also walking. Seeing the mystic walking by, the emperor invited him to take a ride in his chariot. The mystic came and sat in the chariot. But the emperor was very surprised to see that the man was still keeping his bundle, which he had been carrying while he was walking, on his head. The emperor asked, "Why don't you put that bundle down? Are you mad?"

The mystic replied, "No, my mind is as good as yours. I am not putting it down because I feel it is enough that you have asked *me* to sit in your chariot. Now it is not good to put an extra weight on the chariot."

The emperor said, "Looking at your ways, I suspected you have a deranged mind. And then on top of it you say your mind is just like mine! Once you are in the chariot, what difference does it make if you place the bundle on your head or in the chariot? In every sense the chariot is bearing the weight."

The mystic said, "You seem to be an intelligent man. If what you say is the case, then why are you carrying this head above you? Since the divine is carrying everything – life appears and disappears, the waves arise in so many ways and then disperse again – when everything is already happening in his chariot, why are you carrying this head on top of you? I am just carrying the bundle on my head, why are you carrying that head on top of you? And certainly your head is heavier than my bundle."

Our weight is all in the head – nothing is heavier than the head. And one who has lifted off his head becomes weightless; he gains wings, then he can fly in the infinite sky of freedom.

So Kabir says, *I offer my head in the service of my Lord*... Nothing else would work. People are clever. They go to the temple and break open a coconut. A coconut symbolizes the skull – it looks like a human skull with a hair, a beard, a mustache, eyes. People are very cunning. Kabir is saying, *I offer my head*...while other people go and offer coconuts because the coconut *looks* like head. They go and put vermilion in the temple because vermilion looks like blood. But worship can only happen with blood. Worshipping with blood means to offer something from one's being.

What difference will it make applying vermilion? People are clever; they have found substitutes. They save blood and instead apply a red colored mark – they apply vermilion. They save their heads and offer a coconut instead. And even the coconuts they take to offer in the temple are rotten. For years the same coconuts stay in circulation because the coconuts offered by people are sent back to the market by the temple and are sold back to customers again. Many people might have offered the same one before.

Even the coconut *you* offer is not really yours – it is a leftover. It was offered many times before, it was taken away many times before; it keeps circulating. Often, the coconut shop is right in front the temple and is run by a relative of the priest. People offer a coconut in the morning, and by the evening it reaches the shop again. It gets sold again the next morning and is taken back again to the shop in the evening. It gets totally rotten inside.

The idea is to offer your head; instead of doing that you go and find a coconut – and that too a rotten one, a leftover one – which has already been offered by others. No, your honesty is required at the door of the divine; nothing that is borrowed, leftover, alien will ever work there. If you approach the divine with your total self, only then can you be accepted.

*I offer my head in the service of my Lord without any delay.* The latter half of this statement can have two meanings. The first is: I didn't delay and offered my head in serving the divine. This indeed is the path of bhakti – without any hesitation, without waiting for a moment. Let us give some thought to this.

People come to me and they say that they are thinking of taking sannyas. I tell them, there are two ways of taking sannyas. One is taking sannyas after giving it a great deal of thought; then it will cause a delay. Not only will it cause a delay, it will also take away all the charm of taking sannyas. The reason is: the more you think about it, the more you will try to convince your intellectual mind, giving arguments for and against. If the mind decides to go ahead and take it, then that sannyas is worthless because the decision comes from the intellectual mind. And you can never eliminate the intellectual mind with the intellect. The very purpose of sannyas is simply that the intellect is removed. So, if you take sannyas after a long deliberation then its whole meaning will be lost.

There is still another way: by taking a jump. Just take the jump, don't think about it. Set aside your intellectual mind and take the jump. If you put your intellect aside, then a revolution will take place with the taking of sannyas; a transformation will begin. The transformation will begin the moment you take sannyas because you never asked your intellectual mind. This is the first time that you are doing something without the help of the intellect. For the first time you are entering into the unknown, into the dark, into the uncharted.

So there is a jump, which is taken without a moment's delay. That jump has a value. That is truly a jump. If you delay by first weighing up all the pros and cons, finding a ladder, and then climbing down comfortably – then the whole thing will be lost. The whole secret is in taking the jump; in that jump is cutting off of the head.

That's why someone who approaches religion through logic is never able to come close to religion. Beyond logic, beyond reasoning…! There is no question of being logical; it is the domain of mad people. Intellectuals cannot find any entrance – they remain just outsiders. Their intellectual mind becomes the problem. Mad people go ahead and take the jump. Only drunkards can do it. Only people who are not business-like can do it – those who know how to gamble. Only gamblers can do it.

There is a business mind, which goes on thinking and thinking, and by doing so delays, postpones – maybe tomorrow, maybe the day after. Before taking sannyas it will plan, think from all possible angles, make enquiries, try to find out by seeking advice from a thousand and one people whether it would be okay to take sannyas. The whole meaning of sannyas will get lost by going through this exercise.

Sannyas is a leap – a leap of the non-intellect. In that very leap the head drops. So, the first meaning is: …*without any delay*. No hesitation was there, not a moment was wasted. You got it – and took the jump!

The second meaning is: *I offered my head in the service of my Lord without any delay* – I offered my head in service of the divine and yet did not lose anything. On the contrary, I found something …*without any delay*. I offered my head and yet lost absolutely nothing; in fact, I got something. And here I was, unnecessarily afraid that I might lose something.

It is so strange. You possess absolutely nothing and yet you fear you might lose something. What do you have, that you are so afraid of losing it? What is the problem in taking the jump? Your fear would have been justified if you had had anything – but you own nothing. And, whatever you have is worth losing – your misery, worries, tension, and anxiety. You have nothing in terms of wealth; what you have are a lot of troubles. Why are you worried about offering your head? You feel you might lose something. You are like the naked person who never takes a bath because he wonders where he would dry his wet clothes if he took one! And the fact is that the man is not wearing any clothes – he is naked. But just because of this fear where he would dry his clothes if he took a bath, the man never bathes.

It would have made some sense if you had anything to lose. But you never reflect on what you really have in the first place. You are actually afraid that finding yourself empty, having nothing, will cause you pain and anguish. You will feel as though your whole life was a waste – no achievement. It will feel as though you didn't find any shore, you came nowhere close to any destination; you are absolutely hollow from within. You are afraid of looking at that hollowness; you think it will scare you, so you wander around, hither and thither, and never take a look at it. You just go on thinking about taking sannyas, but you will first give some thought to it in case you lose something. No, you have nothing to lose. And the moment you offer your head you will find all that you had wished for and asked for is showering on you.

Jesus has said: He who gives will receive; he who saves will lose. And Jesus has said: To those who have even more will be given; and those who don't have will have more taken away from them... It is a very tough statement but very meaningful because only that which you already have will increase. Nothing in this world ever stops – everything grows, it increases. Remember, if you are miserable, then misery will increase. If you are a loving person, then love will increase. If you are angry, then anger will increase.

In this world nothing ever stops – it goes on increasing. Everything is growing, expanding, evolving. If you decide to delay, then whatever you have is growing – your hell is continuing to grow.

Jesus says: Those who give will find; those who save will lose. What do you really have to save for yourself anyway? You will save nothing but hell. You will lose heaven totally. In saving yourself you will lose God totally. And his next statement is: Those who have shall get more. If God is with you, then more and more of the divine will be available to you because what you have is going to increase. And Jesus says: All those who don't have anything will have everything taken away from them.

*I offer my head in the service of my Lord without any delay*. The head is offered and with that all is given away, yet nothing is lost – everything is gained. For example, a drop falls in the ocean; on the one hand it ceases to be a drop but on the other hand it becomes the ocean. What does it lose? It loses being a drop and gains becoming the ocean. The moment one gives up the ego the drop disappears – one becomes *brahman*, one becomes the ocean. The trivial is lost, the infinite is gained.

What are you really saving? Which moment are you thinking about? What are you waiting for? And why the delay? Kabir is saying: whatsoever you feel like doing… *I offer my head in the service of my Lord without any delay*. There is no need to wait. Immediately, the moment you have understood, the jump can be taken. And only those who jump instantly will be able to attain. Those who postpone will miss because when you postpone, the moment is lost. The door comes closer, but as you postpone the door moves farther away; the opportunity arrives, but as you postpone it moves away. When the opportunity comes, find enough clarity to understand it.

Understanding is not the same as intellect. Understanding means your totality. When your whole being feels it is right then don't miss that moment. You have missed that moment for many lives in the past. At such a moment, don't delay. Offer your head that very moment. You will be losing nothing. The drop will certainly disappear – but the ocean is gained.

Enough for today.

# 7
# Lifting the Veil

**Lift your veil and you will meet the beloved.**
**The Lord dwells in everyone, never use harsh words.**
**Don't be arrogantly proud of wealth and youth,**
**this five-colored body of yours is just a lie.**
**Light a lamp in the shunya palace, and never shift from your posture.**
**Then, with awareness, you will see the shunya palace turned into**
**a palace of joy, and find the priceless beloved.**

Kabir says: **Now there is nothing but bliss**
**and the beating of the endless drum.**

Before we enter into the song, let us understand a few things. The first and the most fundamental thing is that a veil is covering your eyes; but the divine does not have a veil. You have put the veil on yourself – no one else has put it on you. If someone had put it on you, then you would be unable to lift it – then someone else would also have to lift it. And if the divine had been wearing the veil, then, too, you would not be able to lift it because the divine is vast and so his veil would also be vast – beyond your capacity to lift it. The veil is on your eyes and you yourself have put it on. This is the basic thing that needs to be understood. That is why Kabir uses the word *veil*.

Man puts the veil on himself, over his own eyes. That is easy, and convenient too because once your eyes are covered, everything else gets covered. Of course you will need a huge cover to hide the Himalayas, but if you put on a little veil which covers your eyes, the Himalayas will disappear. That is the easiest way. Moreover, you have put it on yourself so you can lift it any time you wish. There is no hindrance, no problem in doing so except your own self. The deeper this understanding goes within you the better.

Ordinarily we think there is a cover hiding the truth; if that were the case, the journey would be very difficult. Then there would be no hope for a weaker person trying to find it. And if indeed the truth is covered, then how will you be able to remove the cover, even though you may try countless times? And if the truth is really covered, then once one person has removed the cover, the truth will be there for all to see.

This is the very difference between religion and science. Once Einstein has discovered a truth then not every scientist, not every student of science needs to discover the same truth again – the veil is lifted. Then it is enough that you read about it in a book. Where Einstein had to make an effort for years, an average student now has to spend just hours.

You may say: "Buddha lifted the veil, Kabir lifted the veil, so what is the need for me to do anything? It is just a matter of getting it, and that's all!" But that is not so. A university can teach science, not religion. Buddha lifted the cover from his own eyes – he did not unveil truth, otherwise it could have been visible for everyone. Then there would have been no person left ignorant in the world. In that case, just as Einstein's principle is written in books – and people read it and there remains no need to discover it again – so Buddha's principle could also have been written in books.

You may find it surprising that science can have scriptures but not religion. How can religion, religiousness, have a scripture? Except you, no one else can lift your veil. And how can that which another person has seen become your vision? As long as your eyes are covered, regardless how much Buddha may try to lift the cover, nothing will happen. What was lifted was the veil that had been covering Buddha's eyes. That is why tradition cannot be created in religion. A religion can never have a tradition. But the sad thing is that long traditions have been created within religion.

A religion cannot be made up of scriptures; religion *is* the scripture. Religion can never be learned from others – you have to search for it yourself. And yet we try to learn from others, so everything has become false. You won't find as much falseness gathered anywhere as around religion.

What could be the reason? Why did religion, which is essentially a search for truth, become surrounded by so many lies? Why did so many scriptures, so many principles, so many philosophies, so many concepts and so many ideas gather around religion? It has happened because the fundamental fact of your eyes being covered by a veil has been forgotten. And each person will have to lift it again; each person will have to lift his veil again from the very beginning. Someone else lifting theirs won't make any difference for you.

Once a person is awakened, becomes a buddha, he will see and disappear – his philosophy, his vision, will disappear with him. When you awaken, see and recognize, your life will also be filled with the "silent drum." But no one else will be able to hear it except you. Your life will be filled with infinite light, but even a person sitting next to you will be unable to see it. Even a wife won't know that a ray of light has entered into her husband's heart; a son won't know that his father has awakened. People may be seated around you and yet no one will be able to suspect you have awakened, the reason being that the veil you have lifted is from your eyes and not from other people's eyes. You can never lift a veil from other people's eyes.

The second thing that you need to understand is that the veil is not external. Had it been external, anyone could have removed it with a little pull. Had this sleep been outward, then anyone could have awakened you by shaking your body. The sleep we are talking about is inner sleep, internal sleep. That is why no matter how much someone may shake you, only the body will move, not your consciousness. So the veil is inside you; it is not an ordinary veil like the one you see covering a woman's eyes. Anyone can lift *that* veil.

This cover, this veil, is covering the inner eye which we may call the third eye. That eye is situated so deep within you that no one else can enter there. Only when you want it, when you are filled with the longing, when your own desire shakes you from within, only then can that cover be removed.

When you have seen the futility of life, when you have seen that – because of the veil – you have banged against many walls and got covered in blood, only then can the cover be lifted. It is lifted when you realize that because of the cover not only are you unable to see the door, but the door itself becomes a wall; when you see that – because of the veil – nothing ever happens in life except conflict, misery, and hell. Not a single moment ever comes when you could say, "I am blissed out!" Not one moment comes in your life when you could jump and dance and say, "I am so grateful that this one moment of bliss compensates for whatever miseries I have been through before; no harm has been done, nothing has been lost. I have attained plenty. Those miseries were of no consequence; to experience this moment of joy, I am willing to bear those same miseries again."

But nothing of this sort ever happens to you. It doesn't happen because neither can an outer storm remove the veil nor can a raging fire burn it. Not even by mistake, or because of some mishap, will the veil ever be disturbed because the veil is covering the inner eye.

There is an inner eye, and the moment it opens the whole of life changes. Then there is an outer eye, and when it is open, life moves along fine – but it never changes. Even a blind person manages; those who have eyes also manage… But there is also a deeper eye than those eyes. This is the eye that opens up when we say an individual has become a buddha, a *jina*; that someone is awakened, has become conscious. And in that moment everything is transformed; when you wake up from within your whole world changes. Then, whatsoever you see, you see it because of you.

One night, Mulla Nasruddin was apprehended by the police. He was drunk. He gave them a lot of trouble and used foul language. But the police managed to drag him to the police station. As Mulla entered the police station he was fuming and said, "What is all this nonsense? Why have you brought me here?"

The inspector of police replied, "You have been brought here for drinking."

Mulla said, "Okay, then that is a different matter!" He was delighted, and then said, "So, when do we start?"

A drunkard will find his own meaning in words. A man wishing and longing for a drink is so unconscious that he will derive his own meaning from whatever he hears. His meaning will come from his unconscious state. The meaning will be his own, but that is natural.

What you see is not the same as what is actually there. You see what you want to see; you hear what you want to hear;

you search for things you want to seek. For example: go on a fast one day and then walk along the same street that you have walked along every day. You will see sweet shops which you never saw before – you will see them for the first time. You will only see those shops; the rest will somehow disappear. Restaurants, hotels, sweet shops, tea stalls, all of these will appear in an intensely visible form.

Just go on a fast for seven days and then walk in the marketplace. You won't be able to see shoe shops, clothing shops anymore – you will just see food shops because your whole consciousness is filled with hunger. Now it is the hunger that will be looking around – not you. That is how our vision creates our outer world.

There is an old story…

There was a saint, Ramdas, in Maharashtra. He wrote the story of Rama. Every day he would write the story and recite it to people. It is said that the tale was so sweet that Hanuman himself would come to listen to it, hiding himself in the crowd.

Since Hanuman himself came to listen to the story it meant there must be some secret behind it. Hanuman had witnessed the entire story of Rama unfolding, so now there could be nothing more left for him to know. But there was something special about the whole thing; while Ramdas was narrating it the one who had been present there – who had witnessed the whole thing – came to listen to the story.

But at one point in the story Hanuman couldn't hold himself back because he himself was being described. Ramdas was saying that when Hanuman went to Ashok Vatika in Lanka he saw white flowers all around. Hanuman interrupted him saying: "Wait, correct that! The flowers were red, not white."

Ramdas said, "Who is this ignorant person wanting me to make a correction in the middle of the story?"

At that point Hanuman appeared and said, "I had to appear in person because I am Hanuman, whose story you are narrating, and I say the flowers were red and not white."

Ramdas replied, "Whoever you might be, just keep quiet! The flowers were white."

It turned into a big argument. Then there was only one way out – to approach Rama. Hanuman said, "So let us go and see Rama. Whatever he says will be the final decision because this is too much. I myself was an eyewitness, and I say that I have seen the flowers. You are telling my story and that, too, after thousands of years. And you are being adamant about such a small matter. What difference does it make if you write that the flowers were red?"

Ramdas said, "It is not a question of what difference it would make; truth is truth – the flowers were white!"

The dispute was brought to Rama's attention and Rama said to Hanuman, "Be quiet! What Ramdas is saying is right. You were so angry at that moment, your eyes were burning red, and so you must have seen the flowers were red. Ramdas is not angry – at least he is looking at the scene in a detached state. The flowers were indeed white; I also know it."

When you see things with angry eyes they will look different. Obviously, if you see through greedy eyes, things will appear differently. When you see things while you are filled with passion and lust, things will appear beautiful when they originally may not have been. When we see things we cover them with our own selves; that's why your vision itself becomes your world. When you change, and when your perception changes, immediately the whole world changes. While you may have seen something as precious before, you will now see it as nothing but garbage; what you may have discarded as meaningless before, you will now find some meaning in; what you may have held dear and thought meaningful before, you will now see as meaningless.

Life is essentially a reflection of your vision; one whose inner sight, inner vision, is asleep is like one who is absent inside – fast asleep. Because the inner eye is closed, you are unable to see the interior aspects of life. The outer can see only the external world. The inner eye will see the internal. For example, you look at me; but if you see me from your outer eyes you will see only my body, not me. You will be able to see me only if you look from your inner eyes. In that case, this body will appear to you like a worn-out garment and you will see the inner consciousness emerging.

If you listen to me with your outer ears, then you will hear only my words, but if your inner ear is awake then you will be able to understand the meaning behind them. Words are merely the outer shell, the body; meaning is the soul. The deeper you are within yourself, the deeper you will be able to see; you will be able to listen that much deeper, your whole experience will be that much deeper. If *you* are shallow, your experience will not go very deep.

There is a Zen story…

A master approached his disciple. The disciple was sitting outside. The master asked: "What is truth?"

The disciple closed his fist and showed him.

Returning after a while, the master said, "The water is very shallow, large boats won't be able to anchor here."

The disciple became very sad even though he had answered very thoughtfully. And that is where the mistake was. He had heard that when this master asked people something he didn't like the answer to be in words. He had also heard an old story that once the master approached such and such a disciple, the disciple closed his fist and the master was quite satisfied with this.

Closing the fist means one, not five, but one; not five elements, just one reality; not five sense organs, just one spirit. So, since he had heard such stories he also closed his fist and showed it to the master. But that fist was a fake one – there was no "one" in it because the fist could have been only as deep as his experience was. He certainly knew of the five elements. He had heard of the "one" – but it was all borrowed, stale; it was not his own understanding.

So the master said, "The water is too shallow; large boats won't be able to anchor here." It certainly hurt the disciple.

After many years, the master returned again. The disciple again closed his fist. The master said: "Great! You have dug well; the water has gone very deep. Now the ship can anchor!"

Those who were watching all this were greatly surprised because in both instances the same thing had happened – the fist was closed, the first time and the second time. People said: "We are at a loss; you have turned the whole thing into a mystery, a puzzle. The first time, too, the disciple had closed that same fist." They asked, "Was it necessary for you to return after twenty years just for this?"

The master replied, "This time there are not five in his fist but one. Before there were five. Previously, although the fist looked closed from the outside, inside it was open. Now the fist is not only closed from the outside but from the inside as well. Now his fist has a meaning – now this fist is not just symbolic, it is an experience."

The words are the same, the symbols are the same, but as you change, the meaning of your words changes – your way of living, the fragrance around you changes. Although everything remains as it is, nothing remains the same. Outwardly, everything will be the same. One day, you will also attain to buddhahood; one day your inner Kabir will certainly awaken. How long will you delay it? And when it happens, outwardly everything will be the same as it is now: you will go to the shops, work at home, raise children, get hungry and eat your meal, feel sleepy and go to bed. Externally, it will all be the same – that's the first fist. But inside everything will change – that's the second fist. You will be transformed and with your transformation the whole meaning of life, the whole poetry of life, the entire experience of life, will be equally transformed.

When the inner eye opens you don't see matter; even if you see matter, it will look transparent. You will begin to see the divine hidden in matter – matter will become just its outer shell.

So keep these two things in mind: the veil is not covering the truth. In fact, you placed it over your own eyes; no one else put it on you. If someone else had put it there, then man would be dependent forever; then it could only be lifted when the other wanted to lift it. But man's being is supremely free – and that is its glory. You have put the veil on yourself. You have gone astray, and that knowingly. If you have gone wrong, then it is because of you. That is why it will be easy for you to reach the right path – you can reach the very day you wish to do so. And the second thing is: the veil is not on the outer eyes, it is covering the inner eye. Keep these things in mind, and then follow Kabir's sutras.

***Lift your veil and you will meet the beloved.***

For Kabir, God – the divine – is the dear one, the beloved one, the lover. When truth is seen through the eyes of love, then truth no longer remains just a dry philosophical idea or concept; then truth becomes the beloved. Then, except for truth, nothing else feels loveable and wherever one finds the truth, the beloved, it becomes loveable.

So make sure you understand one thing: if you search for truth as a dry concept, as science does, then that search will be a dry search. It won't drench the seeker – the seeker will remain unchanged. It doesn't bring transformation, any moisture, any juice, into the seeker's life. The seeker remains dry and juiceless.

For example, a philosopher seeks truth – he gathers arguments, weaves a net of important doctrines and principles, makes all kinds of tests through his thinking process – but his life remains dry and juiceless. He appears like a tree that never grows any green leaves, any flowers. It has only dry branches where nothing grows. The stack of volumes keeps growing; the net of words keeps spreading, but within the energy becomes more and more juiceless. If you decided to listen to a philosopher, his words would give you a feeling, a sense, of a desert – all dry and hot. You will never experience the joy of seeing greenery from his talk.

Kabir is not a philosopher, Kabir is a lover. His words are very juicy. And that juice indicates that those words have emerged from a certain inner juicy source. That's why they have called him a rishi, a sage, a *kavi*, a poet. In Sanskrit, both rishi and *kavi* have the same meaning. Gradually we had to give them separate meanings because there are people who have written poetry without knowing truth. Their poems may sound very appealing but they carry no soul; they are empty from inside. There is a lot of embellishment on the outside, but there is no spirit inside. The mansion looks beautiful, but there is no one living there. The body looks healthy, but it has died – or maybe even never had any life.

In the West, even a dead person is greatly embellished. When a woman dies, lipstick is applied to her lips, mascara is applied on her eyelashes, rouge is applied to her cheeks – the dead woman looks very alive.

The poems poets write are just like this: there is no soul inside, simply an outer embellishment. So always remember one thing: if you ever like a poem written by a certain poet, don't go looking for him, or you will be very disappointed when you meet him. His poetry seems to be of such high quality but the poet himself will appear so ordinary – no height, no depth. So if you happen to like a certain poem, never go to see the poet. You won't find you are in the presence of an individual – he is just skilled, merely has technique. The man will appear knowledgeable about rhythm, verse, words and language and will have the ability to put it all together in such a way that you may get the illusion of certain music emerging from it. But that is all on the surface – lipstick applied to a corpse, mascara applied to a dead body. And the woman looks so beautiful as if she has just returned from visiting Kashmir. But inside, everything is dead; there is no life inside. Don't ever fall in love with this woman. There is no other way than to bury such a woman.

If you ever fall in love with poetry, make sure not to go in search of the poet, otherwise you will get into difficulty. Seeing the poet, even the poetry will look meaningless. There have been great poets in Urdu literature; they have said some very lofty things. But don't go looking for these poets; you will find them even worse than yourself.

This is the difference between a rishi and a poet, a *kavi*. You will find a poet less than his poetry; you will always find a rishi higher than his poetry. If you were to go looking for the rishi and to listen to his song, you would find that actually his song had nothing much to it. If you had been happy with just the song, you would have missed a great opportunity. The source from which the song emerged was infinite, but the song was nothing but its wave – the person was just a "nobody."

Once you have known Kabir, you won't find anything by simply going through his words; the person will have left the words far behind. His poetry will be as if the ocean is left behind and a soft shower of rain has fallen on your house. He is a vast ocean from which many clouds can emerge and shower on infinite houses.

A rishi, a sage, always feels that what he has said has fallen short of what he actually wanted to say. The rishi has truth, and truth is always larger than words. Whenever there is an attempt to convey truth in words, it is like trying to squeeze the whole sky into a narrow space; it is very difficult. The joyful thrill, which is apparent in a rishi's words, is not just because of wordy embellishments. That thrill is just a glimpse of the space of the heart where the words came into being. Just like a breeze passing through a garden carries with it some fragrance of flowers that will envelop a passer-by too – he will also smell the fragrance. That fragrance is an indication of the fact that there is a big garden nearby. The little coolness in the breeze indicates the fact there is a lake nearby.

Kabir is a rishi. What he has said in a poetic way is larger than poetry. When a poet looks at the world, the truth perceived by him no longer appears dry – it becomes juicy. Poetry looks at the world in the same way a lover looks at his beloved. Perhaps you may not find that the beloved is worth anything, but for the lover she is everything. The lover just doesn't look at the beloved – he creates her.

Khalil Gibran has said somewhere that a lover sees in his beloved the woman that God would have created had he had his own way. A lover sees infinite possibilities in his beloved – he sees in her today what she could be in the future – if God had his way. He doesn't see the flower which is right before him; he sees the future of that flower. He sees all the possibilities present in it, this very moment; he sees the whole future existing in the present.

A father doesn't see in his son what he is now – in the present. That's why people get upset when a father goes on talking about his son. They ask him to just stop it because they don't see anything in the son while the father sees everything in him. And all fathers see something in their sons and yet the sons turn out to be ordinary. What does a father see in his son? A father has the precognition of what the son would be like if he were to grow properly. But if the son goes astray, he won't turn out to be as expected. And sons do go astray. The father turns out to be wrong. But the son could have been what the father had seen through his loving eyes.

Every mother sees the best in her son. Of course, he can be the best; he has the potential. This son who looks like a rock can turn out to be a diamond with a little application of a chisel and some polishing – although one cannot be sure whether he will really turn out to be a diamond or not.

Love sees that which you can be if everything else works out well. Hatred sees that which you will become should everything go wrong. Hatred sees hell in you; love sees a paradise in you. Hatred sees the devil in you; love sees the divine in you.

You can get such a glimpse. Even in ordinary love it is not just your imagination. It is the loving eye that uncovers the hidden, which brings out what is lying underneath. It is the eye before which the secret opens its door; the mystery gets unraveled. But when you see the whole world with loving eyes, when you see every particle with loving eyes, and when every bit of this world becomes your lover or your beloved, the infinite that manifests at that moment is God.

That's why Kabir has addressed the divine as the beloved. For Kabir, truth is not just a dry concept – it is the beloved. The relationship between the universe and man is not of logic but of love. That is the reason why a poet can have a glimpse of what a philosopher is unable to find. But while a poet gets a glimpse of it, the rishi becomes one with it.

*Lift your veil and you will find the beloved.* Your eye is covered by a veil. What is this veil? Buddha has said that no one is your greater friend than you yourself and no one is your greater enemy. If you walk with your back toward truth, then you will prove your own greatest enemy; if you walk facing the truth, then you will become your own greatest friend. So what is this veil? You are walking with your back toward life – you are an escapist. You want to somehow avoid life, you don't want to meet life face to face – and that is the veil.

Try to understand this.

You try to escape from where life is happening and yet you wish to attain the divine. The divine is another name for a great, glorious life. But why does a man want to escape from life? There is some fear. The first fear is that life always takes you into the unfamiliar, that which is not known before; it takes you into the unknown and the unknowable. Life is not like a fixed line; it is not like moving in a rut, like going round and round in a groove. Life is not a habit; it is not repetition. Life becomes new every moment. And you are afraid of the new because the old is familiar, you recognize it well. You have lived with the old, the new is not known to you. You have already gone through its pain and pleasure.

It is really strange: rather than attaining new health you would prefer old sickness because the new brings fear – who knows what it will be like? You have been afraid of the new since childhood. And the whole society teaches you to be fearful of the new. When a stranger sits down next to you, immediately you ask his name, where he is heading, what he does, what his religion is. Do you know why you ask him these questions? It is because there is fear as long as the man remains a stranger. If you come to know the person believes in the Hindu religion then the fear relaxes: you are a Hindu, he is a Hindu – now you know each other. You ask: "Do you have children?" because having children makes the person more trustworthy. "Are you from the Congress party or are you a Communist?" You feel it is okay if he is from the Congress party. So, in this way, you work out who he is and get acquainted with him.

The moment a person enters a train compartment people start asking him questions. If he doesn't answer, or if he talks nonsense, you will become suspicious that there may be some danger, you may pull the emergency chain and ask the conductor to inform the police! If, when asked if he is a Hindu or a Mohammedan, first after a little pause he says, "Yes indeed, I am a Hindu" then that will create suspicion – what was there to think about? If you ask him how many children he has and he thinks first and counts them, then that person will look dangerous. Who knows: he might run away with your bedding, he might steal your luggage or he might pick your pocket! He will certainly not look trustworthy. That is why we like to get acquainted with a stranger quickly.

Once, while traveling in a train, Mulla Nasruddin kept staring at the roof of the compartment. After a while, the fellow sitting next to him became a little suspicious. Once or twice, he tried to strike up a conversation with him, to make some attempt to get his attention, but Mulla continued to stare at the ceiling. The man even asked him, "Where are you heading?" but Mulla gave no answer.

Thinking Mulla might be deaf, the man asked in a louder voice, "Where are you from?" There was no answer; Mulla continued staring without blinking. Finally, the man said, "Sir, your scarf is flying out of the window!"

Nasruddin said, "Why don't you keep quiet? Your cigarette is burning a hole in your jacket, yet I never said a word."

Such a man will certainly cause a little suspicion, will cause some fear. Sitting next to him you won't be able to peacefully read a newspaper – he will continue to be in the back of your mind. You will even need to change your seat.

A stranger scares you – why? With people you are acquainted with you feel good – why? We are afraid and we want security. We want to be in a familiar area. That's why you are afraid to enter a forest but you don't feel afraid of entering a garden. A garden is a familiar place, it is man-made. It has a boundary, it has pathways; there is no reason why you would get lost there. A forest has neither a boundary nor pathways; there is every chance of getting lost. It is created by existence – and it is vast. That is the reason why, by and by, man began to live according to the concepts created by human beings – which are like neatly laid-out gardens.

You feel afraid of entering truth; it is found in the vast forest of the divine. Will you be able to survive in it? Will you be able to return from there? It is difficult to say. And even if, having entered truth, you did return, will you be the same person? This, too, is difficult to say. A man who enters truth does not return the same as he was before entering it. We have seen Buddha entering truth and returning. We have seen Mahavira entering and returning. We have become afraid of them. No matter how much we may worship them, place our heads on Mahavira's feet, the fact remains that we have become afraid – because we noticed that the people we had seen entering that path to infinity and then returning were completely transformed. We saw that no kind of relationship was possible between them and us. Our relationship with them broke down – they became the greatest outsiders for us.

Our worshipping Buddha and Mahavira is also one of our tricks – a trick to become acquainted with them. The way we create our acquaintance with them is like this: we say to Mahavira, you are a tirthankara. There are twenty-four tirthankaras and you are the twenty-fourth. Our effort here is to fit Mahavira into our calculations. Now suppose someone were to say he is the twenty-fifth, then a conflict will start because there cannot be more than twenty-four tirthankaras. By saying this, we are creating a structure. We create a system of logic and arithmetic in order to accommodate the unknown dimension that has descended in Mahavira. We place him, as it were, in a pigeonhole: "Okay, you sit here as the twenty-fourth tirthankara… Just perfect!" We say, "Behave like this, because that is how a tirthankara behaves. You should get up like this and sit down like this because that is the way of a tirthankara." When such individuals appear to fit within the structure created by us, we will feel at ease; now there is no reason to be afraid of them.

We worship out of fear. Worshipping is our way of getting to know them. So we worship those who we have abused before. We gradually come to an agreement with the very people we have fought with before; we develop an acquaintance with them. But, by this time, those poor people have already departed. Then we place their images before us and worship them – it seems we are still afraid of them.

I have heard…

God became very tired one day – actually, he must be getting tired every day, not just on that one day. Managing such a vastly complicated business, he must be getting tired. So many troubles! So one of his servants advised, "Maybe, you should go on holiday for a few days. You have not visited the earth now for so long. It would be good to take some rest for a couple of weeks."

God said, "No, I don't feel like visiting the earth because the last I time I visited for a rest, two thousand years ago, I fell in love with a Jewish girl, Mary. People are still talking about it. My son, Jesus, was born there. It was just a short love affair – I was on holiday – and yet people are still talking about it and writing books about it. Someone says, 'Jesus was born to the Virgin Mary,' someone says something else. They still haven't stopped talking about all that nonsense. So, no, I don't want to go there."

What has happened? Why have people continued to meaninglessly discuss this for the last two thousand years? It looks as though we have not yet become familiar with Jesus. We go on discussing him; he is still a puzzle. There are many corners of his life which even now are unknown. We have still not succeeded in understanding him completely. There are still areas of his life which seem to lead us into the dark; that is why the discussion is still going on. New theses, new research, new scriptures are being written. Thousands of books have been written on Jesus and people still continue to write them. It seems that this man will never be understood!

Not so many books have been written about Mahavira because his life is straightforward. He has become familiar to us. The truth is that there is nothing much left to write about Mahavira. There are a few facts and we have already dealt with them. That's why the Jain keep writing the same things again and again; there is nothing else to write.

But Jesus looks more puzzling because it is difficult to fit him into any mold. He stays at a prostitute's house. He is seen with a thief. He becomes friends with gamblers and drunkards; you can never be sure of him. The whole story is very confusing, from the very beginning. He is born of a mother who is a virgin – and here the trouble begins and goes on till the very end. He is born of a virgin mother and the story is sensational right up to the crucifixion – the whole story. And there are corners in that story which have remained untouched; which are difficult to understand.

We have dealt with Mahavira – his is a straightforward life. We have placed him in a mold. We have placed Rama in a mold – also a straightforward life. We couldn't do so with Krishna. That's why so many commentaries are written on the Gita. And Krishna will continue to remain a topic for discussion.

Our whole effort is that the world should not be larger than our field of knowledge. Wherever we find it looks larger than what we know, we come to a halt. And remember, the world is much larger than your knowledge. What do you really know? There is infinity waiting to be known.

If you are afraid of knowing the unfamiliar, the unknown, then you will never be able to know the truth. That's why we put on the veil. Whatsoever falls outside our knowledge, we cover it with a veil. From behind this veil we manage the world of our knowledge, the world of our limitations. Whatever is outside our limits, we exclude with the veil.

Psychologists say that this is the reason why our consciousness is divided into two: one is called the conscious, the second is called the unconscious – and the curtain that exists between the two is the veil. Consciousness is one, but we have cleared just one part of the forest and made it neat and tidy. We have cut the trees, made a boundary and put up a fence. We have made just a small part – a tenth – of our consciousness neat and tidy. It consists of ethics, religions, our ideals, doctrines, scriptures, gurus, temples, worship, prayers… We have put them all together there.

Nine times larger than this – a huge, infinite expanse – is the unconscious inside. We have placed a curtain between this part and consciousness so that it cannot be seen. Our logic is the same as that of an ostrich who, seeing an enemy approaching, puts his head into the sand thinking that that which is not seen does not exist. An ostrich is a die-hard atheist! He hides his head completely in the sand. He says, "If I cannot see the enemy, then it isn't there. If it is there, then show it to me!"

We are afraid of the unconscious, so we have pulled the veil over it. And we exist on neat and tidy ground. Once in a while, the unconscious prods us; once in a while the veil shifts a little. Sometimes the whole system breaks down. Then we call such a person insane and say that the person has gone mad. But we have no idea at all that the person went mad for the very reason that the unknown entered into his sphere of knowledge.

I am reading a book by Eli Vessel – a Jewish philosopher. In the Second World War in Germany his parents, brother and sister were all killed. Somehow, as a young boy, he survived. So in the book he describes the journey, which took them by train to a camp where they were all going to be gassed and then burned. Everyone was apprehensive but there was no way to escape. Hitler gassed millions of people alive and then burned them. He created huge ovens, the like of which had never been made before. What Tamerlane and Genghis Khan did seems like child's play, pales compared with what Hitler did. He made ovens into which ten thousand people could be thrown at one time and within seconds turn into ashes. They were electric ovens.

So the train was moving in that direction. Everyone was tense but everyone was somehow reassuring and comforting themselves that something would happen, that some miracle would happen, that the orders would be revoked, that this might happen or that might happen... People were talking like this while traveling in that closed prison-like train.

Suddenly, a woman went mad. A child's mother became insane. The son tried to console his mother: "Mother, don't be worried; we will soon meet my father. Don't scream, don't cry, soon everything will be alright!" But the woman went on screaming: "Look at the flames! Do you see the chimney rising in the sky?" People, getting scared and not realizing that she was insane, looked out through the bars of the truck. They couldn't see any chimney nor any flames rising. Then they began to scold the woman and told her to be quiet. But her craziness kept growing. People started beating her in an attempt to keep her quiet. Regardless of their beating, she kept on laughing and she said, "No matter how much you beat me, the chimney is there, flames are rising, thousands of people are burning. Don't you smell the stink?"

Afraid, people tried to smell it, but there was no stink. Whenever she would scream, she would also arouse fear in them and their unconscious would also enter the conscious level. They too were obviously scared not knowing what was going to happen next. And this woman was still more trouble. She went on recreating their pain again and again.

Then they had only one course left; they started beating her on her head. Whenever she became unconscious she would go quiet. But once she regained consciousness she would start laughing and say, "Look, be alert and run, there is still time!" But slowly people understood that she had gone mad and so there was no need to pay any attention to her.

The third day, when the train arrived at the camp station and people looked outside, they saw the chimney and the rising flames. And what they saw was exactly how the woman had described it – the same type of chimney, the same type of flames. And she had been regarded as mad while these people thought they themselves were in their right senses.

Often mad people start seeing things that you are not able to see. And often mad people are able to peek into the future which you are not able to do. Mad people realize truths that you are not able to. But no one pays attention to mad people.

New findings have shown that ninety percent of mad people are not really mad. What has happened is that the curtain between their conscious and unconscious has fallen down. And the whole effort in psychology is to restore this curtain so that you become a normal person again. Kabir also asks you to lift this curtain, but there are two ways of lifting this curtain, the veil. One is when the curtain lifts without your knowing it – then you will go mad. If it lifts with your knowing and understanding, then you will become a *paramhansa* – an enlightened one.

If the curtain somehow moved on its own, then the unconscious will crash into your conscious state; your lit house will then fill with darkness. All your boundaries will go haywire; there will be an earthquake. In that case you will go mad. But if you lift your veil consciously, with awareness – taking each step with alertness, knowingly, with understanding – you will be free. With the removal of the veil two things can happen – either going insane or becoming free. Perhaps this is the reason why we are afraid that if the veil is lifted we may go mad.

These meditation techniques I have discovered are here so that you can lift the veil with awareness. They are all techniques for going consciously insane.

People come to me and say, "What is this madness you are making people do?" I tell them I am doing it knowingly. This is precisely your fear: that you might go mad. I am making you go through it deliberately so that you may go mad knowingly, and come back knowingly. Enter your consciousness knowingly and go into your unconscious knowingly so that you may learn the art of lifting the veil that is lying in between. Then you will never go insane.

That is why there is some synchronicity between great sages and insane people. Often great sages are looked upon as insane – it often happens. The reason is that there is a common factor between the two – both their veils were lifted. The veil of the madman was lifted unconsciously; the veil of the *paramhansa* was lifted knowingly. So both have one thing in common – both their veils have been removed.

If you wish to be saved from going insane then there is no other way than to become a *paramhamnsa* because the point at which you are now means that any day the veil may slip. You are standing right in the middle. If you became insane unknowingly, then it would be absolutely impossible to bring you back. So before the madness takes over, it is better that you wake up and pass through the madness. One who passes through madness with awareness becomes a *paramhansa*. Becoming insane consciously is the art of attaining the state of *paramhansa*.

Kabir says:

***Lift your veil and you will meet the beloved.***
***The Lord dwells in everyone, never use harsh words.***

The same resides in each body, in each particle. Life is one. Its manifestations vary. It has appeared as a tree, a rock, as the moon and stars; or it can be seen as animals and birds. It also manifests in human form; in one person it appears in the form of insanity and in someone else as utter freedom. Life is one; its manifestations are many. Hidden within all forms the formless is one. All forms emerge from that formlessness and all ultimately end up in it.

That is why Kabir says: Stop looking for enemies; there are no enemies here. No one is a stranger here; no one is an outsider here. Only *this* is! It is in a thief as much as it is in a monk. It is in a sinner as much as it is in a virtuous person. So don't speak harsh words.

When Kabir says ...*never use harsh words,* he is saying, symbolically, never speak a single nasty word. Don't let anger come in between. Don't bring hatred in between. Don't bring jealousy, malice and enmity in between. After all, who are you going to hate? Who are you going to be angry at? Only "that" – the divine – is.

This is the way we can remove the veil. But what do we do? – we tie the veil even more tightly. Our general perception is that the whole world is our enemy. Whether you think this way knowingly or not, the fact is that you believe the whole world to be your enemy. Now in this vast world made of enemies you have created a small family – a wife, children – they are yours, the rest are all aliens. This family is shrinking day by day. Once, a family used to have about fifty to a hundred members. We saw them as our own people. Now there are only five people left in a family. There is a husband, a wife, children – but we are not sure if they are our own or not because a divorce may happen any day. The wife may leave to be with someone else. The fact is: if you looked closely, you would find that you alone are left to fend with the enemies. The whole world is an enemy and you have to fight against the whole world.

And all this is a result of our education, our culture and the conditionings imposed by society. We are taught to go ahead and compete, fight it out – that you too must have what others are fighting for. Supply is limited so you need to fight. How will you reach, is the question, unless you enter into cutthroat competition. So use the other as a ladder; climb on each other's heads and just go up! The only way to get on is to fight, people say. If you miss even a little, if you become relaxed, humble, and courteous, you are bound to get lost. Then you won't be able to reach. The struggle is difficult, they say, and you must remember that everyone is an enemy.

If everyone looks like an enemy, then certainly the veil will get thicker. And in that case, until you find good reasons you won't consider anyone to be your friend. But enemies are plenty – for no reason. So until it is a proven fact that someone is a friend, you don't accept anyone as your friend. On the other hand, even without any proof, all other people are enemies.

Kabir is saying the total opposite. He is saying that until it is absolutely proven that the other is an enemy – at least until then – see the other person as a friend. But it is so interesting: if one man robs you, you brand the whole of humanity as thieves. From that day on, you lose all your trust in humanity. There are over six billion people in the world, just one man commits robbery and you call all of them thieves – how strange! Now you cannot trust anyone. Of course, you may not want to trust the man who robbed you, but leaving that person aside, the remaining six billion people have not wronged you.

A Mohammedan, for example, does something wrong to you and suddenly you see all Mohammedans as bad people. A Hindu deceives you and suddenly all Hindus are declared bad. A Jain turns out to be dishonest and all Jains are seen as dishonest – it's as if you are just ready to believe everyone is your enemy. If one person is proved to be bad, all are proved bad. But, strangely, on the other hand, if one person is good that does not make everyone else good! This is very interesting: regardless of how much a Mohammedan may be of help to you, how good a person he may be – a saintly person, even willing to put his life on the line – even then not all Mohammedans will be seen as saintly. You will say, "Sure he was a good man, but all the rest are dishonest."

What I want to say is that you function with the assumption that all are enemies. And when you assume this, your veil gets thicker. The only way to tear off this cover is to drop the negative feelings you may have for the other. Dropping negative feelings is what Mahavira calls nonviolence. Giving up ill feelings is what Buddha calls *karuna* or compassion. Christ calls it service. The only difference is in words. One thing is certain: don't see the other as an enemy because the divine dwells in every being. Oneness resides in all beings – look only at that. The beloved is present in everyone – in every heartbeat, in every breath.

> ***...never use harsh words.***
> ***Don't be arrogantly proud of wealth and youth,***
> ***this five-colored body of yours is just a lie.***

Arrogance! – the excuses may be many but it is the same arrogance. Somebody is superior because he is wealthy, another is arrogant because he is in a high position. Someone is full of arrogance because he has a lot of knowledge, while another is showing off because he has renounced everything. Someone acts superior because he is young while someone else is arrogant because he is powerful.

The greater the arrogance the thicker the veil gets. As the ego gets thicker so does the veil. And, in fact, what is there to feel so superior about anyway? When has youth lasted forever? You may have hardly paraded your superiority before youth is gone. It is like a passing breeze – it comes and then goes. What is the point in being superior about something which is not going to last forever?

And it is so interesting that those who have found the eternal never show any arrogance and those who have nothing in their closed fist except air are arrogant. What will you do with your wealth? What will you really achieve through it? You may get nothing but the trivial – that's all you will ever get. You cannot buy this vast universe.

What is this arrogance about? Where can you find a person poorer than a rich man? Of course, he has money, but what else does he have? The wealth is bound to turn into a burden. And how long can it last? Today you may have it, but tomorrow it may be gone. Death will no doubt snatch it away. Take youth: how many people have been young before you? How many people have been arrogant about it and how many must have felt that they were beyond comparison? They must have thought their youth would last forever. And the fact is that youth is nothing more than just a passing breeze, or just a wave. You can see this for yourself at the seashore: a wave rises with great force, it rises with great arrogance, but hardly has it risen when it begins to fall.

You may have hardly begun to be young and old age approaches. It seems as if youth is nothing more than a way of showing you how you are growing old, as if youth is a door through which old age enters. What are you feeling so superior about? Only death follows this life; the whole of life is bound to fall into the abyss of death. All roads may or may not go to Rome but they certainly go to the cemetery!

Kabir has said: "This town of the dead people." Kabir is saying: this town, the village where you dwell, do you think you can call it *living*? What I see is that you are all dead – it's true. All are corpses standing in a queue, waiting for their time to come, which may be sooner or later. Someone who is ahead in the queue may leave earlier. And the interesting thing is that everyone is trying to get ahead and reach to the number one position. All are corpses! If death is inevitable here, then don't call them places to dwell, instead call them cemeteries. It is just a matter of time. When there is no more space left in the cemetery, they have to stand in line. But when your time is up, when it takes no extra effort, the grave will be ready and you will end up there. Except death, you are going nowhere. Paths may be different, the directions may be different, yet what you end up with is nothing but death. So what is there to feel so proud, so superior, about?

*Don't be arrogantly proud of wealth and youth...* because the veil will get thicker if you show such arrogance. But if you see that all achievement is nothing but lines drawn on water – you hardly draw a line and it disappears – when you drop your arrogance, you will find that the veil has begun to shift.

*Don't be arrogantly proud of wealth and youth, this five-colored body of yours is just a lie.* This human body, which is made of five elements, is totally false; it is like a dream. Granted, the dream lasts for many days, maybe for seventy years, but basically it is just a question of time. What does it matter if the dream lasts for seven minutes or for seventy years?

Has it ever occurred to you that while dreaming at night, in seven minutes you may have gone through seventy years? The dream may have lasted for seven minutes but you may have lived all seventy years in that time frame. So how is this different to real life? Waking up in the morning you might say, "This is too much; a whole life from birth to death was completed in seven minutes!" Sometimes, while sitting in a chair, you doze off. Before dozing off you noticed your watch showed it was twelve noon. When you wake up you see the watch showing one minute past twelve. Only one minute has passed, so how did such a long dream occur in such a short time? Even if you verbalized the dream it would take ten minutes; if you described exactly what you saw, it would take at least ten minutes. Then how did it fit into just one minute? The whole of life can be covered in just a moment.

Research done by psychologists shows that it makes no difference how long life is. For example, there are birds that live for five years. Then there are some insects that live for four months. There is a moth that lives for one evening – at the most for twelve hours. But in those twelve hours it lives as much as you live in seventy years. It falls in love, lays eggs, produces children, looks after the family, and goes through anxieties and worries, struggles, fights – and all of this happens in this short span of time. In twelve hours all of this is done – and then the moth dies. If you understand this rightly, then it proves that the moth is more skilled because the work that you do in seventy years it does in twelve hours. Obviously it shows more efficiency. It does everything; nothing is left to be done, everything is completed.

What difference does it make whether the dream lasts for seven seconds or seventy years? A dream is, after all, a dream! The length of a dream cannot make it true. Then what is the difference between a dream and the truth? There is basically one difference: a dream is that which begins at some point and ends at some other point; the truth is that which never begins at any time nor ends at any time.

If you really want to be proud of something then seek truth; feel proud of that seeking. And the fact is: someone who has found truth will never show his pride. But you carry dreams in your hand and feel so superior about it.

> ***Don't be arrogantly proud of wealth and youth,***
> ***this five-colored body of yours is just a lie.***
> ***Light a lamp in the shunya palace, and never shift from your posture.***

These are very significant and precious words. They contain the whole essence of the teachings of all the realized ones. Kabir is saying: *Light a lamp in the shunya palace*... Light the lamp of wisdom in the *shunya*, the void, in that empty space within you. Become awake in the silent void that exists within you.

*Light a lamp in the shunya palace, and never shift from your posture.* There are two essential stages in lighting the lamp. The first is to remain still and not to move from your seat. In Japan, the Zen masters developed a technique they called Zazen. Zazen means just sitting, doing nothing. You just need to be aware of one thing: never to move from your sitting position. This is very significant.

If you become capable of sitting for a while without moving your body, then as the body stops moving the mind also comes to a stop because body and mind are not two, they are two sides of the same coin. How can the mind move if the body does not? Or if the mind stops, then the body stops moving. The point is, start from anywhere but become still. Kabir says: **Don't move from your posture**, from what is known as Zazen. Just sit unmoving and don't do anything. Just make sure there is no tremor of movement in your body. The body should become like a stone statue. The moment the body becomes like a stone statue you will find that first the mind will relax and thoughts will come less and less. Sometimes, when for a moment the body becomes completely still, at the same time thoughts will also disappear. There will be nothing but *shunya*, the void. This is the first stage. Becoming still, you will open the doors of the *shunya* palace.

Now the next stage is when you awake in the *shunya* palace; you attain total wisdom. Watch; keep your awareness. Remain alert! Don't sleep. *Light a lamp in the shunya palace, and never shift from your posture.* It is possible you may go to sleep; if that happens, then you will have missed. If you would attain the state of *shunya* without watching, then it would mean *shunya*, the void, did not become your experience. It would be like your arriving at the door and then getting lost right there, on the steps, so you couldn't enter the palace.

This is what happens in deep sleep: the body becomes still. You may have noticed: when you are unable to sleep you turn from one side to the other. When you get a good night's sleep you change sides less; when you get a really good night's sleep you don't turn sides at all because the whole body becomes still. And when the body becomes still the dreams inside become silent. Then you experience *sushupti*, deep sleep, which is actually a dreamless sleep. Even a moment of that *sushupti* will make you blissful and refreshed. But if someone asked you how you could feel so blissful and refreshed just by sleeping, you wouldn't be able to explain it. You reached the doors of the *shunya* palace but were asleep; you returned from the door and so could not enter inside.

Patanjali has said that both *samadhi* and *sushupti* are the same except for one difference. The difference is that in *sushupti* you are not conscious while in *samadhi* you are fully conscious. Except for this difference, *sushupti*, deep sleep, is almost like *samadhi*. The first stage of both is the same: the body becomes still and the mind becomes *shunya*, absolutely void. And the second stage is you become awake and are fully conscious. Then *sushupti* becomes *samadhi*; then sleeping becomes the ultimate awakening.

> **Light a lamp in the shunya palace, and never shift from your posture.**
> **Then, with awareness, see the shunya palace turned into**
> **a palace of joy, and find the priceless beloved.**

Kabir says, through the device of awareness I found the priceless beloved. Light a lamp in the shunya palace, and never shift from your posture. Then, with awareness, you will see the shunya palace turned into a palace of joy, and find the priceless beloved.

And then, having reached, wake up; see that *shunya* palace with awareness and instantly the *shunya* palace turns into a palace of joy. The moment you are awakened, the palace no longer remains *shunya* or void; suddenly doors open to supreme joy, to supreme bliss. It turns into a palace of joy, of endless enjoyment, because life is a celebration; the divine is always dancing, always singing songs. That dance is the dance of joy and bliss. So the moment you are awakened, the *shunya* palace suddenly becomes the palace of joy.

Then, with awareness, you will see the shunya palace turned into a palace of joy, and find the priceless beloved. Not only does the shunya palace become a palace of joy, but in that palace of joy you meet the beloved.

Kabir says:

> ***Now there is nothing but bliss***
> ***and the beating of the endless drum.***

Kabir is saying, I am in utter bliss; and such drums are beating, such music is sounding; it is *anahad*, endless.

The word *anahad* is very significant. *Anahad* means that which is limitless, that which has no end. That which has always been sounding goes on sounding. Whether you know or not, it is sounding this very moment. It was sounding when you were not and it will continue to sound when you are no more. Celebration is not happening in this world because of you. It has always been going on – eternally. This celebration will continue to go on – day or night, light or darkness, morning or evening. Whether there are stars at night or the sun is shining, this dance goes on. The entire world is drunk with the dance and a drum is sounding endlessly.

What Kabir calls the drum is what the Upanishads call *omkar*. The same sound, the endless sound – a melody, music – is going on without anyone playing it. If someone is playing, then he is bound to get tired at some point. If someone is playing, then he may stop playing sometime. No, the sound, the music, is going on without anyone playing it. There is no one playing it.

It is a very profound concept. And the concept is that no one is dancing and yet the dance is going on. If there were a dancer, then it is possible that the dancer may sometimes get tired, may want to rest for a while. Existence is nothing but a dance, although there is no dancer. Existence is creativity, although there is no creator – there is no person. The day you enter the *shunya* palace, suddenly you will find the endless sound that was always going on – only you were deaf. This *shunya* palace was always a palace of joy – only you were blind. And the beloved was always seated within you. You yourself are the lover and you are also the beloved. You are not going to meet anyone else. You will be meeting your own self.

Kabir says: *Now there is nothing but bliss and the beating of the endless drum*. Never slacken your effort until that moment comes when you can also say there is nothing but bliss. In essence, there is only one effort needed, only one awareness is required: whatsoever you do, do it with alertness. Whatever you do, do it with such awareness that by and by its rays penetrate even your sleep. Then your deep sleep will become *samadhi*. Then even while asleep you become awake. You will be awake even while asleep. Then you will find that you are asleep and yet you are awake. And when this happens, that day you will say: *…now there is nothing but bliss and the beating of the endless drum*.

And never stop until such a moment arrives. It happens that many times even resting places make us feel as if we have arrived at a destination. But until your whole being says, "I am in bliss" and until you have begun to dance and hear the endless drums, and there is joy all around…

Understand it this way. When you begin the spiritual journey you look for peace. Yes, you will find peace, even if you entered in the *shunya* palace in your sleep. But still, it is a resting place, not the destination. One finds peace even having a good sleep. That is why if you are restless, doctors and psychologists give you tranquilizers. If you sleep, it will bring peace. A good sleep will certainly make you experience peace. The same treatment is given to mad people: giving them tranquilizers so that they can sleep. They will become quiet if they get to sleep.

Sleep will bring peace. But peace cannot be the aim of religion. Peace is simply an initial preparation. The goal is the *shunya* palace; when it turns into a palace of joy only then will religion come into being.

So bliss is the goal, not peace. Peace has a negative connotation. Peace means no tension, no worries. But is that enough? Is it enough that you are not worried? How can you say that there is bliss just with this much? What you can say is that you are no longer miserable. But is "not being miserable" a great achievement? It is like having a thorn taken out of your foot – but have flowers showered yet?

Peace is a negative phenomenon; it is just a resting place. Bliss is positive; that is the goal. If you succeed in not moving from your posture, then you will first achieve peace and nothing but peace.

The basic effort in the meditations happening in this camp is to first shake you completely – to utterly exhaust your body to such an extent that no desire for movement is left. If tension or excitement remain in your body, then whether you are standing or sitting the body will feel excitement, it will want to move. So while following all these meditation techniques first move your body totally so that the body's desire is fulfilled. And then, if you are still for even a few seconds, you will have taken the first step toward peace.

But that is half of the journey; the other half still remains. Therefore, each meditation should be done in the spirit of celebration and gratitude. Not only peace but the juice of bliss must flow when doing the meditation, so that you may dance and express your gratitude; so that you may also say: *Now there is nothing but bliss and the beating of the endless drum.*

So peace is the first resting place; bliss is the goal – it is the final destination. There is restlessness and misery where you are now. Restlessness may get removed by finding peace, but misery will not. Buddha talks about the first goal – peace, *shunya*; he doesn't talk about the other part. So Buddha's thought is incomplete. Vedanta, Shankara, talk about wholeness – about bliss and a positive sense of gratitude. So Vedanta's thought goes deeper than Buddha's and is complete. Buddha is the first step while Shankara is the destination. And Kabir has joined both. Kabir is the confluence.

Kabir says, *Light a lamp in the shunya palace.* The word *sunna*, used by Kabir, comes from Buddha; Buddha used that word many times. He says, it is everything, it is the very state of enlightenment. So the word *sunna* is from Buddha. *Light a lamp in the shunya palace...* Here the word *diyana* for lamp is also from Buddha. He also says: "Light a lamp." Even at the time of death, in his last moments, his last words are "*Appa deepo bhava.*" He says to Ananda, "Light your own lamp; be a light unto yourself." So all these words – *sunna, shunya* and *diyana* – have come from Buddha.

Light a lamp in the shunya palace, and never shift from your posture.

The remaining other part is from Vedanta. This part shows the first step – shown by Buddha; the second step is shown by Shankara.

> **Then, with awareness, you will see the shunya palace turned into a palace of joy, and find the priceless beloved.**

> Kabir says: **Now there is nothing but bliss**
> **and the beating of the endless drum.**

Enough for today.

# 8
# Don't Be Asleep While Awake

Seekers! Don't be asleep while awake!
You are neither killed by death nor besieged by misery.
You never grow old.
The opposite happens: the Ganges soaks up the ocean.
It swallows up the sun and the moon.

The ailing person kills the nine planets he thought were afflicting him.
Water catches fire; becomes ignited.
Footless, it runs in all directions and sees the world without eyes.
In contrast, the rabbit eats the lion;
who can ever figure out this puzzle?

One does not drown in a river when holding the pitcher upside down;
but keeping it the right way up, it will fill with water.
Different kinds of people, those who have learned different ways
of keeping the pitcher upside down,
have crossed the river with the master's grace.

Sitting in his cave, he watches the world within
and pays no attention to the world outside.

***Conversely, the arrow, instead of hitting the target,***
***pierces the hunter himself.***
***Only a courageous person can figure this out.***
***He sings and yet sings not;***
***and even while saying not a word, his song continues.***
***He simply watches the drama and the sounds happening all around***
***while rising in love for the infinite.***
***He becomes a witness to his speech and his deeds.***

***All this is a very strange story that cannot be described.***
***Turning back, the earth pierces the sky, so the ancients say.***
***Uncontained elixir showers so much that rivers begin to flow within.***

Kabir says: ***One who is showered with this elixir becomes immortal***
***and keeps tasting the divine endlessly.***

***Seekers! Don't be asleep while awake!***

There are two meanings to this statement. Both are important and worth understanding. We are already familiar with the first one: that we are asleep even while awake. There is no intensity, no urgency, in our waking state. Our waking state is not ablaze; it is more like a glimmering lamp. Sleep is part of our waking state. We get up, sit, walk and do our work – but it's as if someone else were doing it half-asleep.

There is a condition known as somnambulism – sleepwalking. At night a patient with this condition gets out of bed while still asleep and, with his eyes open, does things. He goes into the kitchen, he eats food, he gets back into bed and goes to sleep. In the morning he has no memory of having been to the kitchen the night before; he feels puzzled about what may have happened during the night. If he is living alone in the house, he may think it was ghosts; otherwise who could have eaten that food in the night? Who could have torn his clothes? – which actually he himself tore. Who could have lit the fire? Who could have moved the utensils around? He has no memory of any of these things in the morning.

Our condition is the same as that of this sleepwalking patient – maybe to a lesser degree. But our sleep never breaks, our slumber lingers. We are overwhelmed by a deep indolence. Darkness continues to remain within us. The basic characteristic of this sleep is: whatever we may be doing, we are never present. For example, while having a meal our hands mechanically pick up some food and put it into our mouths. The mind goes on wandering who knows where. It goes on dreaming. The mind is not at all there where we are. We take some food, put it into our mouths, chew it, finish our meal and stand up. An onlooker might say we are doing all of this while awake, but in fact we didn't do it in a wakeful state but in slumber.

A wakeful state is possible only when our total awareness is centered in the given moment, so that whatever we may be doing, our whole mind, our entire consciousness, is present there. Consciousness becoming one with the moment is awakening; and consciousness cut off from the moment is sleep.

We call sleep *sleep* because we are completely cut off from that given moment. You may be lying in bed and imagining you are resting in an emperor's palace. You may be sleeping at home, but dreaming of being in Kolkata or London or New York. And while dreaming, you have no idea that you are actually resting in your own house in Pune. Getting up in the morning you will laugh at how far away you went, how long the journey was.

A dream means going away from where you are, moving away from your actual self, becoming that which you are not, reaching a point where you are not. A dream means that the false appears to be the truth. Awakening means the truth appears as the truth. So we are all asleep. Make sure you understand the first meaning of this sutra rightly. *Seekers! Don't be asleep while awake*. Don't sleep while you are awake!

Once, Mulla Nasruddin went to listen to a lecture. The speaker, a guru, became a little uncomfortable because both Mulla Nasruddin and his wife were seated right in front of him and soon Mulla's wife started snoring. After she had been snoring for some time, Mulla picked up his cane and left. The speaker felt even more hurt.

After the lecture was over he felt it was not proper to ask Mulla's wife: "Was my lecture so boring that you went to sleep?" but he could not resist asking, "I saw your husband leaving. Did I say anything that may have hurt his feelings?"

The wife replied: "Not at all. Please don't worry. Actually, since childhood he has had the habit of sleepwalking."

*Seekers! Don't be asleep while awake!* When you are awake, be fully awake. The result of this will be that when you are asleep you will be totally, fully asleep. As of now you are neither able to remain fully awake nor to fall fully asleep. Your waking includes sleep and your sleep contains waking. It is all mixed up – a confusion. It is all hazy. You are nothing but a hodgepodge; not orderly. That is why those who function in slumber even when awake will lose sleep; when they need to sleep they continue to stay awake. This is naturally so. That is why all around the world people are losing sleep. Today the biggest issue facing man is how to sleep.

There are thousands of tranquilizers available on the market but they are all proving useless. In Russia they have made small electric gadgets, which they are now using. Normally, we only give electric shocks to people who are mentally ill, but these machines give shocks to anyone – but in a very small dosage. At night, the machine is attached to the head and as it keeps giving electric shocks the person is able to sleep. Such machines have been installed in thousands of homes for daily use. And psychologists say that by the end of this century, it will be difficult to find a person, at least in the West, who can sleep naturally – someone who can say he goes to sleep the moment his head touches the pillow.

A hundred years from now people will find it hard to believe there was a time when people went to sleep without doing anything. We also find it hard to believe that Buddha and Mahavira attained enlightenment just by sitting or standing under a tree. And we find it hard to believe when someone says Buddha achieved meditation without doing anything.

The same situation is happening in the case of sleep – in fact it has already happened. A person suffering from insomnia often asks, "How do you get to sleep? – because I can't." You might answer, "I don't do anything in particular. There is no method or technique for going to sleep. I just put my head on the pillow and then I'm asleep." He might then say, "Surely you are lying, because I also put my head on the pillow, but I toss and turn the whole night and can't get to sleep. I am sure there must be some technique that people are hiding from me. There must be some conspiracy going on against me. The whole world is asleep – and here I am, awake!"

What has happened to this man that he cannot sleep at night? He is asleep during the day. He is asleep when he is awake. If sleep comes in when you are awake, then naturally waking will come into your sleeping state. You will become a chaos; nothing will remain orderly in your life. Hate will enter your love; love will enter your hate. You will hate your friend; you will love your enemy. Your life will become an incomprehensible puzzle.

So this is the first meaning: when you are awake, stay awake so that you may sleep at night. A night is a night; a day is a day. Stay fully awake during the day so that you can be totally asleep at night. But nothing in your life is orderly. At home, you think of the office. When in the office, you think of home. You must be crazy: when you are in office just deal with what needs to be done in the office.

I used to be the guest of a high court judge. When I became close to the family, his wife said one day, "My husband adores you. Please make him understand he should stop being a judge when he leaves the court. At night, even in bed, he continues to be a judge. He treats us as if we were clerks or culprits. He never steps down from his position of being a judge. The entire household is going crazy because of this."

You bring your business home. You may be sitting next to your wife but between you there is a safe and a stack of account books. So obviously you are unable to come lovingly close to your wife, to play with your children, to laugh and enjoy. But when you are in the office, your wife and children seem to be around.

Whatsoever you do is always incomplete, so that which remains haunts you like a hangover. Someone who is awake does any kind of work – regardless of how trivial it may be – with total awareness. His whole consciousness is present while he's doing it. When thirsty and drinking water – or just having a cup of tea – he does so with complete awareness. He ends the matter right there and then. He does not keep accounts that need to be settled later. Such a person stays awake totally and also sleeps totally.

A deep silence pervades such a person's life. None of his work ever remains incomplete. Even death will find him ready; when asked he will follow, because he has nothing left to do anymore. Whatsoever he needed to do, he has always done totally.

But if death knocked on your door today, you would not find yourself ready. You might say, "Wait a while. I need to ask someone I insulted yesterday for forgiveness. I need to return money I borrowed from someone the other day. God only knows how many yesterdays have gone by and how many entanglements still remain unresolved. For death, there is no time now."

That is why everyone dies an untimely death. Only an awakened person dies on time – regardless of when he dies. You cannot say Buddha died before his time. A buddha never dies before his time, because no matter at which moment death occurs it is the right time.

There was once a rich man. He had a very precious pet parrot, which he kept in a cage hanging by his door. He had taught the parrot that whenever he went out the parrot should say: "Master! Sir! My Lord! Hurry up – it is already too late!"

In this already fast-moving life, full of hustle and bustle, he had even taught the parrot how to make someone hurry up!

As he came down the stairs, the parrot would immediately say: "Master, hurry up, it is already late!"

Then the man died. As his dead body was being carried out of the house the parrot said: "Master, hurry up, it is already late!"

The parrot had no idea that his master was dead. And his master actually died while hurrying – he couldn't finish anything. Whatever he did, he did in a hurry.

We hardly ever finish one thing before we rush to finish something else. We have hardly finished the second thing before we rush to finish the third. The whole of life turns into just running around – a mad race! And finally we find nothing ever got done.

And remember, if all your acts remain incomplete, then you too remain incomplete. If all your acts get completed, then you too become complete. There is only one totality – when all acts are completed. There is only one kind of contentment and that is when all your work gets done. When this happens a deep silence comes over you, overwhelms you. A silence-filled sky descends on you. That is the sky of utter fulfillment. It is a state of gratification, a deep satisfaction – all the work has been taken care of.

But your acts are never totally finished; even your trivial jobs remain undone. They haunt you. While having your meal you are on the run, but you somehow manage to eat. Then when you are walking down the street, you think of food. While making love, you somehow manage it in a hurry and then you look at other men and women on the street with lust. All and everything you do is unfinished.

Incompleteness is your disease. If you taste your food rightly, you will not have to think of food again. If you make love rightly, your lust will disappear. Whatever we go through in totality, we are then free of it. To be free means to have gone through the experience; a half-hearted experience will keep you in bondage. So, this is the first meaning of *Seekers! Don't be asleep while awake!*

Maybe you will not understand the second meaning right now – because only those who are going deeply into meditation will understand it. A moment comes… As I said yesterday, *samadhi* and *sushupti* are similar, but with one difference: *sushupti* is a deep sleep while *samadhi* is total awareness.

Those of you who are going more deeply into meditation will be able to understand this. A moment arrives when meditation is close to realization, when you are on the border between *sushupti* and *samadhi*. At this point you may go to sleep if you wish, or you may stay awake. Patanjali has discovered a different name for it and that is *yoga nidra*. It is a state where you become totally silent, but where bliss has not yet descended upon you. You cannot yet declare what Kabir says: "…now there is nothing but bliss and the beating of the endless drum." No, drums are not yet beating, bliss has not yet appeared, as yet there is no shower of elixir – but you have become silent. The world has disappeared, but *moksha*, liberation, has not yet happened. The night is over, but the sun has not yet risen. It is early dawn, and you are right in the middle.

The Hindus have called it *sandhya kaal* – the twilight, the meeting point of day and night. They have identified two twilights or *sandhyas*: morning time when the night is over but the sun has not risen yet – which is a moment for prayer – and evening time when the sun has set but the night has not arrived yet. That too is a moment for prayer. These two meeting points are times for prayer.

But they are symbols. A similar kind of *sandhya*, meeting point, occurs within oneself. That is the real meeting point where sleep – the mundane world, darkness – is no longer there, but the sun has not yet risen. Bliss has not yet happened, the drums have not sounded yet. Yes, the worldly noise has disappeared; there is a melody of silence playing within, but the bliss is not there yet. The wrong is left behind, but the right has not yet appeared. This shore is left far behind, but the other shore is still not in sight. One is in midstream.

In this situation there are two possibilities. One is that you end up sleeping – because the peace and silence is so deep that the sleep will be very enjoyable. You may not have had such a sleep before – it will be so deep. And after waking up from that sleep, you will find yourself as refreshed as if you had been asleep for thousands of years – it will be that refreshing. But such sleep is dangerous because although it is pleasant, if you let yourself drown in it, then the phenomenon of bliss – which was so close – will be missed.

*Yoga nidra* or *yoga tandra* is very peaceful but of a negative kind. And it is very difficult to keep control at the time of *yoga nidra*. In fact, even in ordinary sleep you are unable to keep control; when sleep takes over, you begin to yawn, and your eyelids become heavy and begin to close as if they are tied to rocks. At that time it would become difficult if someone asks you to stay awake for just one moment more. If such ordinary sleep is so overpowering, then what can be said about *yoga nidra*, which is so extraordinary.

In that state, your entire body is so peaceful that it is as if you have become a lake of peace. At that time you feel absolutely like going to sleep. And that sleep will be so pleasant that you will forget everything else. Perhaps you may even feel that this is the very bliss that Kabir and Nanak talk about.

Many methods lead only as far as *yoga tandra*. For example, Mahesh Yogi's meditation technique takes you only up to *yoga tandra*. What he calls Transcendental Meditation does not take you beyond *yoga tandra*. That is why, although it had a great effect in the West, it did not make any mark on the East. It affected the West because sleep has become very difficult in the West; sleep has become its biggest problem. That's why America was highly influenced by Mahesh Yogi's meditation technique. People began to fall asleep. This is not a small matter; it is quite precious. People felt very happy because of it.

But happiness is not bliss. Happiness is merely an absence of misery. The disease may no longer be there but health has not come dancing yet. The departure of disease is not the same as being healthy. Health is a positive state. Try to understand this a little.

If you are not ill, then the physician will say, "You are healthy; I don't see any problem. I have checked everything; you have no disease. You are okay." But you know very well that there is a difference between being okay and being healthy. There is one kind of being okay that manifests in well-being, which contains an inner state of joy – as if you are filled with blossoming flowers, as if the stream of life is surging through you, overflowing both of its banks. It makes you ecstatic to be in good health. Each step is a dance; each word rings with music. As you open your eyes they reflect a graceful sweetness. Your energy moves with intensity. So this is one state of being healthy. But then there is another state – which is simply that of being without any illness.

So if a physician does not detect any specific illness, he simply says that you are healthy. But you may be sitting completely limp, like a corpse. Of course, there is no illness – no headache, no stomachache, no broken limbs or any plaster needs applying. You may certainly be sitting there, but without any ecstasy. There is no visible gratitude. Nobody will see in you any feeling to get up and dance or sing a song – nothing of that sort. You are just sitting inertly – just like a dead body.

A corpse never gets sick. You are also not sick. A corpse cannot be ill, and you are not ill. Actually, your "health" is only an absence of illness. Exactly the same situation happens in *yoga nidra*. Tensions disappear, mental stress disappears – there are no concerns, nothing to worry about. One feels great peace. But *yoga nidra* is not *samadhi* – it only brings you to the door of *samadhi*. The real journey begins after that point.

That is why Kabir says, *Seekers! Don't be asleep while awake!* He is addressing seekers, he is talking to sannyasins. That's why, up to now, I did not speak on Kabir – certainly not until I had seekers and sannyasins near me. That is why I remained silent on Kabir.

One can speak on Kabir only when addressing seekers, those who are meditators. Others will not be able to follow. Those who are getting more deeply into meditation here can understand what I am saying. This is an inner experience where everything becomes silent, where you feel happy. But this is not enough; don't stop here. This not the destination; this too is just a resting place. You have to go even further.

*Yoga tandra* is pleasant but it is not a state of enlightenment. It is not the ultimate state. Certainly, the perverted ways of the world are dropped, but the taste of the divine has not been experienced as yet. The meaningless has been left behind, but the meaningful has yet to appear. If you doze off at this moment, you will miss it. Then you will be back again in the world, in samsara. Then you will be back again on the same shore – the other shore will have disappeared.

***Seekers! Don't be asleep while awake!***
***You are neither killed by death nor besieged by misery.***
***You never grow old.***
***The opposite happens: the Ganges soaks up the ocean.***
***It swallows up the sun and the moon.***

***The ailing person kills the nine planets he thought were afflicting him.***
***Water catches fire; becomes ignited.***
***Footless, it runs in all directions and sees the world without eyes.***
***In contrast, the rabbit eats the lion;***
***who can ever figure out this puzzle?***

First you will need to know a particular characteristic of Kabir's statements, and then these words will make sense to you. That particular characteristic is known as *ulatbansi* or upside-down, paradoxical, statements. *Ulatbansi* means an upside-down statement. For example, someone is playing the flute and a moment may come when the flute player becomes the flute and the flute becomes the flute player. Everything goes topsy-turvy between the flute playing and the flute player.

*Ulatbansi* means that the flute begins playing the flute player. A moment comes in life when everything seems to go haywire. Just try to understand this, then it will be easy to follow what Kabir is saying. These statements are symbolic and like puzzles; they appear to us like riddles.

Look at it this way…

As you breathe, the breath goes in and the breath goes out. You think you are breathing. But have you ever thought that if you really are the breather, then you will never die? – because then you can continue to breathe as long as you want.

Mulla Nasruddin turned 100, so people came to congratulate him and to ask him the secret of attaining such a long life. Maybe he could show them the trick; how he managed it.

Nasruddin said: "Just keep breathing!"

But how will you continue breathing? What will you do if it stops? The moment breathing stops you will disappear, you will not survive to take even one more breath. Breathing stopping means you are no longer alive. If you survived even for a moment after taking the last breath, you would be able to take another one. But when breathing stops, you can no longer survive.

You are the breath; breath is your vital energy. The moment your breathing stops, you are no more. You won't have even one moment to realize your breath has stopped and that you will never take another one. There won't be anyone inside you who will know about the breath. Others will know your breathing has stopped, but not you. People in the household will know it, neighbors will begin to scream and cry that your breath has stopped. But you won't come to know it. Had you known it, you would have continued to breathe – how could you have stopped? If you follow rightly what I am saying about breathing, then you will understand that actually *you* are not taking a breath – the breath is happening. *You* are not the taker of breath; you are not the doer.

So Kabir gives us another vision in which he says: simply drop the idea that *you* are breathing. The breath is breathing you. It is not that you are living in the world; the world is living in you. It is wrong to say you are living – existence is living.

Existence is breathing through you. That makes it *ulatbansi*: the one who is breathing is not the breather; rather the breath itself is your life.

Let me explain this so that you will be able to get the idea. Psychologists use a small technique – they call it gestalt. Sometimes, in a children's book, you may have seen a picture of a flower vase. If you look at the vase closely, you will see that, after a while, it disappears and you see the faces of two people facing each other where the vase was. The bend or the curve appears like their noses; part of the vase looks like their heads. The space between the two faces appeared as the vase before. If you look at the two faces closely, after a while the two faces will disappear and the vase will appear again. And if you look even more closely, the vase will disappear again and the two faces will become visible.

These changes will keep on happening. The interesting thing is: when you see the vase you won't see the two faces – although you know very well that the two faces are also hidden in the picture. And when you see the two faces you won't be able to see the vase – although you know very well that the vase is also hidden in the picture. The mind can know only one thing at a time. And the mind is so wavering and unsteady that you cannot even see one vase for a long time. The scene will change. The faces will appear, then the vase, and then again the faces will become visible. The German word for this is *gestalt*. And a whole philosophy developed based on this idea. It is known as Gestalt Psychology. They say that life is a gestalt.

If you believe that "I am breathing," then your entire perspective of life will be that of an atheist; if you believe someone or something is breathing through you, then your whole perspective of life will be that of a religious person. With such a small difference the whole scenario of life will change. If you come to realize that something else is breathing through you, then your whole ego will disappear. If indeed we are unable to take even a breath on our own, then what is the point in claiming credit for the rest of our actions?

For example, you may say "I am in love" but that too is the same as breathing. Loving is happening through you – it is not *your* act. If it was your act… If I said, "Here is a woman, fall in love with her," you might say, "How can I fall in love just like that? I cannot fall in love with just any woman! When it happens, it happens; if it doesn't, then it doesn't – unless you want me to pretend I am falling in love, but then that is a different matter."

But acting is not love. Have you loved, or have you been in love? If you have *loved* then it will be a different matter; then you will think that you are the doer. If it has *happened*, then you will know that you are only the medium, not the doer. It is something else, which has loved through me. If you want to be a doer, you can only love a prostitute and none else. And has anyone ever really been in love with a prostitute!

I have heard…

Once Mulla Nasruddin went to a prostitute. He said to her, "I want to make love to you."

The prostitute said, "Do it."

He said, "I want to make you the light of my life."

The prostitute said, "Make me."

He said, "I want to place you in my heart."

The prostitute said, "Place me."

He said, "I want to die for you."

The prostitute said, "Then die; but whatever you want to do, please do it quickly, because there are other customers waiting outside!"

Acting is one thing, business is a different matter. The more you understand life, the more you will find that you are not the doer.

Things are happening – they are happenings. Love descends – it happens. That's why there is so much trouble with love. People try to make a man understand: "Remember you are a husband, you have a wife and four children, so what kind of craziness is this about falling in love?" The husband also realizes it.

People say, "Look, you are a husband, father of four children, you have a wife, now what kind of madness is this?" The husband also gets the point and makes an effort to come back to his senses: "The matter is simple and clear cut I have four children and a wife, and I have fallen in love with someone else, but what can I do? It simply happened." He knows that it would have been better if this had not happened, he thinks of his wife and children, and yet he feels himself to be helpless in the matter. It happened. We can certainly put the responsibility on him, but that is a misunderstanding.

The phenomenon of love is out of man's control. Until you have attained enlightenment, it is out of your control. When you attain enlightenment a new dimension of love opens up. Then you don't fall in love with someone – you *become* love. Then people receive love from you, you share it, it spreads – but you don't *fall* in love with someone. You have become like a lamp, which continues to burn; whosoever passes by on the street gets its light. You have become like a flower which has blossomed; anyone passing by will receive its fragrance. Then it is no longer your old type of love in which you felt yourself powerless and wondered what to do; although you understood the point, you could comprehend it, your intellect saw the irrationality of it, still you used to fall helplessly.

The intellect has its own logic but the heart does not agree with it. You can repress love and close all your doors. Listening to your mind, you may not get closer to love, but if your heart is beating for someone, then it will continue to beat. You may take care of your wife, massage her feet. You may get worried when she is sick, give her a hug – but you will find it is all fake; that you are doing it all intellectually.

How can you see yourself as the doer? Neither is each breath yours, nor is love truly yours, nor is life really your own.

This is precisely what Krishna is saying to Arjuna in the Gita: "Just become a *nimitta*, a cause, a medium. Drop the idea that you are the doer. These warriors who are standing before us are all dead as far as I am concerned. You are only a means, a channel. These people are standing in front of you like corpses; just push them and they will fall. They are already dead. Their death is certain. You are not going to do the job of killing them; that work will be done by someone else. They are surely going to die. Who kills them is a secondary thing."

If you come to understand that life is a *nimitta*, a channel… This word *nimitta*, meaning channel, or means, is very precious. You cannot find a word comparable to this in any other language. *Nimitta* is a word from the East; it is a word given by the Hindus – and is deeply profound. *Nimitta* means "I am not the reason, nor am I the doer; I am just a pretext, an excuse. I was just a pretext for whatever happened. It is not because of me, it would have happened anyway, someone else would have been the pretext. Whatever was to happen would have happened – the excuse or pretext could have been anyone; anything could have served as a hook. Whatever had to be hung on it would have been hung on it. Whatever was to happen would have happened. I must not bring my ego in."

If you drop your attitude of being the doer, your feeling of being a *nimitta*, a channel, deepens, then that is all that is needed. Then you will understand *ulatbansi* – the paradox – because then everything will look upside down. The whole gestalt will change. Then the world will not look the same to you as before; it will look topsy-turvy. In order to indicate that upside-down reality, Kabir has used metaphors.

Kabir is saying: *You are neither killed by death nor besieged by misery. You never grow old.* This is when you are in the state of being a *nimitta*, a pretext – not the doer. If you are a doer, then death will certainly kill you; then death is bound to happen; then you are sure to die. It is only the attitude that you are the doer which will die – the spirit never dies. But if you believe you are the doer, then you are certain to die.

It is the ego, which is afraid of death, not the soul. As long as you take yourself to be the "I" and nothing but the "I," and repeat your "I-ness," keep embellishing the "I" – dressing it up – death will continue to make you fearful. The more egoistic a person is the more afraid of death he will be. The more egoless a person is the more the fear of death will disappear. And if one attains to the state of being totally egoless, then death will no longer exist because, in that case, what remains will never die at all – the gestalt has changed.

*You are neither killed by death nor besieged by misery.* No pain, no agony will ever take you over. *You never grow old.* And your body will never decay; you will never grow old.

But the body *does* get old. This body is subject to death. This body *does* get destroyed. But you are the body only as long as you believe that "I am." The day you drop the idea that "I am," that very moment your entire consciousness will change. Then you will not be the body, then you will be divine. Then you will see that which is hidden within you.

And remember, you can see only one, not both simultaneously. As long as you believe you are the body, you will not be able to see your being. The day you see you are the being, the body will disappear. That's why the realized ones have said that this samsara, this world, is all maya – an illusion – because the moment *brahman* is seen, samsara becomes invisible. And as long as the world is visible, *brahman* will not be seen. The gestalt is one; only one can be seen at a time. You can know only one; you cannot know both.

You are neither killed by death nor besieged by misery. You never grow old. The opposite happens: the Ganges soaks up the ocean. It swallows up the sun and the moon. The situation becomes totally the reverse. We see the Ganges falling into the ocean; but here Kabir is saying the ocean is falling into the Ganges.

There are two statements by Kabir. One is: "While I was seeking and searching, my friend, Kabir got lost. How can I now find the drop which has fallen into the ocean?" This is one aspect of the gestalt. Kabir is saying that while searching and seeking he got lost, the drop fell into the ocean. Now how can it be brought back? Then there is another statement immediately following it, which says: "While seeking and searching Kabir got lost; the ocean merged with the drop, now how can it be found? The ocean fell into the drop, now how can I find myself?" In one statement he says the drop fell into the ocean, so how can he find himself; in the second one he says the ocean fell into the drop, so how can he find himself. These are the two aspects.

As long as you keep on believing "I am" you will continue to be afraid of the ocean because the drop will disappear into the ocean and then how will it be traced? The day you come to know "I am not" the ocean will dissolve in you. It is the same thing. Whether a drop disappears in the ocean or the ocean disappears in the drop, the phenomenon is the same; only the perception differs. You get scared of disappearing in the ocean. But there will be no fear when the ocean disappears in you; you will feel your treasure has grown. As you go on disappearing into the divine you will be afraid; but when the divine disappears in you, you will dance with joy.

Your mind carries fear, even where godliness is concerned, because you feel you will be lost; that you will not exist anymore. What will happen to your identity? You will lose your name, address – everything! So what is the point of attaining godliness when you are going to lose yourself?

But there is another aspect which is closer to the truth: you don't disappear into the divine; rather the divine disappears in you. Then you don't vanish – you become vast. The drop becomes the ocean.

Kabir says: *The opposite happens: the Ganges soaks up the ocean. It swallows up the sun and the moon.* The Ganges swallows the ocean; it absorbs the sun and the moon into it. This is the outer meaning. Its inner meaning is that the sun and the moon are two metaphors for your two breaths. The sun represents your right-side breathing and the moon represents your left-side breathing. And there are two *naadis,* two ducts, connected inside your body – the *ida* and *pingala*: one is the sun duct and the other is the moon duct. These are symbols of the yogis.

When your consciousness becomes just a channel, a means, when you don't see yourself as the doer, when you drop your ego, when you never say "I" but say "Only *you* are," when you say: "neither 'I' ever was, nor 'I' am now, nor will 'I' ever be in the future." "I" is just an illusion. When you dive deep into this state of being, the ocean falls into the drop. Then your consciousness absorbs both the sun and the moon into itself. Right now you breathe, and you are dependent on breathing. If you stop breathing this moment, you will no longer be alive. At this point breath is your support; you won't be able to survive without breath. In the opposite case, you live through consciousness; the breath is merged into consciousness. That's why a yogi deep in *samadhi* or meditation becomes absolutely breath-less. It becomes difficult to know whether his breath is moving or not.

Those among you who are going deeper into meditation, please let your family members know that they need not be worried if at some moment you become absolutely like a dead person because the breath has stopped completely. Even a doctor can vouch that such a person is dead because although the breath does not stop completely, it stops ninety-nine percent. Just a faint sound remains. And when the breath stops completely, the mind stops absolutely.

You yourself must have experienced the fact that there is a deep connection between your mind and your breathing. Your breathing pattern is different when you get angry; there is stress in the breathing. When you are angry, the breath feels like a car without any shock absorbers moving on an uneven road full of potholes. When you are sexually aroused, the breath moves differently – it goes crazy, you are perspiring. When you are calm, the breath moves slowly – it carries a certain rhythm, there is a certain music in it; it has a rhythmic movement. When you are very happy, the breath moves differently again.

The breathing changes with every mood. If you become a little more alert and change your breathing, your mood will also change because they are connected with each other. Next time when you get angry, watch the speed of your breathing carefully. See how it is moving, get to know it well. When you become calm and silent next time, also watch the nature of your breathing in that peaceful state. When you find yourself cheerful, then also take note of your breathing.

Once you are able to recognize the pace of your breathing – when joyful, when angry, while happy or when you are calm – then you can experiment. For example, as you are about to get angry don't allow your breath to rush with your anger. Simply sit down quietly and let the breathing be as it is when you are calm and silent. You will suddenly find the anger has evaporated!

Once the breathing has changed, anger cannot enter in the body. If you can correctly work out when the breath is in a state of peace and silence, then try to keep that rhythm going for twenty-four hours. You will find that you are filled with deep silence. If you come to know how the breath is when you are happy, then keep it like that and joy will shower upon you and keep flowing within you.

Buddha did great experiments with the mind and breathing. His Anapanasati Yoga is essentially the art of breathing. It is nothing but watching your breath, recognizing the nature of your breath, relating your mental states with your breathing and then dropping those breathing patterns which are associated with the mental states that you wish to get rid of. Then you can hold on to the breathing rhythms of those states that you wish to nourish and support, give momentum to them and slowly let them grow. In that way, with a change in breathing patterns, your entire consciousness will go through a complete transformation. But when the consciousness disappears completely, the breathing will also disappear. Breath is at one end and consciousness is at the other – two ends of the same energy.

So if ever a moment comes in your life when you find your breath is stopping – many sannyasins come to me and say this is happening to them – naturally you will be afraid. But don't be afraid. And make sure people in your family know that this might happen because family members won't listen to you otherwise. If you apparently die and the doctor declares you dead, the family won't listen to you saying that you are still alive!

I have heard…

A man died. He was not really dead; his breathing had just become slow. The doctor said he was dead. His funeral was prepared and the body was taken to the cremation ground. By the time they reached the cremation ground the man had regained consciousness and had begun to move. People became scared. He screamed from inside the funeral pyre: "Let me out! I am alive!"

People said, "This is impossible. A well-known doctor, not an ordinary one, has declared this person dead. Should we believe him or this fool?" About a hundred people had come to the funeral.

The priest, who had come to perform the last rites, said, "Brothers! You were all present; raise your hands and tell us what the doctor said. Whom should we believe? Should we believe this fool who is illiterate and knows not even the *ABC* of life and death and is now telling us that he is alive? Or should we believe the medical expert, who has just returned after being educated in London – he is an F.R.C.S.! He has examined thousands of dead and alive bodies."

The priest started taking people's votes. After all, he was following the democratic process! Everyone raised their hands and said it will be right to listen to the medical expert; how could one trust this other man? He was not trustworthy even when alive, what is the point of trusting him when he is dead?

They burned him.

People believe in experts. So tell people in your family that if such a moment arrives and your breath stops, then there is nothing to fear. No need to shake the body because that can be dangerous. If someone comes and shakes you while your breath is absolutely calm, then the connection between the body and the soul can break – at that moment the connection is very delicate. At that moment you are very far away from your body. Just a very fine thread remains attached; so it can be a problem if someone shakes the body.

So while in meditation, don't have any fear within you – this is exactly the ultimate moment that we are searching for. This is the very moment we are looking for; this is the moment when you will taste the elixir. This is the moment when you will come to know that the body is lying there separately, and you are standing beside it; that you and the body are separate. Once you come to see this, then your life cannot be the same anymore – the gestalt will have changed. Now you will find that the divine alone is breathing in you; the divine alone is living in you; you are no more – only "that" is. You are only a medium for the divine. All life belongs to it. You are just the flute – the divine is the flute player.

Up to now you have been thinking that you are the flute player. You have been thinking that it is you who is singing the song. The fact is: you are simply the medium – existence is the one who is singing. If the flute had a brain – became a little knowledgeable – it would think that it is the one who is singing and that this man, this flute player, is unnecessarily making so much effort. The reasoning is: the song emerges from the flute, so how can the flute believe it comes from this man, this flute player? What has this man got to do with the song? The flute can say, "Show me how you play the song without me! – it is I who is playing the song."

You, too, are simply no more than a flute. Kabir says: "I am nothing but a bamboo flute. The song is yours; the melody is yours! And here I am, believing that the song and the melody are mine. That is why I have developed such vanity." The truth is: one who has become like a bamboo flute has truly become a saint – then there is nothing left to be achieved.

The opposite happens: the Ganges soaks up the ocean. It swallows up the sun and the moon. The ailing person kills the nine planets he thought were afflicting him. Water catches fire; becomes ignited.

Everything turns upside down. The sick person thought he was afflicted by nine planets so he killed them. He believed that nine wrong planets had aligned together and that was why he was in trouble. *The ailing person kills the nine planets he thought he was afflicted with. Water catches fire; becomes ignited.* And everything goes topsy-turvy. Water catches fire and it reflects light.

*Footless, it runs in all directions and sees the world without eyes.* And then comes a moment when you find no need for feet – your consciousness can go without feet in all the ten directions. The body needs feet; consciousness knows no barrier of time and space. It runs in all directions without feet and sees the world without eyes. These eyes are not needed to see the truth.

You can see in the statues that Mahavira's eyes are closed. Jainism has two sects – the Svetambaras and the Digambaras, and they are in conflict with each other over the issue of whether Mahavira's eyes should be left open or kept closed. Svetambaras keep his eyes open while the Digambaras keep them closed. There are Jain temples where both come to worship. So they have divided the time: for half of the day they keep Mahavira's eyes open, for the other half they keep them closed. They stick on artificial eyes that are open.

In this matter the Svetambaras are wrong because there is no point in keeping Mahavira's eyes open. Truth cannot be seen through these physical eyes – these eyes close anyway. There are also inner eyes, but they are not part of the human body – they are the eyes of consciousness, they are the eyes of awakening. *...sees the world without eyes.* There is no need to open these physical eyes; the truth cannot be seen through these eyes anyway. They can see only maya. To look within oneself one needs inner eyes. The eyes are certain to shut; the feet are certain to lose movement; these hands will surely lose strength. None of them will be of any use; only the life energy within you, that can move around in all the ten directions, can see without eyes, can touch without hands.

As far as consciousness or the being is concerned, time and space are no barrier – time and space just don't exist. Both apply only to the body.

Somebody asked Buddha, "After leaving your body, where will you be?" Buddha replied, "I will either be everywhere or nowhere; because it is only the body, which is at some place or in some time." The being neither has any space nor any time. As you go deeper in meditation you will find there is neither space nor time – you are beyond both.

*In contrast, the rabbit eats the lion; who can ever figure out this puzzle?* It is an amazing puzzle: a rabbit eating a lion! ...*who can ever figure out this puzzle?* Although you feel yourself to be a weak person, you suddenly find you have infinite power – the rabbit eating the lion. You, who normally see yourself to be so poor and lowly – living like a beggar your whole life, always asking for something – suddenly find you have become the master; you have become the emperor ...*who can ever figure out this puzzle?*

Swami Ram went to America. He used to call himself an emperor. Though he called himself a king he didn't possess anything except two loincloths and a vessel for carrying water. But he called himself "Emperor Ram."

He used to say, "Emperor Ram is thirsty, please bring him some water." It sounded so strange – and more so to Americans. The American president once said on meeting him, "Everything else is okay, but I don't understand what sort of an emperor you are. You own nothing."

Ram replied, "That's why I am an emperor – because I have no desire, I don't need anything, I am complete as I am. Even your richest person is really poor because he is still asking for something."

Once, there was a Sufi mystic, Junnaid. An emperor came to him. And as he was, after all, an emperor he brought ten thousand gold coins and placed them at Junnaid's feet.

Junnaid asked, "You have plenty, don't you? So you have no desires, you don't need anything more?"

The emperor replied, "Are desires ever finished? That's why I have come to your feet for blessings."

So Junnaid said, "Take these ten thousand gold coins back because you will be poor otherwise; and it makes no difference to my being an emperor. They won't add anything to me, because I am already fulfilled – the water pot is already full. But yours might be a little empty. You are still poor, so take these coins back."

Junnaid was a poor man; he had nothing. What a strange kind of ownership!

Kabir is saying: *In contrast, the rabbit eats the lion; who can ever figure out this puzzle?* Suddenly, with the change in gestalt, as his attention moves away from the body and turns inward, he becomes the master. One who was weak becomes the most powerful; one who was ignorant becomes supremely knowing; one who was in bondage becomes free: *...who can ever figure out this puzzle?* One who was otherwise crying and agonizing to own the trivial has now begun dancing with joy – he has attained the divine: *... who can ever figure out this puzzle?*

Kabir is saying that both are hidden within you. As long as you go on desiring, you will remain poor. As long as you carry the sense of the doer, you will remain poor. As the desiring disappears you will instantly become the master. But that will not happen through satisfying your lust and your desires, because desiring is never satisfied – it is impossible to satisfy it. Buddha has said that desiring is unquenchable. You will not be able to fulfill it. Regardless of how many ways you may try to quench it, no matter how much you may run hither and thither, the craving will not be affected by your running and looking for ways to fulfill it – because by its very nature it is unquenchable.

For example, if you have ten thousand rupees the desire will be to have one hundred thousand rupees, so that all will be well. Then you get one hundred thousand and the desire will be to have one million, so that everything will be okay. Regardless of how much you increase the number, desire will go on asking for ten times more. You have a thousand and then the desire is for ten thousand. You have ten thousand, now you want a hundred thousand. You have one hundred thousand and now you want one million. You have ten million rupees and now the desire is for one hundred million. The distance between you and what you desire remains the same – a tenfold difference. What difference does it make how much you have? Your desire will go on demanding that it is multiplied by ten. That is why the distance between man and his desires is never reduced. Desire always remains unfulfilled; you will always remain poor.

There are two types of poor people in the world: those who have wealth and those who do not have wealth. The two types of poor people are those who have plenty and are poor and those who have nothing and are also poor. The master is born when the outlook changes and the person finds that nothing has been achieved by chasing desires. Then he reverses the flow of the Ganges; he no longer follows outward desire; he turns inward.

And consciousness travels in two directions – either toward outer objects or toward oneself. You can either keep running to find something out there; or you can sit quietly, looking within, to find yourself. He who finds his self finds everything. You may find everything else but miss your self – then you won't have found anything. At the end you will find that you are dying a pauper, that you are dying like a beggar.

**One does not drown in a river when holding the pitcher upside down;**
**but keeping it the right way up, it will fill with water.**
**Different kinds of people, those who have learned different ways**
**of keeping the pitcher upside down,**
**have crossed the river with the master's grace.**

This is a very precious statement: *One does not drown in a river by holding the pitcher upside down...* If you want to cross the river you have to keep the pitcher upside down. The upside-down pitcher becomes helpful because you are able to cross the river with the help of such a pitcher.

*One does not drown in a river by holding the pitcher upside down; but keeping it the right way up, it will fill with water.* If you try to cross the river by keeping the pitcher the right way up, then just because of the pitcher you are sure to drown. Water cannot fill an inverted pitcher, but an upright pitcher gets filled. The way you are now, you are drowning. You must be keeping your pitcher the right way up.

The way you are now, nothing is happening besides the fact that you are drowning. You are drowning every day, every moment. One thing is certain: looking at the way you are drowning, it is clear that your misery is not decreasing, rather it is increasing. Your misery is greater today than it was yesterday – although yesterday you thought that tomorrow it would become less. Your worry is greater today than it was yesterday, and it will be greater again tomorrow. You are drowning, day by day. All your support systems, all your boats, are drowning. One thing is clear: you do not drown in a river when you hold the pitcher upside down, *...but keeping it the right way up, it will fill with water.*

Your pitcher is the right way up – turn it upside down! The direction you are running in now – turn around and run in the opposite direction. Whatever you are doing now, whatever you are thinking now, do just the opposite; think the opposite. If you are on the path of the ego, turn around and follow the path of egolessness. If you are on a thinking track, then move in the direction of no thought.

One does not drown in a river when holding the pitcher upside down; but keeping it the right way up, it will fill with water. Different kinds of people, those who have learned different ways of keeping the pitcher upside down, have crossed the river with the master's grace.

Many of those who learned the art of turning the pitcher upside down were liberated because of the master's grace. Different types of people! *Different kinds of people, those who have learned different ways...* Different types of people, different ways of swimming, different lifestyles – yet they all attain liberation. The essence of it all is: *One does not drown in a river when holding the pitcher upside down; but keeping it the right way up, it will fill with water.* The master's grace made it possible to attain liberation.

But Kabir adds something to that which can be found, in some form or other, in the teachings of all the mystics: even if you have turned your pitcher upside down, if there is no master, you won't be able to transcend the world, be liberated. The first thing is: you simply won't be able to reverse the pitcher without help from the master.

Let us assume that by mistake, accidentally, you managed to turn the pitcher upside down – even then you won't be able to attain liberation. Except the master who else will take away your egoistic standpoint that "I am swimming"? Who else will dismiss your egoistic assertion that "I have reversed the pitcher"? Who else will eliminate your ego that says "now I am not miserable," "now I am peaceful," "now I am in meditation"? And the fact is that this ego can tip the pitcher the right way up again at any moment because the pitcher is reversed only when the ego is no longer there. Then you become an upside-down pitcher. Who else will be concerned about it? Who else will keep a continuous watch over you? Who else will go on drawing your attention, reminding you and waking you?

The master is one who has himself crossed over, one who has attained. He alone can alert you. For example, if ten people are traveling together and are passing through a thick forest and it is dangerous, what will they do? They will take turns staying awake. While nine sleep, one will stay awake so that if there is some danger he can wake up the others. When his turn comes to sleep, he will wake up the next one who has to stay awake. One of them has to stay awake because if there is some danger while they are all asleep no one will know what has happened.

A master means one who is awake and will be helpful while you are asleep. Again and again you will go to sleep. Again and again the pitcher will turn the right way up while you are asleep. You will keep forgetting, keep missing, again and again.

Once it happened...

There was a Sufi mystic. No one knows his real name but he is known by the name of Nassaaj or Khairnassaaj. Once, he was lying under a tree... He was very healthy looking. A man was on his way to find a slave; he wanted to buy a strongly-built slave. Seeing a man reclining under the tree, so relaxed, and wearing torn clothes like that of a beggar, he thought that the man must be a slave who had run away. He looked like a slave on the run, hiding in the forest. He looked like a man who had a strong body and who would be of use. The man approached him and asked if he was a slave on the run.

Nassaaj opened his eyes and told the man he was right. He had run away and he was a slave. What he really meant was that he had run away from God and that had turned him into a slave. He became very famous later on. This is where the difficulty is: there is no meeting point between what a worldly person says and how a mystic speaks. So Nassaaj said: "You are right. I am an escapee and I am a slave."

That man said: "Great! I found you at the right time. I am in search of a slave. I am ready to be your master; come follow me. You are in search of a master, aren't you?"

The "slave" replied, "You are a strange man! That is exactly my search – I am looking for a master."

The man took him home and said: "Now I am your master and you are my slave. Do what I ask you to do."

The "slave" said: "That is exactly what I want, that someone should tell me what I should and should not do. Whatever I do turns out to be of no use. Doing it myself has got me into this mess. I am so glad I met you."

The man began to feel a little suspicious – either the slave was mad or something was wrong somewhere; maybe they were both speaking a different language. But the man thought, "What does it matter? This man is willing and that's enough. Moreover, I got him for free, without any bargaining. And the man is strong and healthy."

The mystic started working for the man. This worldly man found the mystic so kind that he named him Khair. *Khair* means kind, good. The man was a weaver by profession so he taught the slave weaving. His other name became Nassaaj; *Nassaaj* means the cloth weaver. Thus his name became Khairnassaaj. He served his master well for ten years. He served him so well, with such regard, and worked so hard that the master began to feel bothered that he was perhaps exploiting him.

He felt, "I have not spent a penny on him, but have earned so much money because of him. I am actually exploiting him. Now the time has come for me to free him."

He called him and said, "Enough is enough; you have proved yourself to be very useful, but it bothers me that I am exploiting you. I cannot stand this worry anymore. So I hereby set you free. Now you have become your own master."

Nassaaj said, "You have done a great favor in making me my own master. I also learned much. Being with you I learned the art of how to be a servant. And now there is no distance between God and myself. Since the time I learned how to be a slave my ego has broken down. And as the ego broke down my slavery began to disappear too. See, even you are setting me free. I have certainly become freed, but now what do you think about yourself? How long do you wish to remain a slave?"

The language spoken by worldly people and by the mystics may sound the same but it can never be the same. Their gestalt, their perceptions are different. You see one thing while the mystics see something else.

Kabir is saying that you function so sleepily that unless there is someone to keep you constantly awake it will be impossible for you to ever wake up; it will be impossible for your pitcher to always remain upside down. You are bound to sink. And who knows in how many past lives and how many times you have drowned! Slowly, slowly you have become accustomed to drowning. Drowning has become your habit; and now you are not even bothered if you do drown. You think that is how life is.

If a prisoner has spent many years in prison, he believes that that is what life is all about. When long-term prisoners are about to leave the prison, the other prisoners ask them when they plan to come back. Prisoners begin to feel at home in prison; they feel very uncomfortable when they are out of prison. It is just habit. You cannot find anywhere safer than a prison – no hassle, no concerns, no worries. Guarded from all sides – as if you were an emperor. Such huge walls that no one can enter. You can sleep at night, carefree. No worries about food – there is never a famine in a prison. Food will certainly be available. No worry about finding a job; no one there is ever without work. Nobody is jobless in prison. Absolutely no worries – totally safe and sound.

So when someone comes out of prison he is very afraid of the open sky. Try taking your parrot out of his cage and releasing him into the open sky and see how he reacts. You will see the parrot is scared, trembling. He won't stay out long before he comes back to the cage. Leave the cage open and he will fly into it by himself. Try to pull a parrot out of his cage and free him – he will resist and hold on to the cage tightly. He will strike your hand with his beak because he wants you to close the cage door and leave him alone. Where else can such happiness be found as when you are in a cage? To be in the open sky is dangerous.

You have become used to drowning. Prison has become your home and you have decorated it very well. You have painted its inner walls nicely. You have forgotten that where you are now you are actually sinking every day.

And… Different kinds of people, those who have learned different ways of keeping the pitcher upside down, have crossed the river with the master's grace. So it is almost impossible for you to cross over and be liberated merely by your own efforts. You need an awakened person who will keep on alerting you. That is what guru prasad, a master's grace or blessings, means. What is guru prasad? It is prasad or blessing because he does not take anything away from you. In fact, you have nothing you can give him. It is a prasad or blessing because it is an unconditional gift. He gives it to you and it is enough that you accept it; nothing needs to be given back in return. That is why whatsoever a master gives is a blessing. You can never return the favor.

There is an old proverb: "You can repay a debt to your father, you can repay a debt to your mother, you can repay a debt to your teacher, but how can you ever repay the debt to your master?" What in the world will you be able to give in return so that your debt can be repaid?

Ananda, a disciple of Buddha, asked, "What shall we give you so that we can repay our debt to you?"

Buddha replied, "Just do one thing: go and wake up those who are asleep. There is no other way."

There is no other way to repay the debt to the master. That's why we call it *prasad* – whatsoever he gives is *prasad*, a blessing. He gives a pinch of ashes and that becomes a blessing. With his very touch the ashes become like gold. The master gives, and his very giving makes everything precious. Even a pinch of ash given by an awakened person is invaluable. Gold in the hands of an unconscious person is nothing but ashes because the real question is of being awake or being asleep. Being awake everything turns into gold, being asleep everything turns into dust.

Unconsciousness destroys everything; it is nothing but death. Awakening makes everything alive and conscious – it is life, great life.

**Sitting in his cave, he watches the world within**
**and pays no attention to the world outside.**
**Conversely, the arrow, instead of hitting the target,**
**pierces the hunter himself.**
**Only a courageous person can figure this out.**

The seeker sits inside the cave – the heart cave. *Sitting in his cave, he watches the world within and pays no attention to the world outside.* He doesn't look outside; he looks within. The way to awaken is to look within. Close your eyes, shut your ears, keep your hands relaxed, let your body be such as if it doesn't exist – and look within!

Sitting in his cave, he watches the world within and pays no attention to the world outside. Conversely, the arrow, instead of hitting the target, pierces the hunter himself. Only a courageous person can figure this out. And then a phenomenon occurs which only can be understood by someone who is very fearless – only a courageous person, someone who is very brave and daring – only he can make sense out of it. ...the arrow, instead of hitting the target, pierces the hunter himself.

You may shoot an arrow and the arrow, instead of going toward the bird and hitting it, turns back and pierces the hunter. It is an *ulatbansi*, a riddle. Now your consciousness is like an arrow going outward – all your targets are outside. Someone wants to make money – that is his target. Someone wants something else. It is a vast world, there are endless targets, and the arrow of your consciousness is going in the direction of these targets.

There is also a reverse journey where the arrow of your consciousness does not go outward; you close your eyes and it turns inward. You look inside. Your eyes become inward-looking; your way of seeing changes. Your consciousness begins to flow inward as if the Ganges were flowing back toward its source – Gangotri. Your consciousness moves toward its original source – you take it back to where it came from. The very source becomes the target. Then, and only then, does the supreme phenomenon take place; then you experience the ultimate benediction.

But Kabir says: *Only a courageous person can figure this out*. It is not a matter for the cowards; only the brave can do it. That is why we call Mahavira, *Mahavira*. His original name was Vardhamana. The day his arrow turned in the opposite direction we named him Mahavira. Vardhamana died, Mahavira was born. We called him Mahavira because it was an act of ultimate courage.

Remember, religion is not for cowards. You will find cowardly, scared, frightened people in temples – on their knees with folded hands, but they are not religious people. There too, their arrows are going outward. There too, they are asking for worldly things.

It happened…

Vivekananda's father died; they were poor. He had left debts and there was no way to pay them back. On top of this, Vivekananda was lost in a different kind of world – he was overcome by Ramakrishna. So now there was no way out. Vivekananda was spending his time in the spiritual commune, in *satsang* with Ramakrishna or in the company of other seekers.

They had large debts. His widowed mother was at home but because of the situation, meals often didn't get cooked. There were days when, returning home, Vivekananda would find food enough for only one person – either he could eat or his mother. So he would tell his mother he wouldn't be eating at home, he had an invitation for dinner at his friend's home. He would ask her to go ahead and eat the meal. He would go out and walk around in the streets with an empty stomach, drink some water from a nearby tap, and return home smiling and pretending he had had a great dinner. He would enter his home, give a good burp, and describing the dishes, tell his mother how delicious the food had been so that she felt convinced.

When Ramakrishna came to know that the situation was so bad, he said to Vivekananda: "Things cannot go on like this. Are you mad? Why don't you go and ask the mother goddess for what you need? Her statue is in the temple; go and ask her for what you want."

Vivekananda went into the temple while Ramakrishna remained sitting outside. One hour passed. Vivekananda came out blissful, with tears rolling from his eyes. Ramakrishna said, "Did you ask?"

Vivekananda said, "I am glad you reminded me; I completely forgot to ask."

He was sent back inside the temple, came out again after an hour, very happy. Ramakrishna said, "Did you ask?"

Vivekananda said, "I cannot ask because when the mother goddess herself is before me what is there to ask for? And does she not know it already? What is there to ask from God? Let his will be done; we cannot be wiser than him. If the divine wishes it to be this way, then there must be some reason behind it. So if you ask me to, I will go inside again; I cannot say no to you. But once I am there I get lost in ecstasy. I am showered with such joy that I forget my stomach is hungry. No. To hold a begging bowl is not possible. I won't be able to ask for anything."

Ramakrishna said, "I also thought that if you ask then I will know that you are a worldly person and that you will not become spiritual. You can walk this path only if you don't ask."

Only those who are brave and courageous can travel on the spiritual path. *Only a courageous person can figure this out.* Only those who dare to enter into the unknown can walk on this path, those who are willing to drop the trivial and disappear into the infinite. *Only a courageous person can figure this out.*

***He sings and yet sings not;***
***and even while saying not a word, his song continues.***

*He sings and yet sings not...* The seeker sings and yet actually he is not the singer. It is not a song. It is not music. It is simply a joyful state of being. *He sings and yet sings not; and even while saying not a word, his song continues.* The seeker says not a word and yet the song continues.

These are *ulatbansis*, riddles. You may find Meera and Chaitanya singing but Kabir would say they never sing, that there is total silence within them, that not a word is uttered. On the other hand, you find Buddha and Mahavira sitting silently, not saying a word. And Kabir would say, they are singing, there is melody resounding within them – the soundless sound.

This riddle describes the state a mystic is in – he speaks and yet he does not say a word. You don't utter a word and yet you are speaking. Your lack of words is only on the surface; inside you go on talking. A mystic speaks but not a word is uttered by him; speaking happens just outwardly; inwardly there remains a profound silence. A mystic is silent and yet he is saying something; but his way of speaking, even when he is silent, is very different from your talking even when you are silent. When a mystic is silent he speaks through his silence; in that moment he tells you also to be silent. In that moment he is telling you to be just the way he is. In that moment he is telling you that you are invited, the doors are open: enter inside and be silent. And if you can sit silently near a mystic, then you will certainly learn all that is worth learning.

When a mystic speaks the only thing he is saying is: be silent. When a mystic is quiet even then he is saying: be silent. Silence is the door; being free from words in every sense is the path.

> ***He sings and yet sings not;***
> ***and even while saying not a word his song continues.***
> ***He simply watches the drama and the sounds happening all around***
> ***while rising in love for the infinite.***

He looks at the entire scene – all the ups and downs, the whole drama in which people are playing their roles – as if it were nothing but a play. He remains just a watcher … *while rising in love for the infinite.* On the one hand, he sees the whole world as a play; on the other hand, his love for the infinite grows.

As long as you take this world to be real, your love for it will continue to grow, because love grows for that which appears to be real. When you take this world to be just a play... But actually you are facing a great difficulty: you will hardly see this world as a play, in fact, when you go to see a movie you take *that* to be real! What happens in a movie theater? People are wiping away their tears. It is good it is dark and no one can see them. Their handkerchiefs get wet; they carry two handkerchiefs. It is good it is dark so no one can see people quickly wiping their tears and again sitting normally. And actually, it is just a film; there is nothing there except a play of light and shadow.

Mystics say that this whole world is nothing but a play of light and shadow. Mystics turn this world into a play, while you take even a play to be samsara, the world. While watching a play you cry, you laugh, you feel happy. You feel sad if someone in the play is murdered. Or you suddenly sit up straight, seeing someone pushing a dagger into someone else's chest – as if something bad has actually happened. If you see even a drama, a play, as reality, how will you take this world, this samsara, as a play? And the art lies in turning the world into a play.

***He simply watches the drama and the sounds happening all around***
***while rising in love for the infinite.***
***He becomes a witness to his speech and his deeds.***

***All this is a very strange story that cannot be described.***

The mystic looks at the entire play; he not only looks at the play of the world as just a play, but he also looks at his own acts, his behavior, his body, his deeds and his movements: he is a watcher. A mystic also gets hungry, but his feeling hungry is of a different kind. When you get hungry you feel *you* are hungry – "I am hungry." When a mystic gets hungry he knows his body is hungry. He doesn't attach the hunger to himself. When your foot gets hurt, you say you have been hurt. When a mystic gets hurt he simply sees that the foot has been hurt and then does whatever needs to be done – but it is all a play.

A mystic remains a witness – and to have a witnessing consciousness is the most mysterious state in the world. That's why Kabir says, *He becomes a witness to his speech and his deeds. Niju ke johai* means one becomes a watcher. He sees all but with a witnessing consciousness. In that state nothing touches him, nothing binds him. He passes through everything and yet remains untouched. He lives in the world but does not allow the world to enter him. He is in the world but not of the world. That is the characteristic of a seeker, a *sadhu*.

*All this is a very strange story that cannot be described.* And this is a very strange story – it cannot be told. The reason is, the day you come to see the world as a play, how can you *not* enter into the world of mystery? The day you come to know that even your own life is nothing more than a part to be played, then what will be left for you to worry about in life? What suffering, what agony, will there be left in your life? This is all an indescribable story.

**Turning back, the earth inverts and pierces the sky, so the ancients say.**

And the ancients who have known have stated that the earth inverts and pierces the sky. Your consciousness gets inverted and pierces the whole world.

**Uncontained elixir showers so much that rivers begin to flow within.**

Kabir says: **One who is showered with this elixir becomes immortal and keeps tasting the divine endlessly.**

And the elixir showers; it showers all around you in such a way that you don't need a glass to contain it – you get filled with it. With no container, the elixir showers... And when it showers, it doesn't shower into cups and glasses; as it showers, it breaks through all the dams and barriers. It turns into an ocean around you – so much so that *...rivers begin to flow within.* It showers in such a way that rivers inside you get filled – the same as when the rain falls from the sky and the dry riverbeds get filled. It fills you from the inside in the same way, it goes on showering all around.

Kabir says: *One who is showered with this elixir becomes immortal...* And the one on whom this elixir showers lives forever; there is no death anymore, the person: *...becomes immortal and keeps tasting the divine...* And continues to taste the divine forever, for eternity.

There are two kinds of tastes in this world. One taste is that of the body; the other taste is that of the being. The taste that you get while eating food is the taste of the body. What you taste while making love is the taste of the body. The fragrance coming from flowers gives you the taste of the body.

There is still another taste, which you don't get through the physical senses. That taste is the taste of the divine. But that is possible only when your Ganges swallows the ocean; when your arrow turns back and hits you; when you set out on a return journey. That is possible only when: *One does not drown in a river by holding the pitcher upside down; but keeping it the right way up, it fills with water. Different kinds of people, those who have learned different ways of keeping the pitcher upside down, have crossed the river with the master's grace.*

The only secret is to become an upside-down pitcher. The day the waters of the world no longer fill you, on that very day the divine will shower on you. If the pitcher is the right way up, it will get filled with the world and you will be drowned.

You have drowned many times before – now be alert! A long time has already passed – now be aware!

Enough for today.

# 9
# The Tenth Door

**The elixir is continuously flowing in the heavenly cave**
**where, without any instrument, an unstruck sound arises.**
**Only when one understands it properly does one meditate on it.**
**And then one hears the unstruck sound**
**and sees lotuses blossoming without being in the pond.**
**It is then that consciousness will climb onto the lotus and dance.**
**And the swan is playing merrily on top of them.**
**There is a shining light visible without the moon,**
**and the swan is able to see it all around, in all directions.**

**When the evolved person sees that which is at the tenth door,**
**he goes into a deep sleep.**
**At that moment, death does not come close, and lustful desire,**
**anger, pride, and greed burn away.**
**The thirst of many lives is quenched,**
**and all sins and karmas are burned away.**

Kabir says: **Listen, O seekers, it is then that one attains immortality;**
**then there is no death.**

Religion is a search for the elixir.

In man's life nothing is more certain than death. All else is just coincidence – it may happen or it may not. Death is not a coincidence – it is bound to happen. Regardless of how many ways one may find to escape it, they will all prove useless. No one has ever been able to escape from it. Except for man, no animal, bird, plant, or rock is conscious of death. They also die, but they don't know they are going to die. That's why, except man, no other animal can ever give birth to religion.

Religion is born out of an awareness about death. The deeper this awareness is, the more intense the search for religion will be. Religion would be lost if there were no death. If man was never going to die, then all the temples and mosques would collapse. That is why, as he begins to grow old, man starts thinking about religion; as death approaches, he begins to think about it.

In youth, he can forget the temple. At that time, life is at its highest point; life is ascending, life has momentum. He is high on the enjoyment of life. As he begins to climb down the mountain, as old age approaches, he begins to lose confidence. All certainties start crumbling and life seems to be slipping out of his hands. When he hears the steps of death approaching, the search for religion begins.

The search for religion begins because of death, so naturally the search for religion has to be a search for the elixir of life. Until someone has experienced that elixir, he will continue to live in fear, in trembling, regardless of how much he may try to forget death or try to hide it. And we have made great efforts to hide death.

There is one thing that needs to be understood about this. There are two types of cultures in the world: one which represses sex, hides sex, and another which represses death, hides death. The West hides death while it gives full freedom to sex. This freedom increases day by day while death is absolutely swept under the carpet. In the East, it is sex that has been repressed, not death. So these are the two types of cultures.

Sex and death are the two ends of life; sex means birth, sex is the source of birth. If you repress birth, you will have to encounter death. Your eyes will become fixed on death, because there are only two facts in life: either you go on looking at life – and then you can forget about death – or, on the other hand, you look at death and then you can forget about birth, The East has decided to forget about birth, to forget about sex – as if it didn't exist: to arrange life in such a way that man will not come to know that there is anything like sex in life.

Try to understand this: if a Martian suddenly came down to Earth and wandered into Indian towns and villages, interacted with people, and visited shops and offices, he would never know there is something like sex in people's lives. We have kept it hidden in the darkness of the night. The Martian will never come to know about it because it doesn't show anywhere outwardly. We have kept it hidden in our minds.

A culture that hides sex will have to look at death closely. That's why the East became religious, because if you look at death intently, then the search for the elixir will inevitably begin. The West didn't repress sex; it repressed death. That is why so much effort is made there to forget about death. Talking about death is considered improper. In the East, talking about sex is considered improper; if you talk about sex then you are regarded as having no manners, you are uncivilized.

In the West, death is never talked about; death is kept out of discussions. You can talk about sex as much as you like, just never mention death. In the event of someone dying, people have invented expressions to hide death; they say the person has "gone to his heavenly abode." Most of us will actually go to hell, but when someone dies we say he has gone to heaven.

Instead of mentioning death, it sounds sweet to say "gone to his heavenly abode," saying that a person has gone to Vaikuntha, Lord Vishnu's abode, heaven. In that way it appears that the person didn't die – that he is still somewhere. This is a trick to hide death. Sometimes people say someone has "dropped his garments" – as if he just left behind the clothes he was wearing, as if he didn't really die, as if he is somewhere.

We have invented a thousand and one expressions to hide the fact of death – and more so in the West. There, when someone dies, they decorate him with flowers and take the body away with great fanfare and meticulous arrangements – as if nothing like death has happened; as if nothing has happened to cause sorrow or mourning; as if a ceremony. This is a way to forget death. That's why we build cemeteries outside the town. In the West, even at the cemetery, they write on the headstone that such and such a person "is sleeping here"; that is, the person is not really dead – just asleep, in eternal sleep. All these words are simply an effort to hide the fact that something is broken, gone, finished.

Because the West has been hiding death, science was born. Once death is removed from human consciousness, then what remains is birth, sex and life. Then the attention goes toward how life can be made more comfortable, how it can be made more colorful, more aesthetic; how one can build better homes, better roads, better bathrooms – and thus the entire consciousness became engaged in serving life. Death was forgotten, the idea was just to make life more comfortable. That is why science developed in the West.

The East has forgotten sex and so life has remained neglected. There is no concern for how people live. If someone is living in squalor, it is of no concern. Whether someone in a hut is dead or alive, whether someone is hungry or thirsty, whether the hut is stinking, or disease-carrying flies are hovering all around – all this is not of the least concern. The whole thing is taken with the view that after all life – however it is – is nothing but a short play, which will come to an end. Death is the real thing, and it is fast approaching – whether you live in a hut or you live in a palace.

So in the East we hide both life and birth; that is why science did not develop here, but religion did. The day someone sees both with open eyes is the day a revolution will take place in its true sense. If you hide one and look only at the other, you will have a partial understanding – you will remain incomplete. And a half-truth is worse than an untruth because a half-truth appears to be true, but actually it is not the truth at all. Only the whole truth is the truth. And, as yet, no culture in the world has been born, which has seen the whole truth.

I want to make you the carriers of that very culture; that you begin to see the whole truth. Of course, there is birth, and life has to be lived in the right way – knowing that death is bound to occur. Science must be developed so that we may discover the comforts of life; religion has to grow so that through it we may discover the elixir.

Just working with science one is bound to end up finding death. That's the reason why science ended up with the atom bomb and the hydrogen bomb. If you go on searching in this direction you are sure to end up with death. You will find only that which you have been hiding, because while searching you will get what was being repressed. No matter where and how you may have hidden it, you know you have hidden it. No matter how much you may try to forget it, the fact is that you know its whereabouts – and whatever you have hidden will go on affecting your unconscious.

Once a scientist finished his lifelong research. The work he had been engaged in for fifty years was completed. He came running home and saw his little son sitting at the door. He said, "Son, you will be happy to know that my research is over. I have achieved my goal. I have discovered a wonderful thing which I was in search of for a long time."

His son asked, "What is that wonderful thing?"

The father replied, "I have discovered a secret so that, if I wish, I can kill all the people in the world in just one second."

The son said, "Then first show me how you will kill me, Daddy."

His son was very happy and, like children are, always eager to be the first. He asked to be the first one his father demonstrated it on. Hearing this, the scientist became sad.

Today, all scientists are sad because unknowingly they have found death. Actually, they set out to discover life, but ended up finding death. They found what was previously hidden. People in the West have discovered the clue to death: how to kill easily, quickly, speedily and skillfully. Now the entire world can be destroyed in a second. It is so strange – they set out to find life but found death instead!

People in the East went on hiding sex so much that mentally they have become obsessed with sex. They set out searching for celibacy – which they didn't find – and instead they ended up with wicked lust. For twenty-four hours their minds are tuned in to sex. And as long as you are busy with sex, there is no way you can tune in to Kabir. As long as sex is imbedded in every cell of your being, the world Kabir is talking about – that tenth door – will never open.

Sex is the first door; how can someone who is stuck at the first door reach the tenth door? The tenth door is the last one. If you get caught up at the very first door, then how can you reach the tenth door? But what happened is: the more people in the East repressed sex, the more they got obsessed with it; the more people repressed death in the West, the more they encountered death.

What I want to say to you is that whatsoever you hide, it will manifest sooner or later. Don't hide anything. Look at the facts of life. In life, birth is as much a fact as death is. Watch birth as well as death. Then you will be able to transcend both. That which you hide out of fear will keep standing in your way, again and again. No one has ever been free from fear – what is needed is fearlessness.

Romain Rolland has written a very precious statement in his diary. He says: "I know just one kind of fearlessness" – and one who has learned to be fearless has learned everything – "and that is: try to look at life in its totality, neither hide nor add anything to it. Look at life as it is – totally. And live life, experience it fully – as it is. You will be in trouble if you hide it. That will make life incomplete, fragmented. And if you repress it, then again you will be in trouble."

Remember, sex is the source of life and it comes to an end in death. That which begins with birth ends in death; and that which existed before birth will continue to be, even after death.

If you look at birth and death closely, your perception will soon gain such a luminosity and sharpness that you will be able to see beyond them both. If you hide one end, you will be so scared, so afraid, that you will be unable to see anything – your eyes will be filled with fear. And for someone who carries fear in his eyes it is as if his eyes are covered by smoke. Then you will look for a rationalization – and anyone can find a rationalization. But logic and rationalizations do not reflect truth; even insane people can find logical explanations.

Once, Mulla Nasruddin went to a psychiatrist. Just to test how his brain was working, the psychiatrist asked, "Tell me, Nasruddin, what will happen if I cut off one of your ears?"

Nasruddin replied, "Obviously, I will be able to hear only half of what I normally hear; my listening capacity will be cut by half."

The psychiatrist asked, "And what will happen if I cut off your second ear?"

Nasruddin replied, "Then I won't be able to see."

The psychiatrist was puzzled. He said, "What do you mean? You are talking strangely! Why will you be unable to see if I cut off your second ear?"

Nasruddin replied, "You idiot, won't my glasses fall off?"

Eccentric people have their own logic – you cannot beat their arguments. What Nasruddin is saying certainly makes sense. When you hide one thing in life and make another so important, you pay no real attention to either, so a kind of eccentricity enters your heart, your life.

To be eccentric means to be imbalanced; it means you have leaned more toward one side. To have balance means to be in the middle. It is like a man walking on a tightrope: after he leans to the left, he will immediately lean to the right so that he does not lose his balance. He has to maintain his balance every moment. Maintaining balance is not just a one-off thing. It is not as if once you have managed it, it is done forever; you have to manage it every moment. At every step the tightrope walker has to maintain a balance because each step is a new step, it is a new situation. It is not that once you have attained your balance you can then go to sleep.

Life is also like walking a tightrope where you should not make a choice; rather you have to maintain a balance between the two. If you bend too far to the left, you will fall to the left side; if you bend too far to the right, you will fall to the right side. Death is bound to occur whichever side you may fall; you are safe only if you stay in the middle.

So you neither need to get identified with birth nor with death. You do not need to make sex everything, neither do you need to make the desire to be free from death everything. Neither is sex everything nor is *moksha*, liberation, everything. You have to transcend both. No desire should be left – not even that of attaining *moksha*; only then will you be able to go beyond both. And the moment someone goes beyond both, the wonderful events of which Kabir is talking begin to take place in his life.

Such phenomena are beyond logic and will sound very contradictory if expressed in language; whichever way you say it, it will appear incomplete. No matter what you say, a lot will remain unsaid. Whatever you may say, it will feel as if a boundary has been created around that which is unlimited. And no matter what you may say, the listener will think you are talking as if you are drunk because the listener will find no connection between his own experience and what he is hearing.

You have only one experience of life and that is of the first door. Even if you go very deep, still your experience will not go higher than the ninth door. You have no experience of the tenth door.

Our bodies have nine doors: two eyes, two nostrils, a mouth, two ears, an anus, and the sex organ – these are the nine doors. Your whole life is confined to these doors. And all these doors belong to the body. The tenth door is the *sahasrar*. It is in the body and yet not of the body; through these nine doors you connect with other physical bodies. What will you see through your eyes? Obviously, you will see someone else. What will you hear through your ears? You will hear what others are speaking. What will you touch through your hand? You will touch someone else.

The tenth door is the door to the infinite; it is the door of existence. At one end is sex and at the other end is the tenth door. That which is born out of sex meets death and one who goes through the tenth door attains to the immortal. The physical body is born out of sex; the physical body is subject to death. Through the tenth door you get a glimpse of the bodiless which knows no death. That tenth door is in your head and the whole play, the entire drama, takes place between the first and the tenth doors.

You enter the world through the first door; you leave the world through the tenth door. The first door says "Entrance"; the tenth door says "Exit." And one thing is certain: where there is an entrance there will also be an exit. You have entered the world through sex. Sex organs are the door through which you entered this world. This, too, we have forgotten, we never think about this fact. No person ever thinks that he came into this world because his parents made love to each other. You might find it sinful to even think such a thing: your parents making love. You may think, this is only done by the wrong type of people!

Have you ever thought consciously, have you ever paid attention to how you entered in this world? You will find it disgusting even to think about your parents making love. It will cause you great concern just thinking that you have come through a sex organ. We have deliberately forgotten such things. We have kept them hidden. But these are truths and they will not become untrue just by hiding them – they will remain true.

You have never given any thought to how you came into this world. You came through the first door, but if you remain stuck at that very door, then you will always be in this world. There will be no movement in your life if you just remain standing at the entrance. You will simply move round and round like an ox driving a water wheel – and you have been moving like this for countless lives.

Just as there is a door to enter, there is also a door to exit. Searching for this exit is what religion is all about. Religion means searching for the immortal. There is certainly death in this life. As long as you believe that this life is all there is, you will be afraid of death and until death comes you will be sitting on a volcano. Death can happen at any moment – and it certainly will; not even a moment can be trusted!

There was a Sufi mystic, Baijid.

Once he was on his way to make the Hajj pilgrimage. Those were the days when you could buy things cheaply: for one paisa you could buy a day's food and take care of a day's expenses. So as he was about to start his journey with one paisa in his pocket, one of his rich devotees said, "What are you doing? Has anyone ever heard of leaving for the Hajj carrying just one paisa?"

That man had brought a bag filled with gold coins with him. He said, "Please take this with you. Can anyone ever go on the Hajj with just one paisa? It is such a long journey; going and coming back will take at least six months."

Baijid said, "I don't mind taking your bag, but you have to assure me of one thing: that I will live longer than just today. Can you assure me that I will be alive tomorrow? I will accept your bag if you assure me that I will be alive tomorrow."

The rich man said, "How can I assure you that you will be alive tomorrow? Who can be sure of what is going to happen tomorrow?"

Then Baijid replied, "This one paisa is enough for today. If there is no certainty about tomorrow, then what is the point in making any arrangements for it?"

In that crowd there was another mystic present. At this time Baijid had not yet attained enlightenment, though he must have been quite close to it – just on the brink; the jump was yet to happen. That's why he was on his way to the Hajj pilgrimage.

Have you ever heard of wise men going on a pilgrimage? But he was certainly a man of deep understanding and that is why he told the rich man to keep the gold for himself, for his own use. He was willing to worry about the next day only if someone could give him certainty about tomorrow.

So the mystic in the crowd got up and started laughing. Baijid ran after him and asked him why he was laughing. He replied, "If you are certain about this one day then where is the problem with being certain about tomorrow? If you can keep one paisa, then the matter is over – then whether you keep one paisa with you or one crore, what difference does it make? Are you sure of today? And if you have so much trust in one paisa, then how much trust do you have in God? None – you don't have any!"

Baijid dropped that paisa right there and then. And it is said that as the coin dropped Baijid attained enlightenment.

There is no certainty whether you will be alive the next moment and yet you make such elaborate plans and arrangements. The fact is that you will die while still working on your plans. Money, wealth, is like fuel for the journey – it is not the destination. But there are people who just go on accumulating fuel. Their houses are full of fuel. Even when there is no room for them to live inside – because of this accumulation – they will start living outside the house. They keep getting ready for the pilgrimage; obviously, they can set out for the journey only after they have completed all the arrangements. And the fact is that, in this world, nothing ever gets completed, and so people are never able to go on the pilgrimage. They simply die accumulating fuel.

Wealth, money, is not the destination. Money is simply a means of exchange on the road. And your very hold on money shows that you are sure about tomorrow. The fact is: you cannot be sure even for a moment because death can knock on your door at any time. Death is hidden in life itself. Death has entered you from the moment you were born. Right at the time of birth it is determined how you will die and when you will die. The life of each chromosome which makes up your body is decided at that time, whether it will live for seventy years or eighty years. That's all your age will be – though if you live in a reasonably orderly manner then maybe you will live a few years longer than that, and if you live in a disorderedly manner then maybe you will live a few years less. But by and large, the age when death will come is decided at birth. Don't just sit at the entrance; discover the exit too! Buddha has called it the door to nirvana. That is the *sahasrar*.

Hindus grow a lock of hair on the crown of their heads, on the highest point, which simply symbolizes *sahasrar* – that there is a center there. But nothing happens just by growing a lock of hair. People shave their heads, leaving just a lock of hair. The lock of hair was simply meant to show that the tenth door exists there – pay attention to it! Of course, many people grow locks of hair, but no one meditates. Their real attention remains only on the first door regardless of how long their lock of hair may grow. It is called a *choti* because it is at the highest point, the pinnacle.

The crown, the summit of life, remains hidden there; that is why it is called the *choti* – the crown. You may not have thought before why it is called *choti*. It is the peak; it is the Gourishankar. That is where the last door of life is hidden, from where you will be able to enter godliness.

These statements are uttered after having attained to the tenth door. That is why it will be difficult to understand them: your logic will cause difficulty. You will think, "How can this be possible?" But don't be in a hurry to come to a conclusion. Conclude only after experiencing. Then you will also begin dancing as Kabir must have danced.

**The elixir is continuously flowing in the heavenly cave...**

"Heavenly cave" is the name of the tenth door because after that the heavens begin, the infinite sky begins; all boundaries disappear, the limitless begins; the form disappears and the formless begins – hence "heavenly cave." *The elixir is continuously flowing in the heavenly cave*... An endless elixir is flowing, dripping in that heavenly cave.

You have experienced only one kind of juiciness and that is of sexual intercourse, when your semen flows and you feel momentary pleasure. The kind of juiciness that Kabir is talking about is if you imagine that the whole of existence is showering upon you, as if you have taken a shower under it. Every cell of your body is bathing in it and every cell is dancing with joy.

And this is endless; once it starts it never stops. It is eternal; it is not momentary. It is not like it rains now and then there will be a drought. It is showering even at this very moment, but you are not aware of it. It is showering even now but you have not become conscious of it yet. The treasure is available right this moment, but you have not paid any attention to it. It has always been showering – it is the very nature of life that the elixir goes on showering endlessly.

**The elixir is continuously flowing in the heavenly cave**
**where, without any instrument, an unstruck sound arises.**
**Only when one understands it properly does one meditate on it.**

Kabir is saying: ...*where, without any instrument, an unstruck sound arises*. There are two types of sound: one type of sound is *ahat dhvani*, that which is heard when one object strikes another object. For example, when I clap two hands and they strike each other. This sound is called *ahat dhvani* because it happens by striking the two. Whether you play drums, or sitar or any other instrument, there is striking, all are *ahat dhvani*.

But the divine is one, existence is one. There is no other hand to clap, but there, too, a kind of music goes on. That music is unstruck – *anahat*. Hence the mystics go on saying: Find the unstruck, find the *anahat*. So *anahat* means one hand clapping.

Zen mystics in Japan tell their disciples to go and find out how there can be only one hand clapping. This is their special *sadhana* or spiritual discipline. The seeker takes years to figure this out. He thinks up various ways, but the master says: "No, you need not bother to tell me. I will surely hear when the clapping begins to sound. You don't have to tell me; when it begins to sound your whole being will be resonating."

*The elixir is continuously flowing in the heavenly cave where, without any instrument, an unstruck sound arises.* There is no instrument, nothing is sounding, nothing is striking and yet there is an ongoing roar of endless sound. Hindus call this sound *omkar*. Om is the symbol of that sound.

Nanak says: Om alone is the true name. Just that sound of Om alone is the name of truth – there is no other name for it. All other names are invented by man. The word *Om* means nothing. Om is not just a word, it is also a sound.

And whenever a person reaches the tenth door in this world he hears that sound; though, of course, people have written it differently in their own languages. Hindus call it *Om*. Muslims, Jews, and Christians call it *amen*, so their prayer ends with amen. This is another form of Om – the sound heard at the tenth door. Its interpretation may differ because with sound the difficulty is how one will interpret it. For example, when a railway train is moving, how you identify its moving sound will depend on you. How will you say it: chack…chack? Bhak…bhak? Phak… phak? What will you say? It is the same moving train, but if you already have a preconceived idea, then you are bound to hear that sound.

For example, the Hindus believe the sound is *Omkar* – Om. Now if someone has already developed a notion, then whenever he hears the resounding sound he will hear nothing but Om. Whatever concept you may have in mind will give form to the sound. But the mystics all over the world have mentioned the same characteristics for this sound. And the main characteristic is: ...*where, without any instrument, an unstruck sound arises.* The sound is not coming out of anything. Try to understand this a little.

Whatever is born out of something is bound to die, because that which is born out of two things will have a limited range and power. For example, if I clap my two hands it will resound only in proportion to how much power I put into it. As the power runs out, the clapping sound will disappear. Your voice will resound depending on how loudly you scream. The sound of your voice will disappear as the power you have put into it runs out. So the power and limits of whatever is born are determined by birth itself.

Suppose a man and a woman meet and as a hereditary chain their parents, grandparents and great grandparents lived for a hundred years, then the clapping sound coming out of their hands – their child – can live for a hundred years. Then there is another hereditary chain of parents where in their family people died at the age of fifty, so the clapping sound coming out of their hands – their child – will die at the age of fifty.

So, your age-span can be roughly worked out. If the age of your past five or six generations is added together and an average is figured out, then that will be your age; it is not too difficult.

Go back three or four generations and add together the ages of your parents, your mother's parents, your father's parents. Add the ages of ten people and divide them by ten and the answer will give you your approximate age-span. Maybe it will be seventy or seventy-one or maybe sixty-nine – that will be your age. How long the clapping sound of two hands can last will depend upon the power applied by the hands. So whenever anything is born, its end is determined right in its birth. How much power it has...

Unstruck sound will never end because it is not born of anything. That's why we call God eternal, immortal. God is not born of anything. If indeed God had been born, then he too would have to die. Then, Brahma, Vishnu and Mahesh would die because they were born. Then, Rama, Krishna and Buddha would die because they were born. But that which does not die, from which they are born and into which they finally merge after death, that truly is *brahman*. That alone is the one true name – *ek omkar satnam*.

*...where, without any instrument, an unstruck sound arises. Only when one understands it properly does one meditate on it.* When someone begins to understand this, then he begins to meditate on it. The sound Omkar has been going on since eternity; you are that very sound. That sound is still echoing within you; but only when you come to understand it completely, do you pay attention to it. And remember, wherever you bring your attention, that alone becomes the truth.

A young man's foot was hurt while playing hockey and started bleeding. But he was totally engrossed in the game. The spectators could clearly see that his foot was bleeding and also the blood stains on the grass. But the man was lost in the game and did not notice the injury or feel the pain. He didn't see the bleeding.

When the game was over, he suddenly realized what had happened and sat down. His foot was bleeding, his face looked pale. He came to feel the pain for the first time.

What happened? He didn't feel when he got injured. His attention was not there, his attention was on the game. He didn't notice the bleeding, his attention was not there. His attention was focused on the game. You come to know only that which has your attention. That's why different people come to know different things in the world.

If a poet enters a garden, he will see very different things than a scientist will. Nothing will correspond. Listening to them, no one will believe that both have returned from the same garden. The poet will see the beauty. It will bring out the poetry in him; he will return from the garden with a romantic experience. The scientist will return neither with an experience of romance nor with any poetry flowing from him. He may return, perhaps, with more knowledge about some new plants – their names, what kind of plants they are, their classification and from which minerals they are made. Looking at both their notebooks you wouldn't know that they had come from the same garden. It would be impossible to tell.

It is said that when a shoemaker looks at someone, he does not notice the man but his shoes, and from looking at them he finds out what kind of a man he must be. The condition of his shoes introduces the man: how he is doing financially, whether his business is doing well or not, how the relationship between him and his wife is going – shoes tell it all. Shoes have their own story and the shoemaker knows how to read it. When a doctor looks at someone, he doesn't see the man. He notices diseases. As soon as you enter the home of a doctor, just to pay a friendly visit, he begins to notice the disease you may be carrying.

The famous painter, Monet, once did a portrait – a portrait of a poor man, a hungry man in great pain. He invited his doctor friend to see the painting. The doctor went on looking at the painting for ten minutes. Monet was quite puzzled. He said, "I never knew you were so interested in paintings."

The doctor replied, "What painting? This man is suffering from appendicitis. The painting shows he is in pain because of his appendix."

Only a doctor can see what a doctor can see. Only a shoemaker can see what he alone can see. We see that on which our attention is focused. Wherever you focus your attention, that is the only truth for you. Elixir is also flowing within you, but you are too busy with your games. Someone is busy with the game of making money, while someone else is busy with the game of attaining power. You are busy with your games, that is why you are not able to see the elixir flowing inside you. You are busy collecting pebbles. You are involved outwardly. Only when you are finished with your outer involvements will you pay attention to the inner sound. Being finished with outer involvements is what understanding is all about.

Having an understanding doesn't mean being informed about many things. Understanding means having an understanding of these games. Understanding means having an understanding of this outer trouble. Understanding means someone is through with the outer. He has seen enough, now he will close his eyes and look within. Someone has played enough, now he will relax, take a rest; someone has chased enough, now is the time to stop a little. The day you come to see the futility of chasing on the outside – that no matter how much you may have attained, you have got nothing; no matter how much you have collected, it all remains empty, the wealth piles up but you remain poor – the day you come to understand this fact is the very day your attention will turn inside.

Kabir says one pays attention when one comes to an understanding.

***And then one hears the unstruck sound***
***and one sees lotuses blossoming without being in the pond.***
***It is then that consciousness will climb onto the lotus and dance.***

The lotus is seen as a very profound symbol in the East. The lotus flower in itself is very mysterious. And if the outer lotus is so mysterious, you cannot imagine how mysterious the inner lotus must be. Let me explain to you a few characteristics of the outer lotus because the outer lotus also gives a glimpse of the inner lotus.

The first characteristic of the outer lotus is that it grows in dirty soil – and yet there is no other flower as sacred as the lotus is. The lotus grows in a dirty, muddy place, but you cannot find a more sacred petal anywhere – a petal so tender, so fresh, but born in muddy water. A lotus shows the greatest transformation there can ever be. A lotus emerging from the mud is the greatest revolution.

So never be bothered by your own mud. Granted, it is mud – a lot of mud – but pay no attention to it. The lotuses are also growing out of the same mud. Just pay attention to the lotuses. Yes, there is stealing, dishonesty, falsehood, deceit, jealousy, envy, hatred, illusion and emotional bondage – certainly it is a lot of mud. But if the mud is there, then a lotus is also bound to be there.

Simply pay attention to the inner phenomenon – mud on the outside, the lotus inside. And don't get involved with removing the mud; because the lotus is getting nourished by that same mud. Also don't be an enemy of the mud; just look for the lotus. The day you have found and recognized the lotus, you will thank the mud as well. That day you will say, "I am grateful to this body because without it how could this lotus have blossomed?" Had you been only the mud, and nothing but mud, who would there have been to think of changing this mud? Who would have thought of transforming it? Who would have thought of creating a revolution? Who would have thought of setting out on the journey of *satyam, shivam, sundaram* – the good, the truth and the beautiful? This very thinking shows one is in search of the lotus. So pay attention to the inside and you will see lotuses blossoming.

The first outstanding characteristic of a lotus is that the most pure and sacred petals emerge from the dirtiest mud. And if the lotus is hidden in the mud, then similarly the *brahman* is hidden in maya, in our illusionary world, and the being is hidden in the body.

The second characteristic of the lotus is that it remains in the water but the water does not touch it; it stays in the water but is untouched by it. This is exactly the nature of a seeker's journey: he lives in the world and yet remains untouched by it. Although the water is all around, the lotus rises above the water. It leaves behind the mud, the water – everything. It does not run away from it. It stays where it is, but rises above it all. Then even if rain falls or a dewdrop falls, they never touch the lotus. The drop appears and then goes away – it just slips off.

While sitting near a lotus sometimes watch a drop slipping from it, pay attention to it. A drop falls on the lotus and hardly touches it; it just remains distant from it – though so close, right on top of the lotus petal and yet not touching it. The drop does not look as if it is made of water, it looks like a pearl. If the drop touches the petal, it will disintegrate and disperse. There is no touching; the drop remains as closed as it was before falling on the lotus petal. As the drop gains weight, it falls off on its own accord. The lotus remains untouched. The lotus remains distant; it never gets affected by the drop and the drop falls off because of its own weight.

Samsara, the world, will fall away on its own – you need not be bothered about it. Anger will fall because of its own weight – you need not be worried. Greed will fall because of its own weight – you need not be troubled by it. Don't make an effort to drop them. Just become like a lotus; don't let anything touch you.

The next time anger arises, stay untouched inside even though outwardly you may act angrily. It is perhaps sometimes needed in life to do so. It is difficult to continue living without acting out the drama of anger; sometimes it is useful. Go ahead and get angry – just like an actor gets angry in a play – but remain untouched by it inside yourself.

So these are the two unique characteristics of the lotus. Both are equally true about the inner lotus too, except for one difference: *...lotuses blossoming without being in the pond.* There is no pond and yet the lotus blossoms. Ordinarily, the lotus that blossoms in a pond is bound to wither away sooner or later. But the lotus that blossoms without being in a pond, without a cause, will always remain. To be causeless is the key to being eternal.

For example, when you fall in love with someone, if there is any reason behind it, it will come to an end. The reason or the cause may be money, beauty, prestige or status – anything may be the reason. But if love is an outcome of any reason, then it is bound to end. A causeless love will last forever. If you are praying for a reason, then that prayer will also become lifeless. Why would you pray once the cause behind it is fulfilled?

Once I was a guest at a Christian family. The mother of the small boy asked him if he had said his nightly prayer. He said, "There is no need now. All is going well, so why should I pray?" Obviously, when all is going well what reason would you have for praying? If a prayer has arisen for a reason, it will wither away once the cause is fulfilled. So, a causeless prayer...

Have you ever prayed without any cause or reason? If you have, only then will you know the joy of praying. You pray because it gives you such joy – there is no reason behind it. Have you ever loved for no reason? If you do that, then love itself will become a door to the divine. Whatsoever you do without any reason or cause is itself what *sadhana* is, what spirituality is all about.

Let us say a man falls down in the street and you pick him up without any reason. If there were a reason behind it – people may be looking at you and saying how helpful you are – if you carry even this much feeling, then that would not be *sadhana*. Or if, for example, someone is drowning in a river and instantly you jump in and save the drowning person. If, when you do this, you expect that he should thank you and if he doesn't, you feel disappointed, sad, and unhappy; if you feel that despite staking your life the man did not thank you, then that would not be a *sadhana*, a spiritual work. In that case, you would be simply extending your worldly intentions; they have just found new ways of expressing themselves.

I have heard…

A woman drowned in a pond. Mulla Nasruddin who had watched her drowning did not do anything. Later, when the crowd gathered and the dead body was pulled out Nasruddin was asked why he did not save the woman though he was present at the scene.

Nasruddin said, "I have read stories and have watched films too; I could have saved her. But suppose she had proposed marriage to me – which happens in all the films – then who would have saved me from her?"

A cause – maybe this way or that way – will show you are still in the world. Causeless, and you are beyond samsara, beyond this world. There is only one supreme quality of godliness and that is being causeless. It is beyond any purpose or reason. You cannot ask why godliness exists. It is meaningless to ask such a question. You cannot ask why existence is. It just is – there is no cause behind it. So if you become causeless, then you become like existence.

Kabir is pointing to this causelessness: The lotuses are blossoming without being in the pond.

***And the swan is playing merrily on top of them.***

The very day flowers blossom in you without any cause, that day your spirit, your being, will dance merrily upon them like a swan. Your being will begin to dance, your being will attain glory, your being will begin to celebrate only when lotuses blossom in your life without any reason, without purpose. Otherwise, you will always find yourself miserable. Your being, your swan, will keep on crying. If you live for a particular reason, then your being, your soul, will continue longing; its thirst will never be satisfied. But if you live without a cause, then the swan within you is able to play merrily. We have called this merrily-playing swan *paramahansa*. Of course, all swans – *hansa* – are crying and weeping, troubled, suffering unnecessarily, begging unnecessarily but not getting anything. The day a lotus blossoms within you without any reason, that very day your swan, your *hansa*, becomes *paramahansa*.

***There is a shining light visible without the moon,***
***and the swan is able to see it all around, in all directions.***

Your inner eye is able to see to the furthest extent possible – and there is no limit to it, it is endless because there is no barrier for the inner eye. It reaches and covers the whole of existence – and existence is all over, everywhere. Existence never ends; there is no place where you can find a dead end. Existence is endless, infinite. And the eye of the inner swan reaches everywhere; it moves in all directions. *There is a shining light visible without the moon, and the swan is able to see it all around, in all directions.* As far as the eye can see, there is light visible – light which exists without the moon. Try to understand this a little.

There is a light emanating from the sun; it shines but also contains heat. It is warm, it carries heat. Yes, there is light, but it hurts. You cannot bear it for long; you will not be able to even look into the sun. The heat has a painful quality, which can burn your skin. The light of the moon is different; the moon emanates light, but it is cool. You can even look at the moon. You can sit for hours under the moonlight and feel more and more cool, more and more silent. Meditation is not like sunlight; meditation is like moonlight.

Secondly, Kabir says, there is no moon, just the moonlight – without a source, without a cause. Certainly, the moonlight will diminish as the moon sets or as the moon disappears. There will be a full-moon night or sometimes a new-moon night. The moon will be visible sometimes, and at other times it will not be visible. But a light without a source will always be there.

***When the evolved person sees that which is at the tenth door, he goes into a deep sleep.***

This deep sleep at the tenth door… Here, *sahasrar* – the crown of the head – is the tenth door; that is where one goes into *tari*, deep sleep. This word, *tari*, is very sweet. It will not be possible to fully understand what it means by reading the meaning given in the dictionary. The dictionary meaning is: going into sleep. But the word *tari* doesn't mean just sleep. *Tari* means a hypnotic trance. For example, when you look at your beloved – as Majnu must have looked at Laila – that is *tari*. Here, *tari* would mean: consciousness of the rest of the world is dropped, only Laila remained; Majnu became oblivious to rest of the world and was conscious only of Laila.

If you have ever seen a hypnotist, you may have noticed that when he hypnotizes and puts someone to sleep, the person under hypnosis remains asleep toward everything else but stays awake toward the hypnotist. He listens to whatever the hypnotist is saying. If he says, "Get up and run" the person runs. But he won't listen if someone else speaks to him. He remains asleep to everything else; he is only conscious of the hypnotist. His attention remains totally focused on that one person.

*Tari* means you are asleep toward the whole world – as if the world doesn't exist – and your eyes are solely focused on the divine without the eyelids flickering even once. This is bound to happen because when you arrive at the tenth door for the first time, and look at the vast beauty; when you listen to the eternal sound; when you get showered by immortality; when, for the first time, you get the taste of bliss, *tari* happens. As *tari* happens, you become oblivious to the whole world.

It happened to Ramakrishna several times that for six days he would remain unconscious – that was the state of *tari*. He used to go into that state anywhere. For example, while walking along the street, if someone said, saluting him, "Hail Rama!... glory to Rama!" he entered into the state of *tari*; he would just remain standing on the street in a static body posture. People would think he had gone mad. They had to lift him up and take him home. It would take hours before he regained his senses.

When someone asked what happened to him, he would answer, "Hearing the word, *Rama*, I get reminded...and I slip into my inner world." Ramakrishna arrived at the tenth door.

The word *Rama* worked like a key; it instantly opened the tenth door. And when you arrive at the tenth door, you become oblivious of the world, of samsara. If you were standing in the middle of the road, regardless of any traffic hazard – getting hit by a car or a bus – you would have no concern; you would remain standing right there.

When Ramakrishna's disciples escorted him somewhere, they were careful because if on the way someone were to call God's name, big trouble would erupt on the road. People had no idea what was going on; they thought Ramakrishna had gone mad. That is why people did not invite Ramakrishna to attend any celebration or any function because once reaching there Ramakrishna would himself become the event – who could stop someone from saying something or calling God's name?

Once it happened...

One of Ramakrishna's devotees invited him to a wedding at his home. He had requested Ramakrishna to please be careful because it was a special event. But how could one expect Ramakrishna to be careful? Who is there to be careful? Once you have entered into the state of *tari*, then what is the point of being careful? Kabir says he has "gulped the whole tavern" – and you are asking Ramakrishna to be careful? Ramakrishna has not taken just a little wine – he has drunk the whole tavern! So Ramakrishna went to the wedding, and as he went in through the door someone said, "Hail Rama!" and Ramakrishna remained standing right there – for six days. The wedding was instantly put on hold; people forgot all about the bride and the bridegroom. It became necessary to first take care of Ramakrishna. He fell down and then when getting up tears began to roll from his eyes; he got up screaming, "Mother, why are you pushing me away? Why is the door getting shut? Why am I being sent back?" He got up crying.

*Tari* means the hypnotic trance of the tenth door. You see godliness from this point, and the moment anyone sees godliness the world, samsara, disappears. It is very difficult in the beginning. In those early moments you need a companion, a devotee, who can take care of you, otherwise you can die. When Ramakrishna remains unconscious for six days someone has to put water in his mouth, give him milk, fan his body, cover his body – because he himself is totally unaware. He is no longer a part of this world, only a corpse exists. He has flown away to some other world. Kabir says: "O swan, *hansa*! Let us go to that world – the other world. Come let us go to that land."

Once Nanak was passing through a village. As he was standing by a lake he saw a flock of swans flying in the sky and began to run and follow them. His devotee, Mardana, tried to stop him, but Nanak didn't stop. Mardana kept running behind him. Nanak didn't stop until the swans stopped flying. It appeared as if the swans had taken notice of the situation and they stopped. Nanak came close to them. Mardana was afraid that the swans would again fly away the moment Nanak came close to them; but they didn't.

With tears rolling down, Nanak sat among them; and what he said at that moment is very significant. He said: "O swans, you fly in the faraway sky; you must have seen the creator sometimes! You go on long journeys, you must have seen the one who created me. I am in search of him; please give some news about him, his whereabouts!" And just remaining where he was, the tears kept rolling down. He was deeply in ecstasy.

He always took Mardana along with him. Mardana was a musician. The moment Nanak would begin to get lost in his ecstasy, Mardana would start playing his *ektara*, his one-stringed musical instrument. That was his way to bring Nanak back to his conscious state. The moment Nanak heard the sound of that music, he instantly came back to his conscious state. That was the key; otherwise, if he had got stuck at the tenth door, he would have been in the same condition as Ramakrishna was. But Ramakrishna did not have a skilled musician with him like Mardana, who played only that melody, which brought Nanak back. Listening to the melody, Nanak would slowly return from that space, back into his body, back to his normal state. He kept Mardana with him for his whole life.

Mardana was a Muslim; Nanak was a Hindu. He would visit a temple only if Mardana accompanied him because, who knows? He may enter into the state of *tari* in the temple. If a temple forbade any Muslim to enter, then Nanak could not enter.

*Tari* means being on the threshold of the tenth door. There is no state of *tari* for the one who goes beyond it, Buddha and Mahavira didn't enter into that state. When one sees the glory of the infinite while being at this tenth door, one enters into the state of *tari*. So, remember this: the unconscious state that Ramakrishna entered into did not happen in the lives of Buddha and Mahavira. They did not stop and see their being at the tenth door – they just crossed over, and paid no attention to the door. They did not care to see who was beyond the tenth door, they just kept going. They simply became one with *that which is*. In that case there is no possibility of entering into the state of *tari* because it requires duality in order for it to happen. *Tari* happens when one sees the divine. It never happens if one is completely drowned in godliness. Who will then be left to enter into *tari*? The state of *tari* is on the part of the devotee, not the divine.

So this is a greatly puzzling phenomenon. People ask why what happened to Ramakrishna did not happen to Buddha, why it did not happen to Mahavira. Either Ramakrishna is out of order or Buddha and Mahavira are. No, no one is out of order. Ramakrishna has a glimpse of the divine while being at the tenth door; and this is a devotee's state of consciousness.

A devotee says, "O Lord, please be at a distance so that I may see you, so that I may have a taste of you and see your beauty. Please stay at some distance!" A devotee does not want to become God. A devotee says, "Please keep a little distance right until the end. I will come close to your throne but just to touch your feet – that is enough. Let me be your devotee for lives to come."

Certainly, the beauty is vast, and one who knows, a *jnani*, an enlightened one, does not get to see it, but a devotee does – because a devotee keeps a little distance. He says, "You are the lord, I am your devotee; you are my master, I am your servant." That is why Kabir says, again and again, "Says Kabir, the servant" – not a master but a servant. If he may just touch the feet of the Lord – that is his destiny. That is his heaven, his *moksha*.

Devotees of the divine have said in their songs, "I don't want *moksha*, liberation; I just want to be in your service." So the devotee stops at the tenth door. He doesn't go beyond it, because the moment he did so it would mean falling instantly into the ocean. It is like the Ganges staying right where it falls into the ocean and seeing the ocean from that point. This is the state of Nanak, of Kabir and of Ramakrishna.

Buddha and Mahavira go straight into the ocean – they become the ocean. There remains no distance between the devotee and the divine. They themselves become the divine. Then there is no state of *tari* anymore – what kind of state would that be and who would be left to be in that state? As the duality disappears, so does the state of *tari*.

> ***When the evolved person sees that which is at the tenth door,***
> ***he goes into a deep sleep.***
> ***At that moment, death does not come close, and lustful desire,***
> ***anger, pride, and greed burn away.***

Death never approaches at this tenth door because death is possible at the first door; there is immortality at the tenth door. At the first door there are both – life and death. But at the tenth door, where there is life beyond life, there is no birth, no death – simply an immense, exalted life.

*...death does not come close, and lustful desire, anger, pride, and greed burn away.* And now the situation is such that lustful desire, anger, pride, greed all get burned up on their own accord – there is no need to remove them; no need to fight with them. They were basically connected with the first door. Someone who is standing at the first door – the door of lustful desire – will certainly be angry, proud, greedy. As long as there is passionate desire, how can you be free of anger? You are bound to get angry at whosoever comes in the way of your desire. And then how can you be free of pride? If you are really free of pride, free of unconsciousness, then how can you fall into the ditch of lustful desire? Until you are free of desire, how will you be free

of greed? – because greed simply means making preparations to fulfill lustful desire. If you are living in a hut, then naturally you will not be able to find a very beautiful woman. You need a palace to have a beautiful woman. If you are living in a hut, then you will find a woman who would be fit to live in a hut.

So greed simply means preparing things so that lustful desire may be properly fulfilled. As long as there is desire, anger and greed will continue to exist. How will desire disappear? It never goes away by fighting against it. When one's life energy reaches the tenth door, it instantly finds that all has burned away – now there is no more lustful desire, no more anger, nor any greed left.

***The thirst of many lives is quenched...***

The thirst of many, many lives is quenched because what you were looking for in the world is not in the world at all, so the thirst was bound to continue. No matter how much you may drink the water of this world, the thirst will never go away.

It is mentioned in the life of Jesus that once, as he was traveling, he came to a well where a woman was drawing water. It was a hot day, and he had come on a long journey from a faraway village. He said he was very thirsty and asked the woman to give him some water. The woman said, "Forgive me, I am an untouchable, I come from a very low caste. People from higher castes don't drink water touched by me."

Jesus said: "Forget all about that. If you serve me water from this well, then I will let you drink water from such a well that you will never feel thirsty again."

The well Jesus is talking about is the tenth door. For one who arrives at that tenth door then...

***The thirst of many lives is quenched,***
***and all sins and karmas are burned away.***

Kabir says: **Listen, O seekers, it is then that one attains immortality; then there is no death.**

Someone who has known this tenth door becomes immortal. Then there is no death for him.

Religion is a search for the elixir; it is an experience at the tenth door. The purpose of all meditation techniques is for your life energy to rise from the first door and reach the tenth door.

Here, we are working with Kundalini Meditation. This meditation is the way to bring you from the first door to the tenth door. So for the first fifteen minutes let your body shake and vibrate. Shaking the body means letting the energy melt wherever it is repressed; letting the energy flow from where it is blocked. If you shake your body rightly for fifteen minutes, with total feeling, then all the repressed energy will begin to manifest and flow.

The second stage is dancing. Dancing means the energy that has now spread everywhere gets transformed into bliss. Dance as if you are celebrating, as if something tremendous has happened, as if a light has descended into your life. Dance with joy because the more blissful you are, the more the energy moves upward; the more the energy moves upward, the more blissful you become. Suppose you were intoxicated and started dancing as if you had drunk the entire tavern dry, would you dance like a miser? It wouldn't happen. Dancing like a miser would mean dancing as if you have to do it: "What to do, I just got caught here…" Or as if you are just observing, expecting that perhaps something will happen by dancing this way! No, that won't work. Such lukewarm efforts won't work. You need intense passion! Dance like a madman.

Without madness you cannot attain the ultimate. If you move with your mind, then you will remain where you are. You need to go a little beyond your mind. And when your whole energy becomes ecstatic, when it begins to flow upward… To be ecstatic means the energy is moving upward – because a feeling of joy and bliss is experienced once the energy has begun to flow vertically. The more it flows downward, the more one feels miserable, the more life descends into hell. That's why we say hell is below and heaven is above. It simply means that hell is connected with the first door and heaven is connected with the tenth door – *above* and *below* mean nothing else.

When your energy falls down to the first door you create hell for yourself. And when, at the tenth door, your energy flows toward the limitless, you have created a heaven for yourself. Both are hidden within you. When the energy is flowing and you are blissful, stop and either remain standing or sit down so that the energy has a total opportunity to flow. It is useful to sit, so that only the spine remains; the whole body disappears and only the spine remains. The energy moves upward through the spine and all the energy gathers in the spine. Then just lie down, so that it becomes even easier for the gathered energy that is flowing upward to start knocking on the tenth door.

The whole experiment of Kundalini Meditation is all about knocking on the tenth door. And if you do it rightly, you will also be able to say:

**The thirst of many lives is quenched,**
**and all sins and karmas are burned away.**

Kabir says: **Listen, O seekers, it is then that one attains immortality; then there is no death.**

Enough for today.

# 10
# The Silence of the Inner Sky

***Where is the need for words when the mind is in ecstasy?***
***I have found the diamond and wrapped it in my cloak,***
***so why open it again and again?***
***The pan of the scales went up when its load was light;***
***now that it is full, what need is there to weigh it?***

***All the drunkards have gone mad:***
***they drank the whole tavern dry without measuring***
***how much they had taken.***
***The swan has taken flight to the Mansarovar lake,***
***so why should it bother about the pools and ditches anymore?***
***Godliness dwells within you,***
***what need is there to open your eyes outward?***

Kabir says: ***Listen, O seekers, the divine appears***
***exactly when the tiny particle of dust is removed from your eyes.***

After attaining enlightenment, Buddha remained silent for two weeks. The story is that this caused the whole of existence to become sad and unhappy. The gods approached him and, bowing down to him, urged him not to remain silent. They said: "It is after a very long time that someone has attained enlightenment and there are millions of souls who keep wandering around in search of light. You have received it. Please do not hide it; show it to others so that it may brighten up their dark pathways. Please do not let what you have found disappear along with you. Share it with others so that they may have some taste of it. Please do not remain silent. Speak!"

It is said that Buddha replied, "If I do speak, then whatever I may say will not be understood. That is why it is better for me to remain silent; because what I will be saying will be from a totally different world and no one will understand it unless he has already had some taste of it. Without having experienced it, there is no way someone will be able to understand what I will be saying. That is why it is better I remain silent."

But the gods urged Buddha again and said, "Some will follow what you are saying. It will be worth it if only one person gets a little push while on the journey. Even if they are unable to follow the path, some taste of it, some curiosity, some interest and a longing for liberation is worth it."

Buddha replied, "Those who are real seekers will find the truth on their own; there is no need for me to talk to them. And the ones who are not seekers will not listen to me anyway; there is no point in speaking to them."

But Buddha finally gave in to the gods because they said, "There are some people who are just on the borderline. It will take much longer for them to search if they don't hear you. Listening to you, they will take a leap forward. And whether they listen to you or not, please share what you have received."

Compassion is the shadow of wisdom. One who attains to knowing will be filled with great compassion. He will not speak just because he is under any compulsion. There is a difference between our speaking and his speaking. We speak because we can't remain without speaking; we will feel very uneasy if we don't speak. Speaking is our catharsis – as we speak, everything gets flushed out. That's why people go on discussing their miseries – because the more they talk about their miseries the more they feel relieved from them. Their pain and suffering gets dispersed each time they share it. If there is no one around to talk to, then the misery will be stored within, it will become a festering wound.

With ill people, psychiatrists do nothing else but listen. They cure their patients just by listening to them. When the other person listens, you are able to relieve your mind. Someone who speaks everything out empties his mind. We speak because in our sick state we are compelled to do so – or we wouldn't be able to survive. Even if there is nothing to talk about we will go on speaking meaninglessly. For example, we say, "The weather is so nice!" The other person is as able to see that as we are. Or, we say, "Isn't the sun lovely?" The other fellow also has eyes; there is really no need to say it.

It happened that once an emperor told his minister that he wanted to know how many blind people there were in the capital. He asked him to count them.

The minister asked: "Do you want to know the number of really blind people or just of those whose eyes are closed?"

The emperor replied, "What do you mean by those who are really blind? What is the difference between the two?"

The minister said, "If what you really want to know is the number of blind people who are physically unable to see, then the town's doctors can help; the hospital can give us the information. That is not a problem. But if what you really want to know is how many people are functioning as blind then that will be a little difficult; it will need some time."

The next day, the minister sat down in the marketplace and spread some shoes around him. He began mending the shoes. Whosoever passed by would ask, "What are you doing?" The minister would immediately add his name to the list of blind people, because those who were asking him could already see what he is doing – so what was the point in asking? Even the emperor's name was included in the blind people's list, because as he passed by in the afternoon he asked, "What is this you are doing?" The minister immediately wrote down his name.

The list became very long, except that it did not have the names of the children who had passed by – they never bothered to ask. The rest were all blind.

If someone happened to listen to our conversations, he would be very surprised. He would realize we were talking about things which are totally meaningless. For example, we point out things which others can already see. We share information about things which others already know. We speak about things which others have already heard about. We explain things that others have already read about. What are we doing? And the other person goes on tolerating us in the simple hope that in a while, once we become quiet, he will also get a chance to cathart.

We sit and listen until we get a chance – it is just a matter of finding an opportunity. When we *do* listen we are not really listening because we are getting ready to speak. The other person also does not really listen to you – he too is getting ready to speak. We are all talkers – no one is there to listen at all.

If you listen with a witnessing consciousness to two people talking, you will be amazed to see it is not a dialogue but a monologue. Each person is speaking to himself; they simply appear to be connected with the other, but it is just an excuse. In your conversations you select any word from what the other is saying, hook yourself onto that word and get going. Your train moves in some other direction. This is why it is easier for two individuals to have a dispute rather than a dialogue. A dialogue is possible only when a person knows how to listen; we know only how to talk. So even when we arrive at God's temple, we speak; even there we don't allow God to speak.

Real prayer begins when you give God a chance to speak. What is the need for you to speak anyway? Whatever you may say, God knows it all already. Please be quiet; let him speak a little.

But we don't know how to be silent; it is difficult to remain silent. It is the most difficult thing for a sick mind to remain silent. For a healthy mind it is difficult to speak, because once you have become silent then how can you speak? When you become silent, each and every word becomes difficult to utter.

The mystics have spoken but out of compassion. It is not easy for them to speak. It is difficult for those who are rooted in deep silence, in *shunya*, to form even a single word. Even then they create that word just out of compassion, knowing well that the word is not going to matter much; it is because of their compassion that they still go on articulating words. Looking at your face and noticing that, although you have heard the word, you have not understood the meaning, out of compassion they go on speaking in the hope that perhaps it may work out; they may become a cause for someone to wake up.

These words of Kabir are very significant:

***Where is the need for words when the mind is in ecstasy?***

When you have experienced ecstasy, when you are filled with the wine of wisdom, and when you will have become so blissful, then: *Where is the need for words when the mind is in ecstasy?* Then, how will you be able to speak? Then how will it be possible to speak anyway!

What this means is that you will go on talking until you have experienced ecstasy. When a man is happy he becomes quiet; he speaks when he is miserable. When a person is healthy he doesn't talk about health; when he is sick he goes on discussing in great detail about the illness. When you are completely healthy you just forget your body totally; what is the point in talking about the body? You simply become oblivious of the body.

Chuang Tzu says that when the shoe fits, you forget your feet. Only when the shoe pinches do you remember your feet. When your head is well, you forget you have one; it is as if you have become headless. You come to feel the head only when there is a headache; only then are you aware of pain.

That is why, in Sanskrit, the same word is used for misery and for knowledge. *Vedana* means pain or misery and it indicates *veda*, too, which means knowledge. One carries the weight of misery, whereas the state of bliss is like being drunk – one loses all sensation. Misery itself creates sensation. You feel your feet when they are pierced by a thorn; you are oblivious of your feet if no thorn has pierced them. Pain is sensed, but how can a joyful state be sensed? We become so lost in the state of joy that nothing remains to be sensed. It requires a certain distance to feel misery.

So those who know have said that bliss is your self-nature, not misery – because how can something be your self-nature if you cannot become one with it? It hurts when a thorn pierces, because hurting is not our nature. When there is no thorn stuck in your feet there is no pain – you are not even aware of your feet. As you become healthier will there be anything left to be said? When you become totally healthy – when the body, the mind, and the spirit all become silent – then there is nothing left to say.

*Where is the need for words when the mind is in ecstasy?* Talking is part of the world of misery. That's why when someone goes insane, he keeps talking for twenty-four hours. Only a mad person talks for twenty-four hours. He blabbers at night and during the day too. So at one end of the spectrum is lunacy, where the person goes on talking twenty-four hours a day; at the other end is the liberated person who becomes totally silent. There is no one in his inner chamber – all is silence. In his inner dwelling there is no sound, there is nothing to say, and there is no noise – the ultimate nothingness simply exists in a perfect rhythm.

If you just watch and observe a madman you will realize you are mad too. Whether you talk or not, inside you the conversation is going on. The Sufis have a technique which helps stop this inner chatter – and the Sufis say that this internal dialogue is, in itself, the barrier between you and the divine. The moment you become silent inside all curtains between you and existence drop of their own accord. That was the veil. Inside yourself, you go on discussing matters; not a moment passes when the discussion has come to an end. Either you talk with someone on the outside, or, if you don't find anyone, you keep talking to yourself inside – but the talking continues.

Try to look at this a little consciously. This inner dialogue is the veil and you just need to become aware of it with a witnessing consciousness. Create a distance and look at it, and you will find that it is not you but your mind, which is engaged in dialogue. You can watch it from a distance; you can be just a witness. The moment you become a watcher, you will find that, by and by, the inner dialogue will come to an end. In between, you will find some moments where there are gaps. Sometimes you will find the clouds have dispersed and an open sky is visible. It is in that open sky that you will have the first experience of *samadhi*.

You are not made of clouds – you are an empty sky. Clouds come and go, the empty sky always remains as it is. Your nature is not that of the clouds; the empty sky is your innermost nature. That which never changes, which always is – that is your innermost nature! Words are not your nature; *shunyata*, emptiness, is your nature. Words come and go like the clouds do; they rise like waves and disappear. You are not made of words, but you are lost in words twenty-four hours a day. For example, you ask a man to go and see the sky and he brings back news about the clouds; similarly, when you enter within yourself you come out carrying words – you are unable to reach up to the sky.

> ***The pan of the scales went up when its load was light;***
> ***now that it is full, what need is there to weigh it?***

If you are not able to reach the sky, then how will the heavenly cave open up? Unless this happens, how will the elixir flow? Unless this happens, how will you drown yourself in the stream of elixir? And Kabir is right when he says that as one drowns in that stream... *Where is the need for words when the mind is in ecstasy?* The moment one is in bliss, silence sets in.

That is why the mystics have difficulty speaking. They have to make an effort to speak, while you have to make an effort to keep quiet! If you are told to keep two minutes of silence because someone has died, you will feel that those two minutes are like two years; they appear so long. It feels like someone has missed to keep track of time, you want to scream, "Stop now! Those two minutes were over a long time ago." But you remain quiet, even though inside you things keep going – and there is no silence at all.

Can you not be silent for just two minutes? What kind of achievement is this? What kind of intelligence does this take? What kind of skills do you need to do this? And if you cannot be silent for two minutes, then know well you are insane, you are almost mad.

The difference between you and a madman is only that of degrees. You have repressed your madness within; it can explode at any time. It is getting ready. It is collecting like pus inside; it is bound to become a big wound and burst open. It is all just a matter of degrees: someone is ninety degrees mad, another ninety-five degrees and still someone else is one hundred degrees mad. The explosion happens at one hundred degrees – at which point people admit you to a lunatic asylum.

Sit in a corner of your home sometime and on a piece of paper write down whatever is going on in your mind. You will not be ready to show, even to your closest friend, what will appear on that paper because it will look like sheer madness. Write it down on a piece of paper without cheating – write exactly whatever is going on inside. You will be amazed to see how the mind is hopping all over the place!

For example, you see a dog passing by. As you soon as you look at the dog the journey starts: you remember your friend's dog; you remember your friend because of his dog. As you remember your friend you also remember his wife – and the journey goes on.

Now this dog has nothing to do with all of this, but the inner journey starts, the internal dialogue has begun. Now while being on this journey you may see yourself falling in love with your friend's wife, getting married to her, and having children who you are now getting ready for their weddings. If you said to someone all this happened because you saw that dog…

Have you read the stories of Don Quixote? They are your stories. The mind is nothing but a Don Quixote. Don't ever think those stories were written to entertain children; you are doing the same twenty-four hours a day. That is what slumber is; that is what sleep is – about which Kabir says: "Seekers! Don't be asleep while awake." You seem to be outwardly awake, but inside you great dreams are floating around. You are covered by layer upon layer of dreams; layer upon layer of clouds are covering your inner sky. And you go on throwing these piles of madness onto others. That is what your internal dialogue is all about.

*Where is the need for words when the mind is in ecstasy?* But when you are in ecstasy, when you yourself have become the blue sky, when the heavenly cave opens up and the elixir flows continuously, then where will be the need to speak? Then you will become absolutely silent. And yet, those who did become totally silent *have* spoken. But there is a qualitative difference between your speaking and their speaking. They speak because they have known something; you speak out of your madness. They speak because by speaking they want to grant or give something to you. You speak because while doing that you want to throw something out.

Your speaking is harmful to others because you are throwing out your disease. For the realized people, speaking means spreading ultimate goodness, well-being, because they are sharing their own joy. Each and every word spoken by them will carry the sound of their inner music. Each and every word spoken by them will seem filled with a little inner juice. Each and every word spoken by them will manifest a little fragrance of their inner being. You must have noticed: if you hold flowers, they leave their fragrance in your hand. If you pass through a garden, your clothes pick up the fragrance of flowers.

When a word passes through a mystic's *shunya*, it brings along with it a little emptiness, a little freshness of the inner world. That is why if one wants to understand a mystic, then simply listening to him is enough – there is no need to think about anything.

Nanak keeps saying that three things are significant. One is God, about whom we don't know anything. The master is the door to reach God. But we don't know anything about the master either – who is a master? The way to reach him is to be in the company of seekers. Be in the company of seekers in a place where good and kind people are gathered, where good and noble thoughts are being talked about, and where there is talk about the other world. Listening to all such things in the company of seekers you will find a master. And once the master is found you are on your way. A master is found in the company of seekers and God is found in the company of a master. To be in such a place, where noble thoughts are discussed and to listen to them, is of immense value.

But how in the world will you be able to understand the mystics? Understanding them is possible only when you arrive at the same state they are in.

But meanwhile you can experience the elixir that flows from them; you can allow their words to penetrate you. You can be receptive and keep an open mind so that their words can reach inside your being – perhaps these words coming from the unknown world may hit your inner world a little. If you have learned from the mystics how to be ecstatic, you have learned it all.

***Where is the need for words when the mind is in ecstasy?***
***I have found the diamond and wrapped it in my cloak,***
***so why open it again and again?***

Now that you have found the diamond and have wrapped your cloak around it, then why open the cloak and look at it again and again? But you *do* open it. If you found a diamond on the road, you would certainly wrap it up and put it in your cloak; but you would also go on checking it again and again – why? Because, you are doubtful; you are not completely sure that it is possible to find a diamond just like that; you are not completely sure that you have really found a diamond. You are not sure of yourself; you are not sure of the diamond either. You are full of doubts; that is why you keep opening the cloak and looking at it over and over again.

If there is trust, then how can there be any doubt? With trust, you have found a diamond, it is tucked away inside, so why now open the cloak and look at it again and again? When Buddha, Kabir and Nanak become enlightened...they have found the diamond, they have tucked it away; now what is the point in opening the cloak again and again? They don't even talk about it. They remain silent about what they have found; even if they do talk about it sometimes they do it indirectly.

It happened...

A woman was brought to a Sufi mystic, Baijid. She was very fat. Her husband said, "She has been unable to produce children; only if you bless her, please, will it be possible."

Baijid said, "Children? Blessing? Have you gone mad? She is going to die in the next forty days; she will not survive. I can clearly see this by looking at the lines on her forehead. What can I do for her? Nothing can be done about it."

The husband and wife returned full of sadness. She was going to die in forty days! The wife got ill; she stopped eating. But when the forty days were over, she didn't die. This was quite a situation; so they went back to Baijid. Forty days had gone by in crying and weeping, waiting for death – and the wife was still alive.

Baijid said, "Rest assured, now she will be able to bear a child; only her weight needed to be reduced. Speaking of death was just some medicine."

This is the indirect way. Had the woman been told to reduce her weight she wouldn't have agreed. Such straight talk could not have worked. Many doctors, many physicians had already told her to reduce her weight. People come to mystics only when all the doctors and physicians have failed; that's the only reason why they come for blessings. That is their last resort.

Baijid could see clearly that such a fat woman could not produce children. And it was obvious she couldn't be persuaded to lose weight. His talking of death was all fake. But we are such fake people that only some falsehood will work on us. That is why the mystics don't talk about the diamond – they talk about something else which may generate some interest in the diamond. Even if they were to give you the diamond, you would not be able to recognize it because to recognize it you would need to have the experience of it.

It happened...

There was a Sufi mystic, Zunnun. A man came to him and said, "It is all nonsense! I have been to many Sufis; but they are all just talk – there is no substance in it. Such and such a Sufi is a charlatan and you cannot trust the behavior of that other one. And then there is yet another Sufi – he talks big but he has had no experience at all."

Zunnun said, "We will talk more later; I need to do some important work, please help me with it. I have this stone which I would like you to take to the market. Take it to the gold and silver shops and if someone wants to buy it for one gold coin then sell it."

The man went to a nearby market. He went to the gold and silver shops but no one was willing to buy the stone for one gold coin. One person was ready to buy it for one silver coin at the most – and that, too, very reluctantly. So he returned.

He said, "The stone is totally useless. Forget about the gold coin, what you can have is just one silver coin and for that too the man is in doubt; it is not certain if he will want to buy it. What do you want to do now?"

Zunnun said, "Now go to a jeweler's shop but don't sell the stone, just ask how much it can be sold for."

So the man went to the jeweler's. The jeweler was ready to pay one thousand gold coins. When the man refused, he offered ten thousand gold coins. Even then the man refused to sell, so the jeweler asked, "Tell me, how much do you want? I won't let you take this stone away again!"

The man replied, "But the person who owns this stone has not asked me to sell it; he has simply asked me to find out how much it is worth."

The man came back to Zunnun and said, "This is too much! It is good that I did not sell it before or else I would have got just one silver coin. This guy is ready to pay ten thousand gold coins – and is still asking me to name my price!"

The mystic said, "The stone is not to be sold; I just sent you to make an inquiry. One needs to be a jeweler to recognize a diamond. Are you a jeweler who can recognize a Sufi?"

How would a shopkeeper in the business of gold and silver recognize a diamond? – though he may have some idea on seeing the colorful and shining stone and may show some interest in buying it, perhaps for some purpose. If you wanted to sell it to a vegetable vendor, he might say: "OK, give it to me for two pennies; it may be useful for weighing vegetables on the scales."

The mystic said, "Put the stone back; a jeweler is needed to recognize a diamond." Who can recognize a Sufi? Who can recognize a saint, a mystic? The diamond *cannot* be given to you; you won't be able to recognize it. You may even lose it somewhere or give it to children to play with. What is known as the Kohinoor today was once a toy for children within the home of a poor man of Golkonda; he had found it on a farm and his children used to play with it. Only a jeweler knows a diamond; only the wise person knows what wisdom is. Of course the diamond cannot be given to you; you will misuse it even if it were given to you. Hence Kabir says: *I have found the diamond and wrapped it in my cloak, so why open it again and again?* He himself has no doubt because it is his existential experience, which cannot be doubted.

People ask me – in fact they have always asked – how can I be absolutely sure that meditation has happened? How can I be absolutely sure that godliness has been achieved? How can I be absolutely sure that I have attained *samadhi*, ecstasy? I tell them, "How do you come to know you are in pain if someone smashes a stick on your head? Do you go and ask someone whether you are in pain or not?"

If you can experience pain, then why can't you experience joy? If you can feel and recognize pain that also indicates you can feel joy as well, because pain is nothing but an absence of joy. If you come to know sickness, then you can certainly know good health. If you can recognize hell, then you can certainly recognize heaven. So when it is found, you won't have to ask whether you have really got it or not. No, once a diamond is found then... *I have found the diamond and wrapped it in my cloak, so why open it again and again?* There is no room for any doubt – the experience is beyond doubt.

The experience of godliness is beyond doubt. When it happens, it just happens. Then the question does not arise, even if the whole world denies it. Even if the entire world proves it has not happened, still that does not matter. Even if the whole world said that it doesn't exist, it will make no difference. Once you have experienced it, then that itself is proof enough.

An experience of the divine is self-evident – it does not require any other proof. The experience itself is the proof. Once it has happened – then it has happened! But until you have gone through it yourself, it is difficult. You will not be able to figure it out if someone tells you about it; you will come to know it only when it's based on your own experience, not through some other person's experience. So even if Kabir makes frantic efforts, you will not believe what he is saying. You will believe it only when the same happens to you. And then you will also be able to say: *I have found the diamond and wrapped it in my cloak, why open it again and again?*

*The pan of the scales went up when its load was light; now that it is full, what need is there to weigh it?* The pan of the scales stays up only as long as it carries no weight. As it gets heavier, it begins to come down. And when it is at its full weight it touches the floor. Then weighing stops. *The pan of the scales went up when its load was light; now that it is full, what need is there to weigh it?* The weighing comes to an end. Currently in your life you go on weighing and weighing. *Weighing* means comparing. Whatsoever you think, you think it in terms of comparison.

Once, there was a beauty competition; twenty beautiful women from around the country had gathered for the competition. Out of these the most beautiful woman of the whole country was to be selected.

Mulla Nasruddin was also invited as one of the judges. He was an old and very experienced man. He had seen many ups downs in his life. He had seen many women in their relationships, their marriages and divorces – he had seen it all.

When the first young woman appeared, he said, "Mmm..." The second one came, and the third woman came, but he continued to say, "Mmm... mmm..."

Each woman was the best there ever could be; it was difficult to decide who was the prettiest. Those who had invited him felt a little suspicious. The twentieth woman arrived and still he said, "Mmm...mmm..."

So the friends asked, "Nasruddin! You didn't like a single one? You just went on saying, 'Mmm...mmm...'"

Nasruddin replied, "I am not saying that to these women; I was addressing my wife."

He was comparing them with his wife.

Your whole life is full of comparisons. For instance, you are rich... But are you really rich? You cannot be rich except, of course, in comparison to a poor man, then you are rich. But in comparison to a really rich man you are poor. That is why even that really rich man remains poor because someone else will be richer than he is. You cannot get anywhere with comparison. You may have left ten people behind but there will be ten others who are always ahead of you.

Are you good-looking? Yes, of course, in comparison with someone else you must be. But you are also ugly in comparison with another person. Are you healthy? Are you intelligent? Comparison continues all the time – when you say you are healthy, or that you are good-looking, the comparison continues. You can never find peace as long as comparison is happening – because someone is certain to be ahead of you. Then peace will be impossible. And life is so intricate that in one aspect you may get ahead of all the rest. For example, you may collect more wealth than others...

The Nizam of Hyderabad was the wealthiest man in the whole world. He had so many diamonds and so much jewelry from Golkonda that no one was richer than him. He was at the top. Once a year, when he brought out all his gems to place them in the light, he would need seven terraces to spread them all out.

But, before retiring for bed each night, he used to tie an earthen pot filled with salt to one of his feet. He was very scared of ghosts. And keeping salt nearby is one of the tricks; then ghosts don't attack. Because of this fear of ghosts he had become more pitiable than the humblest and the poorest of his servants.

His servants used to laugh at him. They would say, "What is this, Lord, your being so fearful? We are not scared of any type of ghost. Why do you tie such a big earthen pot to your foot?"

He slept with the pot attached to his foot for the whole of his life. His whole life was a misery because of his fear of ghosts. That was his only worry; and often he used to think he would have rather preferred to be a poor man but fearless. What was the point in being the richest man in the world and yet so afraid? He used to feel jealous of wretched beggars, seeing how carefree they were as they walked about, how they would sleep anywhere, without any worry, without any fear.

What to do...?

In these times, the Nizam of Hyderabad had five hundred wives. You may have heard about Krishna – he had sixteen thousand wives. Don't doubt this. If a man can have five hundred in the twentieth century then sixteen thousand is not much – just thirty-two times more! It is possible. He had five hundred wives and yet he lived a miserable life. He was rich but he envied the pauper. He was so scared of death that the very act of living was impossible for him.

Andrew Carnegie was a great millionaire who lived in America. When he was on his deathbed, his secretary asked him, "You own such immense wealth" – he left ten billion dollars cash in the bank – "You must be dying a happy man. Are you leaving this world a happy man?"

Carnegie replied, "What happiness? You cannot find anyone who is more of a failure than I am because my intention was to make one hundred billion dollars, but I could make only ten billion. I am a loser."

He talked about ten billion as someone else would say, "Ten pennies". But for him they were just ten pennies because if someone whose intention was to make one hundred ends up making only ten, then he is naturally a loser – losing by a factor of ninety.

So he was dying a miserable man. His secretary wrote in his biography: "If anyone had offered me to swap places with Andrew Carnegie, I wouldn't have done it. If he had wanted to become the secretary and make me the boss I wouldn't have agreed – because he was not as happy being a boss as I was being his secretary."

He writes further that the office servant would arrive at ten o'clock, the clerk at ten thirty, and the managers would come in at twelve o'clock. The managers would leave at three o'clock, the clerks would take off at four thirty, and the servant would leave at five. But Andrew Carnegie would jump into the office to work at seven in the morning and labor until twelve midnight.

There are stories that Andrew Carnegie could not recognize his own children. When did he have the time? How in the world could a man who is engaged from seven in the morning until twelve at night have recognized his children? He never played with them, never had a conversation with them, never sat down and spent time with them.

You may become wealthy but then there are a thousand and one other things. You may attain a position, status, but even then there are a thousand and one other things. No matter what you may achieve, you will never feel satisfied. As long as there is comparison, the scales will keep weighing you. The day you stop comparing, that very day you will be free. The day you drop the very idea that you need to compare yourself with others, that very day the misery will disappear. That day you come to realize that you are you and the other is the other – the matter is finished.

Once someone asked a Zen master, "Why is there so much joy in your life? Why don't I have it?"

The Zen master said, "I am happy the way I am; you are not happy the way you are."

But the man said, "Yes; but please show us some trick."

The monk replied, "I don't know any trick; just come out with me. Look, this tree is small and that tree is tall. I never saw them having any difficulty because one is small and the other is tall. I never heard them arguing about it, and I have been living here for the last thirty years. The small one is happy in its smallness and the tall one is happy in its tallness. This is because comparison has not found any foothold in their lives – they have not compared yet."

Even a blade of grass sways in the breeze with the same delight as a tall tree does; there is no difference. A flowering grass blossoms with the same joy as a roseflower does – there is no difference at all. *You* make the distinction. You may say, "This is a grass flower and that is a roseflower." But for the grass flower and for the roseflower there is no comparison – both are ecstatic in their own joy. Whoever drops comparison attains ecstasy. And whoever becomes ecstatic becomes free of comparison.

So Kabir says: *The pan of the scales went up when its load was light; now that it is full, what need is there to weigh it?* And now that bliss has showered in its entirety, now that the elixir is flowing from the heavenly cave, what is the need to weigh and measure? The opposite of this is also true: the moment you stop comparing, the doors of the heavenly cave will open. You will become blissful the very moment you stop comparing; or just become blissful and the comparing will stop. They are two sides of the same coin – start from either.

Kabir is right to describe the state of an enlightened mystic, a *siddha*, in this way: as long as the weight was lighter, the scales continued weighing, but now that it has come to its fullness, its fulfillment, what is the point in weighing? But you are not in the same state as the *siddha* is; you are in the state of a seeker – so from where will you begin? I say: just stop comparing; and as you stop comparing the weight will begin to become heavier and heavier. And who has asked you to compare yourself with someone else anyway? You are unique; there is no one else like you. Neither anyone else has an intellect like you do, nor does anyone have a face similar to yours; neither does anyone have eyes like you have, nor hands like you do. Your thumbprint is your very own.

At present there are four billion people in the world, but none of these four billion people has the same thumbprint as you have. You may exhume the bodies of billions and billions of people from their graves and yet you won't find a single person's thumbprint similar to yours. Billions upon billions of people will exist in the future as well and yet you won't find a single individual who has the same thumbprint as you do.

You are absolutely unique – where is the need to compare? You never compare yourself with a cockerel, that he has such a cute comb on his head…and then become sad about it! You never compare yourself with a tree saying, "Look how tall it is, reaching to the sky, while I am only six feet tall. My life is such a waste!" If you don't compare yourself with a cockerel or with a tree, then why do you compare yourself with your neighbor? Why do you compare yourself with anyone?

You will be miserable if you compare because you will just go on comparing. Someone is bound to be different from you; someone is sure to be superior to you, someone… You will come across a thousand kinds of differences and you will go deeper and deeper into misery and frustration. Stop comparing – and the weighing will come to an end. I am saying this in the interests of the seeker. As far as the *siddha*, the awakened one, is concerned Kabir is right: *The pan of the scales went up when its load was light; now that it is full, what need is there to weigh it?*

Remember, you begin from the other end than a *siddha* because what is true about a *siddha* shows the ultimate state of his being – it is not a description of the state you are in now. Where you are now, the scales continue to weigh, and so you become unnecessarily miserable.

***All the drunkards have gone mad:***
***they drank the whole tavern dry without measuring***
***how much they had taken.***

Existentially there is no misery; the misery is in your comparing mind. *All the drunkards have gone mad: they drank the whole tavern dry without measuring how much they had taken.* This is the last thing Kabir is talking about – let it go deep within you.

*All the drunkards have gone mad: they drank the whole tavern dry without measuring how much they had taken.* Kabir is talking about a tavern; the drunkards, who had gathered there, how they drank everything without measuring it – without worrying about how much they had had. Then they all went into ecstasy.

Why are you measuring what you drink? Why are you letting bliss enter you inch by inch? Why are you so scared of bliss? Why don't you allow it to enter you totally? The whole sky is yours! The whole of existence is yours! What is the need to weigh and measure? Is this world some kind of shop? You have not come here to purchase anything. The entire existence is open and available – what are you afraid of? Just go ahead and drink without bothering to weigh and measure.

Try to understand this a little.

Man is not as afraid of misery as he is of bliss because there is a cure when you are in misery – in bliss no cure is possible. There are medicines to cure yourself from being miserable – there is no medicine to cure yourself from bliss. Man is afraid of bliss because bliss is so vast that you can disappear under it; you will not be able to save yourself as you are. You can certainly remain seated on top of your misery. You *do* sit on top of the baggage of your misery – the baggage of bliss on the other hand will sit on top of you! Bliss is so vast.

You are not as afraid of misery as you are of bliss – understand this fact as clearly as possible. Since your very childhood you have been made afraid of joy, of being joyful. For example, if a child is dancing and laughing without any reason, the parents will say, "What's the matter? Why are you laughing?" If a child is jumping and feeling delighted… Actually children do get happy and excited for no reason as the doors of reasoning have not opened yet; the doors of the intellect are closed for the time being. Just very minor things… For example, the child sees a butterfly and gets excited, and starts running after it with such delight. The child finds a red pebble and picks it up as if he has found a diamond and becomes happy. Even when he does not find anything he sits down with great joy.

Once, I was a guest where three children were playing – a boy and a girl of about six years of age. And then there was a small kid who was perhaps three or three-and-a-half years old – all three of them playing. The hosts had gone out to work and I was all alone.

I saw that the boy and the girl were in one room and the youngest child was full of joy sitting on the stairs outside. He was not even a part of the game that was going on. I approached the little kid and asked, "What's the matter, are you not playing with them?"

He said, "Yes, I am playing."

I said, "You are sitting here outside on the stairs but the game is going on inside."

The boy said, "In that game the boy is the daddy and the girl is the mummy. I am the unborn child – I am not born yet!"

He is not born yet but already feeling so excited and joyful. And how long has it been since you were born? – yet you have still to experience that joyful state. When will you feel such a joy? Are you waiting for death to happen? The little child was very happy because soon the wait will be over – the time is coming near.

Children feel happy for no reason and we destroy their happiness, their joy. We try to make them serious. Seriousness is a disease. The father may be reading a newspaper, or busy making calculations, or is lost in counting his money. He thinks he is busy doing some great work. He scolds the child saying, "Keep quiet! I am losing count." You are busy counting bank notes – no other work can be more meaningless than this. You are not going to reach anywhere by counting the notes but you say to the child, "Be quiet!" And the child was enjoying such moments of happiness and joy. He wanted to dance and jump around for no reason in particular. For the sake of something trivial, you stopped something vast from entering.

When a child begins to feel the denials, the restrictions, he slowly begins to become serious. One thing, of course, becomes clear to him: in this society controlling has a value – so control yourself. But the more you control yourself, the more the doors of joy will remain shut, because joy descends in your unrestricted mind, in your free consciousness where there are no restrictions, where all control is put aside. Only then will you be able to drink the whole tavern dry.

Our whole education system is geared toward making the individual useful not joyful. Useful means becoming a clerk somewhere, becoming a teacher in a school, or getting yourself to fit into the office – in the sense of fitting yourself into some piece of machinery. You go on working your whole life, earning money, producing children so that they can also fit themselves in, so that they can also run a factory in the future.

There seems to be no difference: before your father was running a factory, now you are running it. He prepared you first, without himself having experienced any happiness in life – just prepared you to run the factory. And now when you yourself produce children, you get them ready to manage the factory, as if having a factory were such a great thing that the only reason for their being born was to run it. There is no harm if the factory is not running; what difference will it make if it doesn't run? We have turned man into something of less value than the business. As the factory keeps running, man's value becomes less and less.

What is your "utility" anyway? Your utility is that you become useful within the structure of society. All our education is simply to turn the individual into a machine, so he functions like a machine. The more skilled a person is in becoming a machine, the higher he rises in our system. We say that such and such a person is an expert. And the more unskilled a person is, the more he is dropped down to the bottom of our system. But of what value is expertise if it does not bring any joy?

Life is not a business. And, for me, this is the difference between a householder and a sannyasin. Someone who believes life is a business is a householder; someone who takes life as a celebration is a sannyasin. I have asked you to wear red-colored clothes just so that you may understand that red is a natural color for flowers. Someone who lives life expecting it to bear fruit is a householder; the person who wants to be just a flower is a sannyasin.

A result, the outcome, has a utility, but what is the utility of a flower? You can eat a fruit, you can digest it and make blood from it; but what will you do with a flower? A flower has no utility. A flower is non-utilitarian. A flower is like a poem – it has no utilitarian value at all. You can be happy looking at it but you cannot fill your coffers with it. For filling coffers, you need dead currency notes. An alive flower will be of no use; if you fill your coffers with living flowers, they will all die. For that you will need dead banknotes that do not rot. A dead thing never dies again – but whatever is alive will die.

Sannyas means one who sees life as a flower, not like a fruit. This is precisely what Krishna is telling Arjuna in the Bhagavad Gita. Symbols may be different but the story is same; the background is different but the essence is the same. Krishna is saying, "Don't expect any results from your actions; don't worry about the outcome. Just become like a flower. Let whatever is happening happen. Do whatever you can, but don't make it your ultimate purpose – simply function as a medium."

To be like a flower means you have given space to celebration in your life – you will dance, you will sing, you will be in sheer delight. But if I ask you to dance, you will ask, "Why? How will I profit?"

People come to me and they ask how meditation will be profitable. I wonder: will you ever come out of your banks? Will you ever come out of your shops – always working for gain and profit? Your whole mindset is tied to rupees. If I tell these people, "When you attain *samadhi*, instantly a thousand rupee note appears before you," they will say, "Then it is worth pursuing; please give us a technique. Why did you wait so long?" But if I tell them, "Bliss will shower upon you; a moment may come..." Then they will say, "We cannot afford it!" or "The timing is not right yet anyway!" They would rather wait till death approaches them.

People suddenly become religious at the moment of death. They keep procrastinating till the last moment of their lives. That is why you hear people saying: "Go and listen to the saints when you grow old. You are still young; this is not the time." So, people come to me...

Once an old man came to see me. His son had taken sannyas – the son was fifty years of age, not just a young lad. The man must have been about seventy-five years old. He said, "What are you doing giving sannyas to young boys? Is this the right age to enter sannyas? And I am still alive! As long as the father is alive, the son is nothing more than a young lad. And you gave him sannyas? Sannyas has to be the last thing!"

I said, "Now that you have come, let us forget all that has happened. Let us suppose I made a mistake, but I am not going to make the second mistake."

He asked, "What do you mean?"

I said, "Now, sannyas for you…!"

He began smiling, though it was more of a fake smile.

He said, "I will give some thought to it; then I will come."

I said, "Now, what is the delay for?"

He continued, "No, I did not come to you with that purpose in mind. That is not the issue."

I said, "Your view is that sannyas be given at a later age. So in that case, you are already too late. Seventy years are enough. You have already lived the maximum. You have finished with the original deposit; now you are living on its interest! Even then you have no courage to enter into sannyas."

He said again, "I will give some thought to it. And even then, there is a lot of work to be done, problems to be sorted out; my grandchildren need to be settled in marriage. But I will surely come someday."

He said all of this, but the day never came – because he died. A few days ago a letter from his son informed me that the man had passed away.

Don't die while you are still in business. Life is certainly meant to be enjoyed and celebrated. That does not mean you should not do business, but when you are doing it, do it just for fun and celebration. Even when you earn, be prepared to lose it. Even when you collect, do it for giving it away. Even if you save, do it for sharing with others. Happiness must remain your target; to flower should be the aim – a flowering that spreads fragrance all around.

*All the drunkards have gone mad: they drank the whole tavern dry without measuring how much they had taken.* Don't drink joy and happiness by weighing or measuring it – drink it without any concern for how much you have had. You don't have to make any monetary payment – bliss has no price tag. You won't need to pay anything. Just the willingness to drink it is enough – and the doors of the tavern are open.

One night, Mulla Nasruddin made a phone call to the owner of a tavern, at around three in the morning, asking him at what time the tavern would open.

The owner said, "Sir, is this the time to ask – in the middle of the night? You woke me up unnecessarily! The tavern will open as it always does, at nine o'clock in the morning, not a minute before. So go back to sleep."

After five or ten minutes the phone rang again. The owner picked it up with great anger. Nasruddin asked, "When will the tavern open?"

The owner said, "I have told you once: not even one minute before nine in the morning. Now be quiet and go back to sleep!"

The phone rang again after fifteen minutes. The owner was already furious with Mulla for not allowing him to sleep. He said, "What's the matter? Are you completely drunk or what?"

Nasruddin said, "Yes, I am drunk; but the point is that I am locked inside the tavern – I am not outside. So I want to get out, not get in. When will the tavern open?"

You may also be thinking he must have had too much to drink; when the tavern closed he must have been left inside and obviously, without the owner's presence, he had the whole tavern to himself!

You must also drink bliss like this, not by purchasing it. There is no question of purchasing – why do you drink bliss measuring and weighing it? Why does man drink joy and happiness in bits and pieces? He is afraid, that's why.

People come to me and say, "If we begin to really dance, we become afraid that perhaps we may lose control. The control that we have held onto might be lost. As we enter into meditation, a moment comes when an explosion seems imminent – and that's when fear takes over." They say, "When we arrive at that point it feels like we might lose ourselves." They have somehow managed to stay in control until then.

What is this fear of losing control? The fear is because the society has taught you to repress. You have repressed so many things that you are afraid of losing control over yourself. You are afraid that all that is repressed within you may become manifest. You have pushed so many things down inside. And if you drink bliss openly, then whatever you have repressed may come out. Then it will be a problem; it will become very difficult to handle it.

When a seeker approached Gurdjieff, the first thing Gurdjieff would do was to get the person drunk. He was a very strange master – but of immense value...

Only strange people are of some use. The dead people that you worship are of no use. But you worship them precisely because they are totally dead. They don't destroy your controlling in any way; on the contrary, they cooperate with your controlling. They are supportive of your misery; they add to your misery, they arrange it properly for you.

When you approach your gurus, someone may say, "Stop drinking tea"; someone else may say, "Stop smoking cigarettes";

or someone else may say, "Take the vow of celibacy." Someone may suggest this, and someone may suggest that. As it is, you are already so miserable; as it is you are so tied up, have put so many controls upon yourself – and they will add some more; they will put more chains on you. They will not encourage you to be happy, but will encourage you to get more into bondage. And it is true that as joy and happiness descend, all other trivial things which keep holding you back will disappear. The trivial holds you back simply because there is no joy in your life.

If a man is an alcoholic, then there are two ways to make him free of drink. One way is to ask him to take a vow, to make him promise; or order him and make him swear he will not drink anymore. This way you put one more chain on him. The second way is to show him how to get drunk with the divine. And the day he gets drunk with the divine, the alcohol will drop on its own accord. This is how you bring the person toward bliss, freedom – you don't put more chains on him, rather you just break all his chains.

This person will certainly drop alcohol. Once you have tasted the drink of the divine, the other alcohol will begin to stink. When you get drunk on the divine, the other alcohol will begin to taste like dirty water from the drain. Once you have experienced divine love, celibacy will automatically happen; there will be no need to make it happen. And once you have attained all the wealth of the divine, then pushing to gain worldly treasures – the cowries, the small seashells of this world – will drop of its own accord. Attain the divine so that one day you may drop this samsara, this material world. Exactly this is the eternal message from all the enlightened mystics.

But the kind of dead people that you are worshipping will put more chains around you. They are the ones who have put on the chains; or maybe their forefathers have. And they have chained you from all sides. For example, you are unable to laugh openly because then people may say you are uncultured. They will say: "Is this the way – laughing so loudly?" You laugh only superficially; your laughter does not reach your belly because there is fear. All repression gets into the belly. That is where repressed sexual energy is. If your laughter goes to your belly, instantly you will find lust arising; so you remain afraid. You laugh just on the surface; you don't even breathe fully.

Psychologists say you will be able to breathe fully only when you have dropped your conflict with sex. You breathe very superficially, you breathe at the upper level of your chest and not all the way down. When the breath goes deep within it hits the sex center. When people have been doing Dynamic Meditation for some time, some of them come to me and say, "What's going on? We believed meditation would help us become celibate, but instead sexual passion is coming up!" I tell them, "You have repressed it for so long, now it is bound to manifest – but let it be so, don't be afraid. Let it arise and manifest so that the fear disappears. Just pass through it and continue with meditation because only when the sexual energy rises upward will it transform into celibacy."

Celibacy is not an enemy of sex – rather it is a transformation of sex. For such transformation to take place it is necessary for the sex energy to arise. For the transformation of the power of sexuality, sexual energy is needed; how can there be a transformation without energy? So don't be afraid. Your saints and mahatmas cause fear in you from all sides. Remember one thing as a principle: stay away from anyone who causes fear in you. Go to the one who makes you fearless.

So when anyone approached Gurdjieff, the first thing he would do was to get the person drunk; so much so that people would ask, "Why does he do that?" He would ask the person to just sit and would observe how the person's entire behavior changed after drinking. Whatever was repressed within him would start manifesting. Before the person was drunk, he may have been saying, "Rama, Rama, Rama..." but then he would start being abusive.

Are you familiar with drunkards? People say, "He is such a good man, but after having a drink..." You are saying he is behaving badly because he is drunk, but drink can never produce abusive language. No chemistry can prove that alcohol produces abusive language. The fact is: abusive language, insults are already repressed inside – alcohol removes the barrier and the abuse surfaces. Now the man does not repeat "Rama, Rama, Rama..." Instead, he throws away the piece of paper that was wrapped around him and printed with "Rama, Rama, Rama..."! Until that moment he appeared to be very quiet but then suddenly he gets angry. If you ever visit a pub, you will see the real picture of man – and that is exactly *your* real picture. But you are hiding it; and that's why you are afraid of drinking – because then your true character will manifest.

Have you ever tried *bhang* – a marijuana drink? After drinking it, people begin to talk nonsense. It was all lying within; how can *bhang* create it? *Bhang* simply removes the barriers and you forget all about your society, upbringing, your civilized ways – everything. You appear purely as a human being – as you truly are within. The true man hiding inside begins to manifest. For example, you are conscious while welcoming someone and you say: "I am so obliged you have come. It is a good omen! Your visit to our house is very auspicious. Just seeing your face there is happiness all around." Then as you get drunk, you start saying, "Get out of here! I have had to look at your face since this morning! Whenever I see your face my whole day is ruined!" What is hidden inside bursts out!

Gurdjieff used to bring out the person hiding within. He says that it is first necessary to know how the man is from within; then, accordingly, meditation techniques can be figured out.

When you do Dynamic Meditation, Kundalini Meditation and other such meditations, it brings out all that is repressed inside you. Gurdjieff used to make a person drunk – I don't find that is necessary. Dynamic Meditation brings out all that is lying inside you. You can see for yourself. In Dynamic Meditation you will find someone screaming and shouting who otherwise looked so calm and quiet. Someone who before looked like a good, harmless man, suddenly begins to throw his fists in the air and is fighting with another person as if he wants to kill him. This is the real man – not the one who appeared to be so kind and harmless.

There is no need for alcohol; you just need to be uncontrolled and all your inner reality will come out. And that is the only thing which has to be transformed. What appears on the outside is all false. It is just make-up, cosmetics; it has no value, it is meaningless. Just making some changes to that will make no difference at all. What is needed is to transform the real, which is within, because that is our source of energy.

*All the drunkards have gone mad: they drank the whole tavern dry without measuring how much they had taken.* You are afraid of becoming happy because of control. Wake up! Forget all about control; take care of joy and happiness. As joy and happiness begin to enter your life, the control will go away of its own accord. That doesn't mean you will become uncontrolled. This also does not mean you will become an anti-social element or that you will begin doing wrong things. No! Now you are living in fear; when joy and happiness enter, fear will have no place. As you are now, you can commit an anti-social act at any time.

When you read stories about people who committed murders, no one could have predicted that any of them was the sort of person that could kill somebody. They were people who were just as kind and well-behaved as you are; and yet, one day, they killed someone. Psychologists have arrived at a very strange conclusion. They say: the man who shows a little bit of anger every day can never kill anyone. He is a good man because his anger is released every day. The man who maintains a peaceful facade every day and keeps collecting anger within, that man can commit a murder any day.

A lot of fire is needed for an explosion to take place. What explosion can there be if sparks are released every day? That is why the type of husband, the type of a wife, who within twenty-four hours once in a while fights, is better. A husband who always remains like a buddha is dangerous when his wife starts a fight! He is dangerous because he can strangle her any day – he won't settle for anything less. He will have accumulated so much anger that one day he will surely kill her.

So, beware of *sadhus* or godly men; they become killers! You can see what happens when the Hindu–Muslim riots break out. Good people – those who up to that time were minding their shops, going to the market, buying and selling things – were friends, and suddenly it is all over. The very person who visited the mosque every day, prayed five times a day, and another person who visited the temple every day, wrapping a piece of cloth printed with the name of Rama around him – these very people set fire to each other's homes, kill each other, even kill small children.

How can all this happen? It is because of all that is repressed within. The way you are, you are dangerous! You just need an excuse to explode and the fire breaks out. That is why psychologists say a world war is needed every ten years – because people accumulate so much inside that if it does not find an outlet in a war then everyday living will become difficult. So, some type of craziness is needed, for whatever reason, with whatever excuse. For example, you see people watching a football match; it is so strange, thousands come to watch it. The players on the field are doing nothing significant except kicking a ball from one side to the other. And the spectators are roasting themselves in the sun and jumping up and down more than the players do. And it may all turn into quarrels or even fights!

Or see horse racing; people bet on them. Sometimes they are very thrilled, sometimes they are unhappy; sometimes crying or sometimes laughing. If you watch them closely, you will be amazed what kind of craziness is going on. One thing is for sure: you won't be able to persuade a horse to watch such a race. You may make humans race, but horses will never come to watch it! Horses will wonder what kind of craziness this is. Even donkeys won't come to watch such a race – forget about horses. But horses run and people just stand there watching. And these are the elite of society – sensible, rich, in a high position, everything! They are intelligent, so why are they doing this? Obviously, there is some element of insanity that needs to find an outlet.

There are people who are engaged in cockfights. These are the high profile VIPs, sitting and watching a cockfight. They are releasing their violence through such a cockfight. If one person's cockerel kills the other person's cockerel then it becomes symbolic: one has destroyed the other. So the cockfight just serves as an excuse. The one who loses the fight will not be able to sleep the whole night – it was a defeat.

Then again, cockfights and the like are expensive; so people use cheaper means such as a game of chess. They place horses, elephants – of course artificial – on the board; having real ones would be very expensive! The days of the rajas and maharajas have gone; so, instead, the game of chess. People get lost sitting and playing the game. And these are the kind of people for whom Kabir seems to have said these words: *All the drunkards have gone mad: they drank the whole tavern dry without measuring how much they had taken*. They drank the whole tavern dry without weighing how much they had had.

Violence, anger – all are released through the game of chess. Our games are nothing but abridged editions, manifestations, of violence. In every way we are filled with garbage. You will have to get rid of it, otherwise you will always remain afraid of joy and happiness. And if you are afraid of joy, you are simply ruined because the whole journey of life knows only this: *All the drunkards have gone mad: they drank the whole tavern dry without measuring how much they had taken.*

This sutra is of great significance:

> **The swan has taken flight to the Mansarovar lake,**
> **so why should it bother about the pools and ditches anymore?**

Now that the swan has found the *Mansarovar* – the Himalayan lake – why would it stray into pools and ditches? Why would anyone who has already attained the divine wander in the trivial? Why would anyone who has found the ultimate tavern bother to go into these worldly pubs? Even his visits to these pubs are for nothing else than to search for the real one.

You are searching for the same love in your wife that you can achieve only through prayer; in your husband, too, you are searching for the same love that no husband can give – only the divine can. In money you are looking for that which you can find only through attaining the ultimate wealth. In seeking status you are actually seeking that which is found when you reach the ultimate state. So in the world you are really searching for precisely that which is not in the world at all.

*The swan has taken flight to the Mansarovar lake, so why should it bother about the pools and ditches anymore?* The real issue is not of abandoning the pools and the ditches; rather, it is of searching for the *Mansarovar* lake. The question is not that you drop the low and the trivial – the trivial is not even worth dropping, it is so trivial! It is pointless even to talk about it. If you busy yourself with dropping it, you will end up giving it great importance – and it is not worth giving it that importance. Simply go and search for the vast!

There is no need to give up the world, rather attain godliness. This the most profound of messages from Kabir and Nanak. That is why they did not initiate sannyasins. Their sannyasin is a householder – he is in the house. What is the point in abandoning the world? It is not even worth it. Godliness is to be attained; what barriers can the world create for the one who has found godliness? Let the world be; let the pools and the ditches remain what they are. One who has found the lake will have no interest in the pools and the ditches anymore. There is no need to escape from the pools and the ditches. There is no need to destroy them either. Leave something for those who have not found the lake; leave at least the pools and the ditches for those who have not found it yet.

There are two ways of living: one is the negative way and the other is the positive way. One way says, drop all that is wrong – this is a negative way. And the other way says find all that is right – this is a positive way. Avoid the negative because the negative takes you nowhere but closer to death.

I don't ask you to give up wealth. I don't ask you to escape from your home. I ask you to wake up! This home is not enough for you – look for a larger home. Even when the larger one is found, you will continue to live in this house but like a lotus untouched by the dirty water. This home will not affect you. You will continue to be within the world and yet outside the same world – the world will not enter you.

***The swan has taken flight to the Mansarovar lake,***
***so why should it bother about the pools and ditches anymore?***
***Godliness dwells within you,***
***what need is there to open your eyes outward?***

Kabir says: ***Listen, O seekers, the divine appears exactly when the tiny particle of dust is removed from your eyes.***

Kabir says: *Godliness dwells within you, what need is there to open your eyes outward? Samsara*, or the world, means: we search outside for that which is lying within. *Dharma*, or religion, means: we are searching for it where it actually is.

There was a Sufi woman, Rabia – very precious! In the history of mankind very few women have reached the point where Rabia is. One day people found her looking for something outside her house. She was an old woman, so other people also joined her in the search.

This is an old story; nowadays no one comes forward to help like this. It was a small village so neighbors came out to help her. They asked Rabia, "What have you lost?"

She said, "I have lost my needle."

So they continued looking for it. The sun was about to set and darkness was approaching.

Then one man asked, "A needle is a very small thing and the road is quite wide; where did it fall? If you give us the exact location, we may be able to find it; otherwise nightfall is close."

Rabia said, "Don't ask me where it was dropped because actually it fell inside the house."

People started laughing and said, "Rabia, have you gone mad? If the needle fell inside the house, then why are you looking for it outside?"

Rabia said, "What to do? I am helpless; there is no light in the house, it is dark. What is the point of searching for it in the dark? So I look for it outside; at least some daylight is still left. You can search for it only where there is light."

People said, "You crazy woman! Yes, it is true that you can search for it only where there is light, but if you have not lost it where you are looking for it, then what can light do? The light is not going to create the needle for you. It is better, Rabia, that we bring some light inside the house, because a thing can be found only where it is actually lost."

Rabia said, "You people are very intelligent! But you have not applied the same principle in your own lives. And I am doing exactly what you have been doing in your lives. You are searching outside for that which you have lost inside. So I thought, since this is your logic and since I live in your neighborhood, it is better that I follow the same logic. And you are calling *me* mad!"

Have you ever wondered where your joy went? You have lost your joy in cars, in big houses, in big safes. Do you ever remember that when you came into this world you did not bring any safes with you, any big cars or any big houses with you? What did you bring with you, really? You certainly brought joy with you – you were happy. You were tremendously happy, like a child is, utterly delighted. You brought your joy with you.

It is essential to understand this: how can we search for something that we have not tasted yet? Everybody is searching for joy and happiness. That means, at some time or another, you have known what joy is, you have had some taste of joy. How can you search for it otherwise? Every child is born with joy. Each child arrives from the world of joy. Each child is in tune with joy from within. Then, slowly, slowly we control and dominate him and society conditions the child.

This is the reason you cannot remember anything before the age of four. Try and dig into your past – you can remember only as far back as three, four or five years of age. Before that the memory stops. Why? What is the reason? If you were alive, then the memory has to be there. But you were so happy and the memory is made up of misery, not of joy and happiness. When the shoe fits rightly, there is no pain, so how can there be any memory of it? You are unable to recall anything from before the age of four or five because you were so happy, you were so joyous, that no memory occurred at all. Since there was no misery, there was no trace of memory – your mind remained as blank as ever.

Joy, happiness, leaves no trace: it is like birds soaring in the sky leaving no footprints behind. That is why you are unable to remember. And yet, some unknown melody continues to hum within you. This is the reason why a very old person says that childhood was so great; he recalls his childhood with such fondness.

Jesus says: unless you become like a child, you will not enter the kingdom of God. This certainly means that children have already had some glimpse of the kingdom of God before. Certainly! Joy was flowing within, but society placed its shadow on it. Education and conditioning repressed it all. If you want to find and experience the same inner joy now, you will have to cut through your education and your conditioning.

Godliness dwells within you, what need is there to open your eyes outward? Kabir says: Listen, O seekers, the divine appears exactly when the tiny particle of dust is removed from your eyes.

When you see the Himalayas with open eyes – the vast Himalayas – the high peaks, the wide open arms touching the sky… You can see the snow-clad Himalayas; your small eye is able to see the gigantic Himalayas. But if one wanted to hide the Himalayas from your eyes, what would be the best way? Dropping just a small particle of dust in your eyes would be enough. No need to hide the Himalayas; just putting a small particle of dust into your eyes is all that is required. That's it; the eyes will get irritated and the Himalayas will disappear. The Himalayas get hidden under the cover of the dust particle; a speck of dust in the eyes and the Himalayas will disappear. Such huge and vast Himalayas get hidden by a tiny grain of dust!

Kabir says: this is exactly how the divine has disappeared. Just a tiny particle, a tiny speck of dust has fallen into your eyes and it is hiding the divine which is of such vast proportions. So in order to search for godliness you don't have to do anything except to just clean your eyes, to just remove the dust particle. As the eyes get clear, godliness appears – it has always been present.

Kabir says: *Listen, O seekers, the divine appears exactly when the tiny particle of dust is removed from your eyes.* Godliness, the master, the divine, is hiding just behind that speck of dust. No need to go and search for it far away – it is just a matter of removing that tiny speck of dust from your eyes.

What is that dust particle? About which eyes and which speck of dust is Kabir talking? Your ego is lying in your eyes like the dust particle. "I am" – this is the dust particle. And that which is, is hiding underneath it. The moment you remove "I am" – when it is gone – instantly the meeting with the divine takes place. As soon as the "I" disappears, godliness is attained. As long as "you" are, you won't be able to find the divine within. The very moment you are ready to lose yourself, that very moment godliness will surely be attained. It was already there, you had never lost it – it was just because of that speck of dust.

Let me repeat the entire song again so that it can continue to echo in your hearts…

***Where is the need for words when the mind is in ecstasy?***
***I have found the diamond and wrapped it in my cloak,***
***so why open it again and again?***
***The pan of the scales went up when its load was light;***
***now that it is full, what need is there to weigh it?***

***All the drunkards have gone mad:***
***they drank the whole tavern dry without measuring***
***how much they had taken.***
***The swan has taken flight to the Mansarovar lake,***
***so why should it bother about the pools and ditches anymore?***
***Godliness dwells within you,***
***what need is there to open your eyes outward?***

Kabir says: ***Listen, O seekers, the divine appears***
***exactly when the tiny particle of dust is removed from your eyes.***

Enough for today.

# About Osho

Osho's unique contribution to the understanding of who we are defies categorization. Mystic and scientist, a rebellious spirit whose sole interest is to alert humanity to the urgent need to discover a new way of living. To continue as before is to invite threats to our very survival on this unique and beautiful planet.

His essential point is that only by changing ourselves, one individual at a time, can the outcome of all our "selves" – our societies, our cultures, our beliefs, our world – also change. The doorway to that change is meditation.

Osho the scientist has experimented and scrutinized all the approaches of the past and examined their effects on the modern human being and responded to their shortcomings by creating a new starting point for the hyperactive twenty-first century mind: OSHO Active Meditations.

Once the agitation of a modern lifetime has started to settle, "activity" can melt into "passivity," a key starting point of real meditation. To support this next step, Osho has transformed the ancient "art of listening" into a subtle contemporary methodology: the OSHO Talks. Here words become music, the listener discovers who is listening, and the awareness moves from what is being heard to the individual doing the listening. Magically, as silence arises, what needs to be heard is understood directly, free from the distraction of a mind that can only interrupt and interfere with this delicate process.

These thousands of talks cover everything from the individual quest for meaning to the most urgent social and political issues facing society today. Osho's books are not written but are transcribed from audio and video recordings of these extemporaneous talks to international audiences. As he puts it, "So remember: whatever I am saying is not just for you...I am talking also for the future generations."

Osho has been described by *The Sunday Times* in London as one of the "1000 Makers of the 20th Century" and by American author Tom Robbins as "the most dangerous man since Jesus Christ." *Sunday Mid-Day* (India) has selected Osho as one of ten people – along with Gandhi, Nehru and Buddha – who have changed the destiny of India.

About his own work Osho has said that he is helping to create the conditions for the birth of a new kind of human being. He often characterizes this new human being as "Zorba the Buddha" – capable both of enjoying the earthy pleasures of a Zorba the Greek and the silent serenity of a Gautama the Buddha.

Running like a thread through all aspects of Osho's talks and meditations is a vision that encompasses both the timeless wisdom of all ages past and the highest potential of today's (and tomorrow's) science and technology.

Osho is known for his revolutionary contribution to the science of inner transformation, with an approach to meditation that acknowledges the accelerated pace of contemporary life. His unique OSHO Active Meditations™ are designed to first release the accumulated stresses of body and mind, so that it is then easier to take an experience of stillness and thought-free relaxation into daily life.

Two autobiographical works by the author are available:

***Autobiography of a Spiritually Incorrect Mystic***, St Martins Press, New York (book and eBook)

***Glimpses of a Golden Childhood***, OSHO Media International, Pune, India (book and eBook)

# Osho International Meditation Resort

Each year the Meditation Resort welcomes thousands of people from more than 100 countries. The unique campus provides an opportunity for a direct personal experience of a new way of living – with more awareness, relaxation, celebration and creativity. A great variety of around-the-clock and around-the-year program options are available. Doing nothing and just relaxing is one of them!

All of the programs are based on Osho's vision of "Zorba the Buddha" – a qualitatively new kind of human being who is able *both* to participate creatively in everyday life *and* to relax into silence and meditation.

**Location**

Located 100 miles southeast of Mumbai in the thriving modern city of Pune, India, the OSHO International Meditation Resort is a holiday destination with a difference. The Meditation Resort is spread over 28 acres of spectacular gardens in a beautiful tree-lined residential area.

**OSHO Meditations**

A full daily schedule of meditations for every type of person includes both traditional and revolutionary methods, and particularly the OSHO Active Meditations™. The daily meditation program takes place in what must be the world's largest meditation hall, the OSHO Auditorium.

**OSHO Multiversity**

Individual sessions, courses and workshops cover everything from creative arts to holistic health, personal transformation, relationship and life transition, transforming meditation into a lifestyle for life and work, esoteric sciences, and the "Zen" approach to sports and recreation. The secret of the OSHO Multiversity's success lies in the fact that all its programs are combined with meditation, supporting the understanding that as human beings we are far more than the sum of our parts.

**OSHO Basho Spa**

The luxurious Basho Spa provides for leisurely open-air swimming surrounded by trees and tropical green. The uniquely styled, spacious Jacuzzi, the saunas, gym, tennis courts...all these are enhanced by their stunningly beautiful setting.

**Cuisine**

A variety of different eating areas serve delicious Western, Asian and Indian vegetarian food – most of it organically grown especially for the Meditation Resort. Breads and cakes are baked in the resort's own bakery.

**Night life**

There are many evening events to choose from – dancing being at the top of the list! Other activities include full-moon meditations beneath the stars, variety shows, music performances and meditations for daily life.

**Facilities**

You can buy all of your basic necessities and toiletries in the Galleria. The Multimedia Gallery sells a large range of OSHO media products. There is also a bank, a travel agency and a Cyber Café on-campus. For those who enjoy shopping, Pune provides all the options, ranging from traditional and ethnic Indian products to all of the global brand-name stores.

**Accommodation**

You can choose to stay in the elegant rooms of the OSHO Guesthouse, or for longer stays on campus you can select one of the OSHO Living-In programs. Additionally there is a plentiful variety of nearby hotels and serviced apartments.

www.osho.com/meditationresort
www.osho.com/guesthouse
www.osho.com/livingin

# Books by Osho in English

**Early Discourses and Writings**
The Art of Living
Astrology
Breaking All Boundaries
Compassion and Revolution
A Cup of Tea
Dimensions beyond the Known
Earthen Lamps
The Eternal Quest
Flowers of Love
From Sex to Superconsciousness
The Great Challenge
Hidden Mysteries
I Am the Gate
The Independent Mind
Into the Void
Keys to a New Life
Life Is a Soap Bubble
Love Letters to Life
New Dimensions of Yoga
The Path of Meditation
The Psychology of the Esoteric
Religion's Expiration Date
The Search for Peace
Seeds of Wisdom
Silence: The Message of Your Being
Work Is Love Made Visible
Three Steps to Awakening
Into the Void

*Meditation*
And Now and Here
In Search of the Miraculous
Meditation: The Art of Ecstasy
Meditation: The First and Last Freedom
The Inner Journey
The Perfect Way

*Buddha and Buddhist Masters*
The Book of Wisdom
The Dhammapada: The Way of the Buddha(Vols 1-12)
The Diamond Sutra
The Discipline of Transcendence (Vols 1-4)
The Heart Sutra

*Indian Mystics*
Bliss:Living beyond Happiness and Misery (Shiv Sutras)
Die O Yogi Die (Gorakh)
Enlightenment: The Only Revolution (Ashtavakra)
Krishna: The Man and His Philosophy
Showering without Clouds (Sahajo)
The True Name (Vols 1&2) (Nanak)
The Last Morning Star (Daya)
The Song of Ecstasy (Adi Shankara)

*Baul Mystics*
The Beloved (Vols 1 & 2)

*Kabir*
The Divine Melody
Ecstasy: The Forgotten Language
The Fabric of Life
The Fish in the Sea Is Not Thirsty
The Great Secret
The Guest
The Path of Love
The Revolution

*Jesus and Christian Mystics*
Come Follow to You (Vols 1-4)
I Say Unto You (Vols 1 & 2)
The Mustard Seed
Theologia Mystica

*Jewish Mystics*
The Art of Dying
The True Sage

*Western Mystics*
Guida Spirituale (*Desiderata*)
The Great Challenge (Treatise of St. Dionysius)
The Hidden Harmony (Heraclitus)
The New Alchemy: To Turn You On (Mabel Collins' *Light on the Path*)
Philosophia Perennis (Vols 1 & 2) (*The Golden Verses of Pythagoras*)
Reflections on Kahlil Gibran's *The Prophet*
Theologica Mystica
Zarathustra: A God That Can Dance (Nietzsche's *Thus Spake Zarathustra*)
Zarathustra: The Laughing Prophet (Nietzsche's *Thus Spake Zarathustra*)
The Voice of Silence (Mabel Collins' *Light on the Path*)

*Sufism*
Just Like That
The Perfect Master (Vols 1 & 2)
The Secret
Sufis: The People of the Path (Vols 1 & 2)
Unio Mystica (Vols 1 & 2)
Until You Die
The Wisdom of the Sands (Vols 1 & 2)

*Tantra*
Tantra: The Supreme Understanding
The Tantra Experience: The Royal Song of Saraha (same as Tantra Vision, Vol. 1)
Tantric Transformation: The Royal Song of Saraha (same as Tantra Vision, Vol. 2)
The Book of Secrets: Vigyan Bhairav Tantra

*The Upanishads*
Behind a Thousand Names (Nirvana Upanishad)
Finger Pointing to the Moon (Adhyatma Upanishad)
Flight of the Alone to the Alone (Kaivalya Upanishad)
The Heartbeat of the Absolute (Ishavasya Upanishad)
I Am That (Isa Upanishad)
The Message beyond Words (Kathopanishad)
Philosophia Ultima (Mandukya Upanishad)
The Supreme Doctrine (Kenopanishad)
That Art Thou (Sarvasar Upanishad, Kaivalya Upanishad, Adhyatma Upanishad)
The Ultimate Alchemy (Vols 1 & 2) (Atma Pooja Upanishad)
Vedanta: Seven Steps to Samadhi (Akshaya Upanishad)
The Way beyond Any Way (Sarvasar Upanishad)

*Tao*
The Empty Boat

The Secret of Secrets
Tao: The Golden Gate (Vols 1 & 2)
Tao: The Pathless Path (Vols 1 & 2)
Tao: The Three Treasures (Vols 1-4)
When the Shoe Fits

*Yoga*
Yoga: The Science of the Soul (Vols 1-10)
The Path of Yoga (Vol.1)
The Heart of Yoga (Vol.2)
Yoga: The Mystery beyond Mind (Vol.3)
The Alchemy of Yoga (Vol.4)
Yoga: A New Direction (Vol.5)
Essence of Yoga (Vol.6)
Yoga: The Science of Living (Vol.7)
Secrets of Yoga (Vol.8)
Yoga: The Path to Liberation (Vol.9)
Yoga: The Supreme Science (Vol.10)

*Zen and Zen Masters*
Ah, This!
Ancient Music in the Pines
And the Flowers Showered...
And the Grass Grows By Itself...
A Bird on the Wing
Bodhidharma: The Greatest Zen Master
The Buddha: The Emptiness of the Heart
Christianity, the Deadliest Poison and Zen, the Antidote to All Poisons
Communism and Zen Fire, Zen Wind
Dang Dang Doko Dang
The First Principle
God Is Dead: Now Zen Is the Only Living Truth
The Great Zen Master Ta Hui
Hsin Hsin Ming: The Book of Nothing
I Celebrate Myself: God Is No Where, Life Is Now Here
Kyozan: A True Man of Zen
The Language of Existence
Live Zen
The Miracle
Nirvana: The Last Nightmare
No Mind: The Flowers of Eternity
No Water, No Moon
One Seed Makes the Whole Earth Green
The Original Man
Returning to the Source
The Search: Talks on the 10 Bulls of Zen
A Sudden Clash of Thunder
The Sun Rises in the Evening
Take it Easy
This. This. A Thousand Times This
This Very Body the Buddha
Turning In
Walking in Zen, Sitting in Zen
The White Lotus
Yakusan: Straight to the Point of Enlightenment
The Zen Manifesto: Freedom from Oneself
Zen: The Diamond Thunderbolt
Zen: The Mystery and the Poetry of the Beyond
Zen: The Path of Paradox (Vols 1-3)
Zen: The Quantum Leap from Mind to No-Mind
Zen: The Solitary Bird, Cuckoo of the Forest
Zen: The Special Transmission

**Osho: On the Ancient Masters of Zen**
Dogen: The Zen Master
Hyakujo: The Everest of Zen – With Basho's haikus
Isan: No Footprints in the Blue Sky
Joshu: The Lion's Roar

Ma Tzu: The Empty Mirror
Nansen: The Point of Departure
Rinzai: Master of the Irrational

*Responses to Questions*
Be Still and Know
Beyond Enlightenment (Talks in Bombay)
Beyond Psychology (Talks in Uruguay)
Come, Come, Yet Again Come
From Bondage to Freedom
From Darkness to Light
From Death to Deathlessness
From Ignorance to Innocence
From Misery to Enlightenment
From Personality to Individuality
From the False to the Truth
From Unconsciousness to Consciousness
The Goose Is Out
The Great Pilgrimage: From Here to Here
The Invitation
Light on the Path (Talks in the Himalayas)
My Way: The Way of the White Clouds
Nowhere to Go but In
The Osho Upanishad (Talks in Bombay)
The Path of the Mystic (Talks in Uruguay)
The Razor's Edge
Sermons in Stones (Talks in Bombay)
Socrates Poisoned Again After 25 Centuries (Talks in Greece)
The Sword and the Lotus (Talks in the Himalayas)
Transmission of the Lamp (Talks in Uruguay)
Walk without Feet, Fly without Wings and Think without Mind
The Wild Geese and the Water
Yaa-Hoo! The Mystic Rose
Zen: Zest, Zip, Zap and Zing

*Osho's Vision for the World*
The Golden Future
The Hidden Splendor
The New Dawn
The Rebel
The Rebellious Spirit

*The Mantra Series*
Hari Om Tat Sat
Om Mani Padme Hum
Om Shantih Shantih Shantih
Sat Chit Anand
Satyam Shivam Sundaram

*Personal Glimpses*
Books I Have Loved
Glimpses of a Golden Childhood
Notes of a Madman

**Interviews with the World Press**
The Man of Truth: A Majority of One

For any information about OSHO Books, please contact:

**OSHO Media International**
17 Koregaon Park, Pune – 411001, MS, India
Phone: +91-20-66019999 Fax: +91-20-66019990
E-mail: distribution@osho.net
Website: http://www.osho.com

# For More Information

For a full selection of OSHO multilingual online destinations, see osho.com/allaboutosho

The official and comprehensive website of OSHO International is osho.com

For more OSHO unique content and formats see:

- OSHO Active Meditations: osho.com/meditate
- iOsho, a bouquet of digital OSHO experiences featuring OSHO Zen Tarot, TV, Library, Horoscope, eGreetings and Radio. Please take a moment to do a one time registration which will allow you a universal login. Registration is free and open to anyone with a valid email address: osho.com/iosho
- The OSHO online shop: osho.com/shop
- Visit the OSHO International Meditation Resort: osho.com/visit
- Contribute in the OSHO Translation Project:oshotalks.com
- Read the OSHO Newsletters: osho.com/NewsLetters
- Watch OSHO on YouTube: youtube.com/user/OSHOInternational
- Follow OSHO on Facebook: facebook.com/osho.international.meditation.resort
- and Twitter: twitter.com/OSHO

Thank you for buying this OSHO book.